SAGE was founded in 1965 by Sara Miller McCune to support the dissemination of usable knowledge by publishing innovative and high-quality research and teaching content. Today, we publish more than 850 journals, including those of more than 300 learned societies, more than 800 new books per year, and a growing range of library products including archives, data, case studies, reports, conference highlights, and video. SAGE remains majority-owned by our founder, and after Sara's lifetime will become owned by a charitable trust that secures our continued independence.

Los Angeles | London | New Delhi | Singapore | Washington DC

India, China
and
Sub-regional
Connectivities
in
South Asia

Bulk Sales

SAGE India offers special discounts
for purchase of books in bulk.
We also make available special imprints
and excerpts from our books on demand.

For orders and enquiries, write to us at

Marketing Department
SAGE Publications India Pvt Ltd
B1/I-1, Mohan Cooperative Industrial Area
Mathura Road, Post Bag 7
New Delhi 110044, India

E-mail us at **marketing@sagepub.in**

Get to know more about SAGE

Be invited to SAGE events, get on our mailing list.
Write today to **marketing@sagepub.in**

This book is also available as an e-book.

India, China

and

Sub-regional Connectivities in

South Asia

Edited by
D. Suba Chandran
Bhavna Singh

$SAGE www.sagepublications.com
Los Angeles • London • New Delhi • Singapore • Washington DC

First published in 2015 by

 SAGE Publications India Pvt Ltd
B1/I-1 Mohan Cooperative Industrial Area
Mathura Road, New Delhi 110 044, India
www.sagepub.in

SAGE Publications Inc
2455 Teller Road
Thousand Oaks, California 91320, USA

SAGE Publications Ltd
1 Oliver's Yard, 55 City Road
London EC1Y 1SP, United Kingdom

SAGE Publications Asia-Pacific Pte Ltd
3 Church Street
#10-04 Samsung Hub
Singapore 049483

Published by Vivek Mehra for SAGE Publications India Pvt. Ltd, typeset in 10/12pt Book Antiqua by Diligent Typesetter, Delhi and printed at Sai Print-o-Pack, New Delhi.

Library of Congress Cataloging-in-Publication Data

India, China and sub-regional connectivities in South Asia/edited by D. Suba Chandran, Bhavna Singh.
    pages cm
    Includes bibliographical references and index.
    1. South Asia—Commerce. 2. South Asia—Foreign economic relations—China. 3. China—Foreign economic relations—South Asia. 4. South Asia—Foreign economic relations—India. 5. India—Foreign economic relations—South Asia. 6. Regional economics—South Asia. I. Suba Chandran, D., editor. II. Singh, Bhavna, editor.
    HF1586.5.I53   337.1'54—dc23   2015   2015027855

ISBN: 978-93-515-0327-9 (HB)

The SAGE Team: N. Unni Nair, Alekha Chandra Jena, Anju Saxena and Vinitha Nair

Contents

List of Tables

List of Figures

List of Abbreviations

AAI	Airports Authority of India
ACIS	Advanced Cargo Information System
ADB	Asian Development Bank
ADC	Autonomous District Council
AH	Asian Highway
AJK	Azad Jammu and Kashmir
ALTID	Asian Land Transport Infrastructure Development
ASEAN	Association of Southeast Asian Nations
ASYCUDA	Automated Systems for Customs Data
ATM	Automatic Teller Machine
BADP	Border Area Development Programme
BBIMN	Bangladesh–Bhutan–India–Myanmar–Nepal
BCIM	Bangladesh–China–India–Myanmar Forum for Regional Cooperation
BIMSTEC	Bay of Bengal Initiative for Multi-Sectoral Technical and Economic Cooperation
BIS	Bureau of Indian Standards
BLO	Border Line Officer
BNP	Bangladesh Nationalist Party
BOT	Build–Operate–Transfer
BRO	Border Roads Organisation
BRTF	Border Roads Task Force
BSNL	Bharat Sanchar Nigam Limited
BSTI	Bangladesh Standards Testing Institute
C&F	Clearing and Forwarding Agents
CBM	Confidence-building Measures

CCEA	Cabinet Committee on Economic Affairs
CCTV	Closed Circuit Television
CFL	Central Food Laboratory
CII	Confederation of Indian Industry
CKD	Completely Knocked Down
CNPO	Chandel Naga People's Organization
CPA	Commonwealth Parliamentary Association
CPAPD	Chinese People's Association for Peace and Disarmament
CPC	Communist Party of China
CPD	Centre for Policy Dialogue
CTMS	Container Terminal Management System
DBO	Daulat Beg Oldi
DC	District Collector
DGFT	Directorate General of Foreign Trade
DIG	Deputy Inspector General of Police
ESCWA	Economic and Social Commission for Western Asia
EU	European Union
FDI	Foreign Direct Investment
GATT	General Agreement on Tariffs and Trade
GDP	Gross Domestic Product
GMS	Greater Mekong Sub-region
GOI	Government of India
GSDP	Gross State Domestic Product
HTC	Hill Tribe Council
ICD	Inland Clearance Depot
ICP	Integrated Check Post
ICT	Information and Communication Technology
ILP	Inner Line Permit
IMF	International Monetary Fund
IMU	Islamic Movement of Uzbekistan
INCB	International Narcotics Control Board
IPCS	Institute of Peace and Conflict Studies
ISAS	Institute of South Asian Studies
IT	Information Technology
ITBP	Indo-Tibetan Border Police
J&K	Jammu and Kashmir
KKH	Karakoram Highway
KNA	Kuki National Army
KRI	Key Research Institute

LAC	Line of Actual Control
LCS	Land Customs Station
LDC	Least Developed Countries
LEP	Look East Policy
LoC	Line of Control
LTK	Ladakh–Tibet–Kashgar
MCM	Meitei Council Moreh
MoU	Memorandum of Understanding
MPA	Maritime and Port Authority
MRP	Maximum Retail Price
NCT	New Mooring Container Terminal
NEC	Northeastern Council
NEFA	Northeast Frontier Agency
NFR	Northeast Frontier Railways
NGO	Non-governmental Organization
NH	National Highway
NHAI	National Highways Authority of India
NHPC	National Hydroelectric Power Corporation
NICCI	Nepal–India Chamber of Commerce and Industry
NLCPR	Non-lapsable Central Pool of Resource Scheme
NRB	Non-resident Bangladeshi
NSUC	Naga Students Union Chandel
NWUC	Naga Women Union Chandel
PGCB	Power Grid Company of Bangladesh
PGCI	Power Grid Company of India
PLA	People's Liberation Army
PMGSY	Prime Minister's Gram Sadak Yojana
PRC	People's Republic of China
PWD	Public Works Department
QPR	Quarterly Progress Report
RAP	Restricted Area Permission
RMB	Renminbi
RMG	Ready-made Garment
RoO	Rules of Origin
SAARC	South Asian Association for Regional Cooperation
SAFTA	South Asian Free Trade Area
SAGQ	South Asian Growth Quadrangle
SAPTA	SAARC Preferential Trade Arrangement
SARDP-NE	Special Accelerated Road Development Programme in Northeast

SASEC	South Asia Sub-regional Economic Cooperation
SD	Subdivision
SDMO	Subdivisional Magistrate Office
SKD	Semi-knocked Down
SLEPC	State-level Export Promotion Committee
SLOC	Sea Lines of Communications
SRMTS	SAARC Regional Multimodal Transport Study
TAR	Tibet Autonomous Region
TSP	Triple Superphosphate
UC	Utilization Certificate
UN	United Nations
UNDCP	United Nations Drug Control Program
UNESCAP	United Nations Economic and Social Commission for Asia and Pacific
UNLF	United National Liberation Front
VAT	Value-added Tax
VDC	Village Development Committee
WTCM	World Trade Centre Mumbai
WTO	World Trade Organization
WY	World's Yours

Preface

This volume by the Institute of Peace and Conflict Studies (IPCS) is a part of a project under the Asian Security Initiative of the John D. and Catherine T. MacArthur Foundation. Since its inception in 2009, the project has aimed at developing a framework for regional cooperation in Southern Asia by which India and China and other South Asian countries could cooperate on key challenges in the military, economic and infrastructure realms.

The first volume focusing on 'Military Confidence-building and India-China Relations: Fighting Distrust' edited by Maj. Gen. Dipankar Banerjee and Dr Jabin T. Jacob was released in 2013. This book remarkably shaped the foci of the project and set the prelude for the current volume which looks at the remaining two core areas identified under the project: expanding economic activity along the Sino-Indian border areas and developing infrastructure for connectivity between India and China.

Based on field research in Jammu and Kashmir, Himachal Pradesh, Nepal, Sikkim, Arunachal Pradesh, Manipur and Bangladesh along with similar studies across China, scholars prepared their first drafts that were discussed at a conference in Chengdu, China. These essays were subsequently revised after another round of discussion amongst the Indian scholars held in Gangtok, Sikkim.

Though the project was conceived and implemented based on extensive field trips all over South Asia, especially along border regions, there have been recent developments which are likely to shape the future course in this region. China's 'One Belt One Road' strategy along with its push for the Maritime Silk Road (MSR) was outlined at a time when the drafts of this volume were at an advanced stage. While these are significant developments, the essays in this volume predate this new Chinese push.

While most chapters outline political exigencies, economic hurdles, topographical advantages and disadvantages, the findings and recommendations are substantiated by extensive field trip inferences. The larger attempt has been to formulate recommendations and implementation strategies for respective decision-makers to take advantage of the window of opportunity that exists in South Asia today. Timely initiatives from these participating countries can immensely help to capitalize and consolidate the economic growth of the South Asian region.

It has been attempted to identify innovative ways of how bordering regions in South Asia can engage with each other for effective coordination in transport infrastructure and enhancement of trade activities. While there are obvious comparisons on the national level, there is also an attempt to look for regional solutions and enhanced engagement of the smaller administrative units of these countries in a more autonomous manner, for instance, envisaging a particular 'Sichuan model'.

It is most opportune to express our sincere gratitude to Maj. Gen. Dipankar Banerjee, Former Director of the Institute, along with Dr Jabin T. Jacob, who conceived this project. We are tremendously thankful to both of them for their support. We are also grateful to the John D. and Catherine T. MacArthur Foundation for entrusting this study to the IPCS. We express our sincere gratitude to all the Indian, Chinese, Nepalese and Bangladeshi participants at the Chengdu conference and to the Chinese People's Association for Peace and Disarmament (CPAPD) which helped with organizing and hosting the conference in China. Thanks are also due to Dr Mallika Joseph who helped at several stages of the project and IPCS researchers for helping with the editing and proofreading, especially Nayantara Shaunik, and Teshu Singh for her support in facilitating the book during the final stages.

We are also grateful to the Central University of Sikkim in Gangtok for helping us with facilitating a dialogue at the national level. As an extended part of this study, the Institute also constituted a Task Force led by Amb TCA Rangachari, Mr Jayadeva Ranada and Professor Madhu Bhalla, which held meetings in New Delhi and Gangtok, including a field trip to Nathu La.

The Task Force came out with a report titled 'Trans-Himalayan Trade 2020: Looking beyond Nathu La' besides which a series of essays titled *Nathu La Papers* were published by the Institute separately.

The editors are also immensely grateful to the publisher and his team for their patience and support in making this work possible.

D. Suba Chandran
Bhavna Singh

Border Trade as a Means of Integration in South Asia

1

Perspectives on Regional Cooperation: Envisaging a Sichuan Model

Li Tao*

Introduction

China's western development strategy presents a historic opportunity not only for Sichuan's development in general but also for Sichuan–South Asian regional cooperation in particular. As a major forerunner of China's western development strategy in this era of globalization and regional integration, Sichuan's economic relations and trade cooperation with its South Asian neighbours have become a matter of vital importance. Given its strategic position, Sichuan needs to make a comprehensive assessment and take concrete measures to enhance its engagement and cooperation with the South Asian countries in the political, economic and cultural realms in order to ensure rapid and sustainable economic development.

* This chapter was completed by the joint efforts of Li Tao, Wen Fude, Zhang Li, Chen Jidong, Yang Wenwu, Zhang Wei, Dai Yonghong, Yin Xi'nan, Song Zhihui, Zhang Lii, Ou Dongming, Xiang Yuanjun, Huang Zhengduo, Zeng Xiangyu, Tang Pengqi, Li Li, Chen Xiaoping, Huang Yunsong, Lei Ming, Li Jianjun and so on from the ISAS, Sichuan University. The author is grateful for their comments and contribution.

Sichuan's capability to embark on the path of becoming regional centre is highly predisposed given the fact that it is the only member of a one-trillion-yuan gross domestic product (GDP) club. Its market economy ranks first among the 12 provinces of western China and its GDP ranks ninth overall among provinces. These favourable indices are likely to be enhanced by the grand development strategy announced by the state for west China. In addition, Sichuan is likely to play a leading role in promoting the economic development of west China, and facilitating the southward opening up of China through its considerable advantages in infrastructure, transportation and a highly qualified human resource pool.

Sichuan's nodal role in China's western development strategy and attractive prospects of its cooperation with South Asia have received wide attention from abroad, especially from South Asia. It can also offer an effective model for South–South cooperation. All the above-mentioned factors suggest the importance of China–South Asia cooperation on the one hand, and Sichuan's significant role in this process on the other hand.

Significance of Sichuan-South Asia Cooperation

1. **Capitalizing Opportunities Presented by Economic Globalization and Regional Integration.** Globalization and regional integration have become universally accepted apertures for economic development. The grand transformation of world economy calls for enhanced regional and sub-regional cooperation between China and South Asia.
2. **Lack of Regional Cooperative Mechanism Exists between China and South Asia.** China has managed to develop a variety of regional and sub-regional cooperative mechanism (such as '10 Plus 3', '10 Plus 1'). However, there is no such mechanism covering both China and South Asia as yet. Such a stipulation logically suggests the pressing need to set up effective cooperative mechanisms and institutions.
3. **Economic Upsurge in China and Other South Asian Countries.** Rapid economic growth of China and South Asia (India in particular) has attracted worldwide attention.

Thus, further cooperation between these two Asian giants becomes essential in the context of global economic power transfer scenario (from the Atlantic region to the Asia–Pacific region).

4. **Sichuan as a Hinterland Zone for China's Western Development Strategy and Its Southward Development Initiative.** Given its geographic location as a backbone of China's coastal regions and their main connecting link with the western regions, China's western development strategy stipulates a central role for Sichuan, especially for its southwestern provinces, and considers it a major element of China's comprehensive opening-up strategy.

5. **Sichuan as a Bridge for China–South Asia Cooperation.** Besides being a bridge between east China and west China, on the one hand, and a hinterland special economic zone, on the other hand, Sichuan's cooperation with South Asian countries is also significant for defence and security reasons of the Chinese border and the stability and prosperity of its ethnic minority-inhabited regions.

Advantages from Sichuan-South Asia Cooperation

1. **Geographical Proximity.** Sichuan enjoys a favourable geographical location for developing cooperation with South Asia: it lies just next to the Bay of Bengal and has proximity to the Indian Ocean region and South Asia. The land transportation route from Sichuan to Myanmar and India is 3,000 km shorter than the maritime route via the Malacca Straits. Moreover, recent developments, such as the opening up of the Nathu La, establishment and operation of the Qinghai–Tibet railway and Yunnan–South Asia international transportation corridor, massive upgradation of the China–Nepal road network and the recently operationalized airline between China and South Asia, have considerably improved the transportation scenario between China and South Asia and offered brighter prospects for trade cooperation among them.

2. **Historical and Cultural Linkages.** Sichuan has developed economic and cultural exchanges and friendly connections

with South Asia from ancient times. Sichuanese merchants established business links with South Asia along the 'Southern Silk Road' as early as 300 BC. They travelled from Chengdu to Yunnan and subsequently Myanmar and did business with the Indian traders. The Indian businessmen picked up Sichuanese products and sold them in the Indian markets, while their Sichuanese counterparts took jewelleries and jades for their markets back home. Thus, a long-lasting history of bilateral trade laid sound foundations for the resumption of such business linkages in present times.

3. **Economic Complementarities.** Sichuan and South Asia have close complementarities in natural resources, industrial structure, structure of consumer demands and so on. These can provide a great platform for improving Sichuan–South Asia regional cooperation. For instance, Sichuan enjoys advantages in the industrial sector; its industrial products are considered competitive in the South Asian market in terms of quality and quantity. However, South Asia (India in particular) enjoys advantages in the financial sector, software, education and medical services and so forth. In other words, South Asia's advantages in the service sector and Sichuan's advantages in the industrial sector can meet the urgent needs of the other side and accelerate economic development of both.

4. **Human Resources.** Sichuan's leading role in the economic development of southwest China can be illustrated by its rapid economic growth rate, partly attributed to Sichuan's remarkable human resources advantage. In 2008 alone, about 270,000 professionals, comprising 2,000 with doctor's degree, 14,000 with master's degree, 114,000 undergraduates, 140,000 senior national school students, graduated from around 100 higher educational institutions in Sichuan. Institutions of higher education such as the Sichuan University are quite active in international programmes, offering educational services to a large number of international students (South Asian students in particular) each year, whose presence and efforts after returning to their original countries will greatly enhance Sichuan–South Asia economic cooperation.

5. **Institutional Patronage.** Sichuan enjoys intellectual support from major policy think tanks, especially the Institute of

South Asian Studies (ISAS), Sichuan University, in its endeavour towards enhancing cooperation with South Asia. The ISAS, Sichuan University, was founded in 1978, revamping the erstwhile India Studies Office (established in 1964 under late premier Zhou Enlai's instruction to revive the focus on foreign affairs). As a Key Research Institute (KRI) of humanities and social sciences at universities and the only Chinese higher educational institute specializing in South Asian studies, ISAS managed to build itself into an effective and influential South Asian studies agency with a fair reputation at home and abroad. Envisioning the principle of 'servicing Sichuan, going towards South Asia, deliberating globally', ISAS has done a tremendous work on framing a comprehensive opening-up strategy for China, striking a balance between sea and land, and the eastern and western regions. The ISAS also strives hard to become a vital think tank for Sichuan's Provincial Government and Communist Party of China's (CPC) Sichuan Committee. It has made great efforts to stimulate Sichuan–South Asian economic and trade cooperation and offer relevant advice and intellectual support, particularly in the following ways:

a. *Envisioning a Market Strategy for Sichuan.* The ISAS suggested a go-to South Asia market strategy for Sichuan, as early as 1986. ISAS paid attention to Sino-India economic and trade cooperation since earlier times and compiled the *Sino-Indian Economy and Trade Guidebook* in the 1990s and published *Researches on Sichuan-South Asia Economic and Trade Cooperation; Go to South Asia: A Guidance to Economic and Trade Cooperation with South Asia; A Study on Regional Cooperation among China, India, Myanmar and Bangladesh*; and *Strategy for Developing South Asian Market: A Case Study of Tibet and Its Uniqueness*. It has completed relevant projects, such as *Sichuan-South Asian Economic and Trade Cooperation Studies; Sichuan-South Asia Regional Cooperation: Prospects and Strategy; China's International Economic Cooperation: A Case Study of the Sichuan Province; China-ASEAN Free Trade Zone: Options for Sichuan; A Study on South Asia and West China Cooperation and Development; China's Cooperation with South Asia; A Study on Regional*

  Cooperation among China, India, Myanmar and Bangladesh and other works.

b. *Research Centres as Motors of Sichuan–South Asia Cooperation.* The ISAS has set up three centres, namely, the Centre for South Asia–West China Cooperation and Development Studies, Pakistan Studies Centre and the Centre for Tibetology and South Asia Research, conducting intensive research on all sorts of relevant issues. The three centres also facilitate frequent visits of officials and scholars from South Asia, furthering Sichuan–South Asia cooperation in a thorough manner.

c. *Functioning as Information and Service Centre for Enterprises.* The ISAS also did intensive work for enhancing the economic and trade linkages between Sichuan and South Asia. The ISAS faculty extended consultative services to officials, businessmen and scholars from South Asia on issues concerning bilateral and regional cooperation. The institute also held a series of important international conferences and invited entrepreneurs from South Asia and within China (Sichuan in particular). Such events and relevant dialogues, sodalities, discussions and meetings have effectively stimulated the economic and trade cooperation and friendly engagement between western China and Southern Asia.

In December 2003, ISAS hosted the International Conference on 'China's Western Development Strategy and South Asia: The Road Ahead'. Ambassadors from India, Pakistan, Nepal and Bangladesh and experts from think tanks, business elite and government agencies participated in the conference. Challenging issues such as 'potentials and prospects of West China–South Asia Cooperation' were discussed, and consensus on various issues was reached. Business dialogues between ambassadors and Sichuanese businessmen took place on the sidelines of the conference. Similar events also took place during the international conference on 'China-Pakistan Economic and Trade Cooperation: Present and Prospects', and 'China-Bangladesh Business Dialogue'. The ISAS also continues to make strenuous efforts to reinforce a two-way understanding between China and South Asia through its official website.

Major Hurdles to Sichuan–South Asia Cooperation

1. **Divergences in Sino-Indian Relations.** As rising Asian powers, the roles of both India and China affect the nature of cooperation in South Asia. From 2004 to 2007, China's trade with India alone amounted to 69.47 per cent, 70.08 per cent, 71.38 per cent and 76.33 per cent, respectively, of China's total trade with South Asian Association for Regional Cooperation (SAARC). While the China–Pakistan trade contributed to only 15.63 per cent, 15.96 per cent, 15.06 per cent and 12.92 per cent, respectively, from 2004 to 2007, the quantity of China–Bangladesh trade amounted to just 10.02 per cent, 9.296 per cent, 9.16 per cent and 6.795 per cent, respectively during the same period. Thus, a lack of understanding between China and India on significant issues hinders cooperation in the region at large. It is possible to argue that India's domination in SAARC impedes China–SAARC cooperation in general and Sichuan–SAARC cooperation in particular.

2. **Unstable Political, Economic and Security Conditions in South Asia.** Most South Asian countries are undergoing major political and economic transformations, and their growth is slowed down by unstable political, economic and security conditions. Poverty, ethnic/religious conflicts, territorial disputes and terrorism are some such issues which hinder cooperation between Sichuan and South Asia.

3. **Insufficient Infrastructure.** Competent infrastructure in transportation, energy and communication sectors is a prerequisite for successful economic cooperation. However, South Asia suffers from inadequate number of highways, inefficient working of railways and airports and severe shortages of power supply. Huge investments and considerable construction period are required to improve the condition of these sectors.

4. **Information and Regulation Gap.** Sichuan's foreign trade itself suffers from certain inherent institutional obstacles, for instance, unsound market system, which leads to uncertainties in Sichuan–South Asia cooperation. These irregularities need to be timely rectified to avoid any increase in transaction costs and transaction exposures.

Despite the above-mentioned impediments, Sino-Indian economic and trade cooperation presents huge opportunities for regional cooperation, and Sichuan can play a unique role in China's efforts to handle such opportunities and challenges. Therefore, it is significant to enhance Sichuan–South Asia cooperation and build Sichuan as an economic engine for China's southward development initiative as well as a cornerstone for regional security, and a propeller for the stability and development of China's minority-populated regions.

Recommendations for Intensifying Sichuan-South Asia Cooperation

Both Sichuan and the South Asian countries can benefit tremendously from the opportunities provided by the expanding nature of trade in this region. Towards this aim, they need to bolster their economic and cultural milieu by promoting sustainable and rapid economic growth by the following means:

1. **Setting Up a Regional Mechanism for China–South Asia Cooperation.** China–South Asia relations (Sino-Indian relations in particular) and India–Pakistan relations are progressively improving. A working mechanism for opening up western China is being institutionalized. Further, constructing a China–South Asia regional economic community will help in transforming Sichuan's geographical disadvantage of non-access to the Pacific into advantage through access to the Indian Ocean. As an inevitable choice of Sichuan's 'southward opening up', the proposed community will cover a land area of more than 10 million km^2 with a population of around 2.6 billion. By reducing the geographical inaccessibility or semi-inaccessibility for the tri-junctions of west China, South Asia and Southeast Asia, it will aid the formation of a consciousness of 'Chindia', cultivating political trust between China and India. This would tremendously increase the prospects for building a 'Harmonious Asia' and peace and stability across the Chinese frontier.

Institutional mechanisms for regional coordination, interest sharing and interest compensation among stakeholders at varying levels need to be set up. Sichuan must use its advantages and actively participate in the process of mechanism building for Sichuan–South Asia economic cooperation.

a. *International Fairs as a Mode of Economic Cooperation.* Setting up programmes such as the 'China-South Asia Economic Cooperation Forum' during the Western China International Fair held annually in Chengdu can bolster economic linkages. Since these informal forums are attended by high-level dignitaries such as politicians, businessmen and experts from South Asia, speeding up held-up issues could result in swifter cooperation.

b. *Setting Up Headquarters in Chengdu.* Considering its geographical position, Sichuan could be made the centre of 'China-South Asia Economic Cooperation Community'. The regional countries would also benefit by reaching consensus on the 'China-South Asia Economic Integration Framework Agreement', and setting up 'China-South Asia Economic Cooperation Organization' which can offer better institutional frameworks.

c. *China–South Asia Unconventional Security Mechanism.* A regional arrangement also requires cooperation on unconventional security matters, such as drug smuggling, human trafficking, illegal immigration, piracy, terrorism, arms smuggling, money laundering, international economic crimes, cybercrimes and environmental protection. China and other South Asian countries need to take concrete and workable measures to motivate cooperation for upgrading their capabilities to meet unconventional security challenges and safeguarding regional peace and security.

2. **Strengthening Logistical Support.** An open communication, information and logistics system linking the coastal areas to the interregional trade centres must be built for consolidating Sichuan–South Asia regional cooperation. It will undoubtedly facilitate economic development of all the provinces falling within the circuit of cooperation.

Sichuan must join hands with Yunnan, Tibet and Xinjiang to construct international passageways for facilitating Sichuan–South Asia regional cooperation. The suggestion to construct '1 Bridge Plus 3 Lines' and '2 Old Airlines Plus 4 New Airlines' put forward in this regard, aiming to linking Sichuan with Indian Ocean, will assist in establishing a multimodal land, flight and freight transportation system between Sichuan and the rest of South Asia.

a. *Land Transportation: The 1 Bridge Plus 3 Routes Model.* Within this model, '1 bridge' refers to the South Asian land bridge, while '3 routes' refer to the eastern route, middle route and western route along the land bridge.

The eastern route of the South Asian land bridge (constructed in collaboration with Yunnan) would span through Chengdu–Kunming–Dali–Ruili–Mandalay–Sittwe and to the Indian Ocean. This would shorten the transport route between the Middle East, Africa, Europe and Sichuan by 5,000 km, securing the route for China's oil imports.

The middle route of the South Asian land bridge (constructed in collaboration with Tibet) would connect Chengdu to Ya'an–Kangding–Litang–Bowo–Nyingchi–Lhasa–Camphor Wood–Kathmandu–Calcutta–New Delhi–Mumbai, as well as New Delhi and Calcutta (Kolkata). This route will effectively benefit the minority regions in China and enhance the stability of China's southern frontiers.

The western route of the South Asian land bridge (constructed in collaboration with Xinjiang) would connect Chengdu to Karachi (Pakistan) via Lanzhou–Urumqi–Kashgar–Khunjerab, Havelian and Islamabad. This would enhance economic development in Tibet, Xinjiang and other parts of South Asia.

b. *Air Transportation: 2 Existing Airlines Plus 4 New Airlines.* The proposed air transportation system between China and South Asia will comprise the previously existing Chengdu–Lhasa–Kathmandu airline and the Chengdu–Karachi airline, along with four recently inaugurated airlines, namely, the Chengdu–Kunming–Calcutta airline, the Chengdu–Colombo airline, the Chengdu–Dhaka and

the Chengdu–Bangalore airlines. The Chengdu–Lhasa–
Kathmandu airline (1,854 km, two hours flight time)
would aid Sichuan's trade with India and Nepal, and
boost intraregional tourism. The Chengdu–Karachi airline (4,600 km) will provide another major stimulus for
Sichuan's economic and trade cooperation with South
Asia as well as the Middle East, within which Karachi's
potential as an intermediary linking Sichuan and the
Middle East and Africa could be fully explored.

The 1,200-km Chengdu–Kunming–Calcutta airline
will be a major step towards operationalizing the flight
and freight multimodal transportation system between
China and India, thereby greatly augmenting Sichuan–
India business links. The 3,350-km Chengdu–Bangalore
airline (operational since 2010) is considered another
major stimulus for Sichuan–South Asia cooperation,
especially in the information technology (IT) and tourism sectors. The 1,154-km Chengdu–Dhaka airline will
prove to be a critical link for Sichuan–Bangladesh business links, and a platform for flight and freight multimodal transportation between them. In addition, the
Chengdu–Colombo airline (extending 3,651 km) would
accelerate Sichuan–Sri Lanka economic and trade cooperation. These air transportation systems will ensure
a systematic connection between Chengdu and the
capitals/economic hubs of South Asian countries, and
Chengdu would thus become a major logistical hub for
China–South Asia engagement.

c. *Substantiating the Existing Links with Upgraded Information Systems.* Considered the Silicon Valley of western
China, Chengdu has the potential to develop itself into
a world-class IT hub on the models of the Indian IT
industry having its hub at Bengaluru. A positive move
towards building a regional IT zone would be to establish a direct air link between Chengdu and Bengaluru.

3. **Instituting a Pan-Himalayan Water Regulation Mechanism.**
The Tibetan Plateau, known as the 'water tower of Asia', is
the source of the Indus, the Ganges, the Yangtze River, the
Yellow River and many other major rivers of Asia. Hence,
this region becomes crucial to the lifeline of China and other

South Asian countries. However, this region is especially amenable to environmental hazards and climate change. The drastic rise in temperatures in the pan-Himalayan region has led many scholars to predict an impending complete glacier meltdown in the Himalayas by 2035. Thus, climate change posits a very serious challenge to the ecology of South Asia and most parts of western China, including Nepal and Sichuan. In case of any adversity, the freshwater resources of 1.3 billion Asians will be seriously threatened.

Threats to the South Asian ecology are already noticeable in the lower-altitude countries of South Asia, such as Bangladesh and Maldives, where rise in the water levels of the Indian Ocean has led to immersion of portions of their land. Even in western China, damage and degradation of the ecosystems and biodiversity losses have raised alarms. However, threats to the Himalayan ecology are by no means widely noticed or a matter of debate in the academic circles.

Therefore, constructing a pan-Himalayan water resource-regulation mechanism and protecting the 'water tower of Asia' have to be the major thrust areas of cooperation between China and South Asia. And being the biggest economy with geographical proximity to South Asia, Sichuan should actively participate in China–South Asia cooperation and promote the establishment of this mechanism:

a. *Implementing Ecological Protection Projects.* As a joint strategic response to climate change, the following measures can help in regional cooperation: cross-border biodiversity conservation, rationalization of grassland utilization and protection of grassland, rationalization of forestry utilization and protection of forestry and wetland protection and wildlife management.

   The southern slope of Himalayas will result in serious soil erosion and geological disasters in general because of its huge hydraulic, thermal and gravity gradients, and floods and sedimentation along with damages to natural plants in South Asian countries in particular. The 'Three Rivers ecological protection project', mainly operated from Sichuan and Qinghai, would be highly constructive for the improvement of the ecological system in

South Asia. The Sichuan–South Asia cooperation to protect the ecosystem in Tibetan Plateau is very promising in this regard. In addition, Sichuan could participate in the ecological construction and protection programme of the 'Source of Three Rivers National Nature Reserve', safeguarding the birthplace of the Mekong River and taking care of the interests and concerns of downstream countries.

b. *Cooperation on Regulation and Development of Transnational Rivers.* Enhancing mutual trust to establish hydrological information-sharing system, rationalizing the utilization of water resources, co-regulating and jointly developing transnational rivers would be some of the major areas of cooperation under this mechanism.

A Shared Vision for the 21st century between China and India (signed on January 2008) explicitly mentions that 'the two sides agree that this (sharing hydrological data) has contributed positively to building mutual understanding and trust'. Therefore, both countries should deepen understanding, expand common consensus, enhance mutual trust and promote sharing of hydrological data and cooperation on cross-border rivers in the region.

c. *Poverty-relief Cooperation.* This would entail sharing experiences in poverty relief; adopting 'technology-oriented poverty reduction, knowledge-oriented poverty reduction and industry-oriented poverty reduction' and other forms of cooperation to alleviate poverty in the pan-Himalayan region.

The unusual geographical environment in the Tibetan Plateau and Himalayan region has resulted in very poor human living conditions. Poverty is the largest obstacle to ecology protection in this region. Alleviating poverty, promoting rational exploitation and utilization of resources, as well as realizing regional sustainable development have become a major challenge as well as opportunity for cooperation among relevant parties. Sichuan and the South Asian countries should join hands to eradicate poverty.

d. *Personnel Training and Technological Cooperation.* Technical personnel, planning and input are major elements for solving ecological problems. Cooperation on environment-protection technology, personnel training and investment management; access to each other's experiences and lessons on ecological environment protection; as well as establishing personnel exchanges mechanism can help in increasing mutual understanding and trust.

Sichuan and South Asian countries should learn from each other in combating common challenges to ecological environment. India can benefit from China's support in its 'Himalayan ecological protection plan', especially in technology and human resource.

4. **Cooperation through Educational Exchanges.** As an important premise for Sichuan–South Asian economic and trade cooperation, educational cooperation can provide a major impetus for deepening sustainable cooperation. It can play a pivotal role in the paradigm shift from 'geopolitics to geo-civilization'. Sichuan and South Asia enjoy a solid historical basis for educational and cultural exchanges. The renowned universities in China such as Sichuan University, University of Electronic Science and Technology of China and so on can provide superior educational resources for transnational educational cooperation. The higher educational institutes in South Asian countries also have their own advantages.

In order to strengthen the educational cooperation between Sichuan and South Asian countries, the chapter proposes:

a. *Setting Up Sichuan–South Asia Educational Leadership Exchange Mechanism.* In order to promote Sichuan–South Asia educational exchange and cooperation, we suggest that the leadership mechanism should be led by the respective Education Department and Foreign Affairs Office of Sichuan's Provincial Government. Major universities of Sichuan, such as the Sichuan University, should participate in the mechanism. Needless to say, educational counsellors from all South Asian consulates, for instance, in Chengdu and other related personnel, need to be included within the process.

b. *Setting Up Relevant Higher Education Associations.* A close relationship between the major universities of South

Asia and Sichuan calls for a stable and workable Higher Education Cooperation Association. Such an association would promote China–South Asia personnel (international students and scholars) and academic exchange and cooperation.

c. *Learning from the '1 Plus 2 Plus 1' System between Sichuan University and the University of Washington.* Setting up international students exchanging mechanism and carrying out a 'Sichuan-South Asia Thousand Youth Exchange Programme' will further such associations.

d. *Promoting Exchanges in Leading Sectors of Education.* It is advisable to introduce services of superior educational sectors of South Asian countries (such as the IT education of India) to Sichuan Province, even to cooperate for running educational institutions in Sichuan. Another option is to export China's competitive educational service in certain sectors (such as education in medical science) to South Asia and enhance linkages.

e. *Promoting Cooperation in Distant Education.* Cooperation in distant education would require great efforts by making use of IT, such as computers, Internet and so on. Both sides can select each other's leading projects to establish collaboration on educational enrolment and training.

f. *Linking Up Educational Cooperation with Business Cooperation.* Targeted training sessions can be offered to employees from both Sichuan and South Asian countries. Another approach for educational cooperation would be to transform relevant companies into demonstration centres of economic collaboration, which can integrate a number of elements, such as talent exchange and training, creative production, research and development operations as well as exhibition and trade.

5. **Capitalizing on the Cultural Resources in Sichuan through Sichuan–South Asia Cultural/Religious Dialogue Mechanisms.** Sichuan is the birthplace of Taoism and thus a huge reservoir of South Asian culture and capable of deeply imprinting on cultural ties. Buddhism is another cultural belief that significantly bonds China with South Asia. Sichuan also boasts a huge Buddhist legacy through cultural relics such

as the Daci Temple that Xuanzang visited. The ISAS and the Institute of Taoist and Religious Studies at the Sichuan University are committed to comprehensive research on culture and religion in South Asia. They could become the major think tanks in conceptualizing civilizational and religious mechanisms for the region.

Such cultural mechanisms would enable Sichuan to take the initiative when developing Sichuan–South Asia relations and re-examine the current situation of its communication with South Asian countries, as well as to conceptualize the prospects in a better way. The basic elements of such a communication should cover the following main aspects:

a. *Setting Up Institutionalized Cultural/Religious Forum; Promoting Cultural Exchanges and Academic Communications.* Issues such as homogeneity and heterogeneity of the Chinese and Indian civilizations, cultural exchanges between China and South Asia in ancient times, Buddhist scriptures translations, backflow of Buddhism, Tao Te Ching's spread in South Asia, comparisons between the thought of Taoism and Hinduism and so on can be discussed at length to look for scope of cooperation. International scholars and people from religious circles could be invited to pay visits to renowned Buddhist temples and Taoist temples in Sichuan, or to the famous scenic spots which are rich in Buddhist and Taoist culture, such as Mount Emei and Mount Qingcheng. This would help in clarifying and enhancing perceptual understanding on Chinese culture and the cultural geography of Sichuan. Domestic and overseas prominent persons and eminent scholars from renowned South Asian universities could be invited to deliver academic speeches in universities in Sichuan or government agencies.

b. *Reinforcing Confucius Institutes/Gandhi Institutes.* Setting up these institutes would be helpful in deepening the impact of Chinese soft power in South Asian countries, and will enable its people to have better understanding of the history, culture and customs of South Asia. It will help to cultivate a solid cultural foundation for future generations between China and South Asian countries.

c. *Enhancing Sichuan–South Asia Media and Communication.* In order to create a positive atmosphere about the ties and for an overall deepened understanding between China and South Asian countries, both sides should strengthen media conversation and communication and build a positive public opinion. Both sides should be encouraged to set up press stations in each other's territorial units.

d. *Organizing Sichuan–South Asia Cultural Exchange Weeks.* Sichuan could hold events such as the Chinese Film Week, the Chinese Photography Week, the Chinese Kung Fu Culture Week, the Chinese Tourism Week, the Chinese Cuisine Week and the Chinese Book Fair in major cities across South Asian countries, such as New Delhi, Bangalore, Calcutta, Bombay, Madras, Islamabad, Karachi, Colombo, Kathmandu, Dhaka and Thimphu. Sichuan could invite related agencies of the South Asian countries to Chengdu, Mianyang, Leshan and other major cities around Sichuan to hold influential events, such an Indian Film Week, an Indian Yoga Week, an Indian Dance Week, an Indian Photography Week, a Pakistani Film Week, a Pakistani Cultural Week, a Sri Lankan Cultural Week, a Sri Lankan Tourism Week, a Sri Lankan Photography Week, a Bangladeshi Film Week, a Nepalese Tourism Week, a Bhutanese Tourism Week and a Maldivian Tourism Week and so forth.

2

Border Trade in Ladakh, Tibet and Kashgar (LTK): Premature or Political Investment?

D. Suba Chandran

Introduction

India and China commenced limited border trade across the Nathu La in 2006; according to the government, 29 items are to be exported from India, and 14 items are to be imported from China.[1] This border trade takes place primarily between Sikkim and Tibet Autonomous Region (TAR), which remained a part of a feeder Silk Route until 1962. Can India and China consider opening a similar border trade between Ladakh, Tibet and Kashgar (LTK), which were also part of a feeder Silk Route until 1962? The following sets of questions need to be addressed, if a proposal to open border trade in this region should be projected. What would be the political objectives of allowing border trade in the LTK sector? What would be the economic objectives of border trade in the LTK? What was the nature of trade in these sectors before the closure of the Silk Route in 1962? Does the situation in 2010, almost after five

---

[1] For the complete list of items, see 'Indo-China Border Trade through Nathu La Pass', Online Web URL: http://sikkimindustries.gov.in/report%20on%20 nathula%20trade.pdf.

decades of the closure, warrant the opening of border trade, from an economic perspective? What items could be traded if the LTK region is opened for border trade? Are there sufficient goods to be traded, or will this go the cross-Line of Control (LoC) trade way? Are the economies complementary? What is the nature of existing infrastructure? Is there adequate infrastructure in terms of roads, markets, business communities and so forth which could facilitate border trade? Should the focus of trade be on the movement of goods only or should it include trade in services as well? How would this border trade help local communities in the LTK? What are the likely challenges and fallouts of a border trade in the LTK?

Border Trade in the LTK: Understanding the Political and Economic Objectives

What is the primary objective behind projecting a proposal for border trade in the LTK region? Is the objective a popular one — based on local expectations, aimed at improving the peripheries of India and China to interact more closely and reinvent their historical ties? Is the objective a political one — based on existing political problems in these border regions, aimed at bringing peace and stability in the LTK through border trade? Is the objective a strategic one — based on the larger issue of the India–China relationship itself, aimed at strengthening and expanding ties at every level between the two countries?

One should be clear regarding the objectives; for, some may be relatively achievable and some may be difficult to pursue. Once the objectives are clear, it would be easier to propose strategies to pursue them. This chapter intends to explore the above-mentioned three objectives, along with their limitations and fallouts.

First, the economic objectives of border trade in the LTK region should remain limited, for various reasons explained subsequently. From an Indian perspective, in terms of border trade in Ladakh, not much can be traded with the other side.[2] Even if trade

---

[2] This will depend on how border trade is defined in the Sino-Indian context; if it primarily refers to goods produced within the border regions and 'traded to' the other side, it will have limited impact. If it means goods 'traded through' the border regions, it may, however, have a different impact.

is allowed to be of a 'transit' nature, meaning, goods produced outside these three regions are allowed to be traded through the LTK, again from an Indian perspective, it will be limited. Ladakh has serious problems of connectivity with the rest of India. As of now, there are only two routes that link the region with the rest of India: the first one is through Zoji La, in the Kashmir Valley, and the second is through the Baralacha La, from Himachal Pradesh. Both routes are treacherous and are susceptible to rough weather conditions: the Srinagar–Kargil–Leh route through Zoji La is closed for six months during the year and the Manali–Keylong–Leh route is closed for nine months. Even when they are opened, both these routes are not easy even for the movement of people in smaller vehicles, let alone goods in trucks.

Second, precisely for the above reasons, border trade is unlikely to provide a fillip to the overall Sino-Indian economic relationship. Hence, the primary objective of border trade cannot be aimed at the larger goal of economic integration. Neither can there be many fallouts for the local economy unless both countries decide to open this region for bilateral trade and use it as a transit point. The only option, which cannot be a publicly stated objective, is to follow the cross-LoC trade model between India and Pakistan. Though both countries initiated the cross-LoC trade as an unofficial border trade,[3] in reality, both India and Pakistan selectively close their eyes to the movement of non-Kashmiri goods.[4] Unless New Delhi and Beijing also pursue a similar strategy in terms of opening border trade for local items, while simultaneously closing their eyes when goods are traded from the rest of India and China, the possibility of a substantial border trade in the LTK will remain a pipe dream.[5]

---

[3] Though cross-LoC trade cannot technically be called border trade, the primary objective of this trade is to allow the movement of goods between the two sub-regions of J&K.

[4] Garlic and coconuts are the most traded items in the cross-LoC trade; the former comes from China, through the Northern Areas along the Karakoram Highway (KKH), and the latter from south India through Punjab.

[5] A distinction needs to be made here, in terms of the economic fallouts of the border trade to Ladakh and the rest of the two regions in the LTK. While it may be beneficial to Tibet and Kashgar whether this trade remains primarily a border trade or has certain aspects of transit trade—officially or unofficially, Ladakh may have less advantages to take out of this.

Third, perhaps, because of the above two reasons, the objectives of border trade need to be a mixture of political–strategic–economic, aimed at bringing peace and stability in the LTK region. In this case, border trade, primarily in goods, may not make economic sense but can strengthen a larger political–strategic objective, especially if the economic interaction of the region has a 'transit' aspect and involves trade in services.

Border Trade in the LTK over the Ages: Reviving the Silk Route

The name Silk Route, immortalized and romanticized by historians, anthropologists, travellers and treasure hunters, is an anomaly. First, it was never a single route; though it linked modern-day China and Europe, in reality, it was a series of routes supplanted by multiple feeders. While the feeders linked regional economies with the main arteries of the European and Chinese land mass, at times, depending on the season and political situation along the arteries, trade was in fact carried out through the feeders. It was actually a network of routes. Second, it was called a 'Silk Route' only in the 19th century; silk was one of the many commodities that travelled along these routes.

Four empires — Roman, Persian, Indian and Han — interacted in the beginning; in fact, it was because of the political stability that these four empires provided that merchants and traders could commute from one region to another. Not only traders but also religious ideas moved along these routes; Buddhism, Islam and Christianity — all three religions — moved across the above four empires and their successors. Invaders, from Genghis Khan to Tamerlane, also traversed the Silk Route.

While Kashgar was a part of the primary artery, Tibet and Ladakh were a part of the feeders, in both senses. The regional economies of Tibet, Ladakh, Kashmir and Punjab tried to link to the main artery mainly through the Kargil–Gilgit axis; at times, because of political problems in Xinjiang and Central Asia, primary trade was carried out using this feeder route. Most of Yarkand's trade through this axis via the Karakoram Pass was primarily a result of the exchange of religious ideas.

In the LTK sector, the following four features could be observed in the Silk Route. First, not all the three regions mentioned here had the same level of productivity and contribution in the Silk Route. For instance, Tibet's indigenous goods were limited primarily to gold, rock, salt, borax, musk, yak tails and wool, while it imported shawls, saffron and dried fruits from the Kashmir Valley via Ladakh.[6] Even today, agricultural productivity in Ladakh is limited and not self-sufficient; from salt to wheat, everything has always been procured from outside Ladakh. Neither has Ladakh produced raw materials or finished goods in abundance. The only exception has been animal husbandry, especially the rearing of sheep. According to the Animal Husbandry Department of the Jammu and Kashmir (J&K) Government,

> Ladakh region has the distinction of having the most Pashmina producing goats. Pashmina fibre has a unique position among animal fibres for its fineness, warmth, lightness, softness and ability to absorb dyes and moisture. Since olden times, Kashmir has brought Pashmina, commonly termed as *Cashmere wool,* to the world by producing woven garments of extremely fine quality.[7]

Second, Leh and Kargil in Ladakh were merely trading depots/hubs in the routes, as most of the goods that originated from India came from Srinagar, Amritsar and Hoshiarpur.[8] Besides the wool and salt from Changthang, Ladakh did not have much to offer that could be traded in the Silk Route.[9] The rural economy in

---

[6] Janet Rizvi, *Trans-Himalayan Caravans: Merchant Princes and Peasant Traders in Ladakh* (New Delhi: Oxford, 1999), 9–10. According to Rizvi, 'a peculiar feature of Tibet's trade was that much of it—particularly with other Buddhist countries like Ladakh and Bhutan, also with China—was carried on under the guise of official religious missions, in which the commodities exchanged were designated as a "tribute" from lesser power and "presents" from a greater one'.

[7] Department of Sheep Husbandry, Government of J&K, Online web URL: http://www.jkanimalhusbandry.net/sheep.htm#Historical%20Background.

[8] Outside modern-day India, goods from the then Mughal and British India also originated from Shikarpur, Peshawar, Quetta, Jalalabad and Kabul, feeding into the Silk Route via Leh and Kargil.

[9] The Changpas, the nomads of the Changthang region, reared livestock. Their wool, meat, cashmere and some milk products were primarily used for local consumption.

Ladakh was mostly a subsistent one; the best example being that of the salt of the Changthang region.[10]

Third, the local communities in Leh and Kargil were never a part of the big business groups; to refer to Janet Rizvi's phrase, they were more 'peasant traders' and less 'merchant princes'.[11] The involvement of local people in Leh and Kargil was limited to transporting goods from Leh and Kargil up to Skardu and Gilgit, Srinagar, Zanskar, Amritsar and Lhasa. While the Shia Muslims of the Kargil region primarily transported goods in ponies towards the north and the west, the Buddhists of the Leh region primarily transported to Lhasa and Karakoram Pass.[12]

Fourth, more than the products, there was a substantial movement of ideas and armies along the Silk Route, primarily between Ladakh and Tibet. Both Buddhism and the armies of Tibet and Ladakh travelled on both sides, during different periods of history.[13] The monasteries and the legends of this region highlight this movement along the Silk Route between Ladakh and Tibet.

The quantum of illegal trade is small and takes place primarily along the Tibet–Ladakh border. First, the illegal trade between Kashgar and Ladakh is not heard of, primarily, because Kashgar is better connected with the Gilgit-Baltistan region, which is under Pakistan's control. The Kargil–Skardu sector has not been opened yet across the LoC; hence, the level of smuggling or movement of illegal goods across the LoC in Kargil–Skardu–Gilgit–Kashgar sector is irrelevant. Second, there is a strong monitoring of this sector by the Indian and Pakistani militaries, which makes any movement difficult. Third, in terms of topography, the LoC is not porous or easily breachable.

---

[10] The Changthang region also had numerous lakes: Tso Kar, Tso Moriri and Pangong Tso. Salt was primarily procured from the Tso Kar, which was sold in the rest of Ladakh; due to the laborious process and inferior quality, Changthang salt has become irrelevant, namely, the bigger market. Today, mainland iodized salts have taken over the local markets.

[11] Janet Rizvi, *Trans-Himalayan Caravans: Merchant Princes and Peasant Traders in Ladakh* (New Delhi: Oxford, 1999).

[12] Interviews with former transporters (who are now really old and few) and their descendants.

[13] Janet Rizvi, *Ladakh: Crossroads of High Asia* (New Delhi: Oxford, 1996); Jacqueline Fewkes, *Trade and Contemporary Society along the Silk Road: An Ethnohistory of Ladakh* (London: Routledge, 2008).

On the other hand, in the Ladakh–Tibet sector, a small section is engaged in illegal trade, mostly as couriers, to transport smuggled goods from Tibet into Ladakh. In most cases, Tibetan refugees undertake smuggling with some local support. Chinese crockery and quilts are the most smuggled items, primarily for local consumption, in Ladakh. Besides, there are minor items, mainly trekking gear, from shoes to tents, which are smuggled from (and through) Tibet.[14] One can see these items openly displayed and sold in the markets of Ladakh; the state is silent on the issue, for it neither accepts nor denies the presence of this smuggling.[15] Officials on the Indian side ignore this (unofficially, of course) trade for three reasons: first, they consider it insignificant and not affecting the overall trade basket in Ladakh; second, they believe it feeds into the local tourism economy; and third, given the remoteness of this region, this illegal trade, in fact, is beneficial for the local community.

Border Trade: Lessons, Threats and Challenges

Border trade in Ladakh is not very new to J&K either in the past or in recent years. While the past has been explained in the previous section, an analysis of recent developments in J&K relating to border trade should be taken into consideration. It is important to understand the negative fallouts; else, this initiative will create multiple expectations with few achievements at the ground.

First, since 2008, India and Pakistan have allowed the movement of goods through the LoC; this followed the opening of the LoC for the limited movement of divided families.[16] The primary problem of the cross-LoC trade is linked to the lack of necessary infrastructure; there is a lack of a proper banking system and communication network, and even today, it continues to exist primarily as a barter trade. Any border trade in the LTK sector should consider this important problem to avoid it by ensuring

---

[14] Interviews and personal observations.

[15] Some officials, though they agree that smuggling is inevitable, consider it is primarily used for local consumption and hardly goes beyond J&K.

[16] See D. Suba Chandran, 'Expanding Cross-LoC Interactions', *IPCS Issue Brief* (September 2009).

sufficient infrastructure for uninterrupted trade.[17] Second, traders in the cross-LoC trade are frustrated because of the difference in the objectives of trade when compared to what the governments of India and Pakistan expect out of this economic initiative.

While the government designed this as a 'trade to other Kashmir', the traders expected it to be a 'trade through other Kashmir'. Kashmiri traders expected this as a transit trade, resulting in goods from J&K reaching the Gulf and Europe via Rawalpindi and Karachi. On the other hand, the governments wanted this to be a nominal and token trade as a confidence-building measure (CBM). In fact, the governments see it as a political CBM rather than an economic CBM. Third, since this is a zero-duty trade, non-Kashmiri traders, primarily from Punjab (on both sides of the Indo-Pak international border) and even from Gujarat and Sindh, jumped into the trade and started exploiting the 'no duty' provision. All they had to do was to find 'proxy traders' in J&K who act as agents taking a percentage of the trade. Today, cross-LoC trade is more a proxy trade.

What are the possibilities that the above-mentioned mistakes observed in the cross-LoC trade will also be reflected in Ladakh's border trade in the LTK region? First and foremost, business establishments in Ladakh are poorly developed to organize successful border trade. Neither are there successful business communities and traders, nor are there adequate agricultural and manufacturing goods to trade. Whatever little the Silk Route could develop, in terms of cultivating a small group of business families, their descendants have found alternative means today after the closure of the Silk Route in 1962.[18] While the Silk Route families fondly remember 'those days' and would be willing to do business if the road is reopened, it is more out of romanticism than cold economic calculations.[19] Today, the economies of Kargil and Leh districts are more integrated with the rest of India.

[17] One should also consider the reverberations of opening border trade in the LTK region with basic infrastructure on the cross-LoC trade.

[18] Most business groups have migrated from Ladakh or have found alternative opportunities.

[19] Preliminary findings of an ongoing anthropological study on 'Silk Route Families' conducted by this researcher researched on what happened to those families who traded along the Silk Route. Today, their descendants are settled in Kargil, Leh, Srinagar, Jammu, Chandigarh, Amritsar, Hoshiarpur and New Delhi and are engaged in different occupations.

Second, thanks to the boom in the tourism industry in the last two decades, Ladakh has almost shifted from a land-based economy to a services-based economy largely thriving on the tourism sector.[20] Even the nomads of Changthang region, who are known for their sheep rearing, are shifting professions and crowding Leh to engage themselves in tourism-related activities, as cooks, guides and assistants to trekkers.[21] Besides, there is also mounting pressure from environmentalists to protect natural resources, which affects nomadic life.[22] The recent announcement of creating a wildlife sanctuary in the entire Changthang region by the government of J&K, according to the nomads, is likely to affect their livelihood further.

Third, if Ladakh is opened for border trade without adequate infrastructure and capacity building, there is a greater chance of non-Ladakhis making use of and profiting from it. As of now, the local community in Leh believes that their market has been completely taken over by Kashmiri traders' shops. Tibetan refugees have numerous exclusive shops and markets in Leh, mostly selling smuggled goods and small ornaments. One of the primary complaints of Kashmiri traders now engaged in cross-LoC trade is related to the hijacking of the trade by Punjabi traders from Amritsar and New Delhi. The size, contacts and trade basket of these traders from outside J&K — and in the case of LTK region, from outside Ladakh — are too big for the local business communities to compete.

Fourth, the political boundaries and popular sentiments therein should be taken into account while opening the LTK region for border trade. Ladakh on the Indian side is not a monolithic region — in terms of both population and geography. It consists of two districts: Leh and Kargil; the former is a Buddhist majority, while the latter is a Shia majority district. People from the Kargil district are more interested in opening the Kargil–Skardu–Gilgit road for the movement of both people and goods, while the people of Leh are keener in opening the Leh–Kailash Mansarovar route, more for the movement of people than for the goods.

---

[20] See Ladakh Autonomous Hill Council, 'Ladakh 2025: A Road Map for Progress and Prosperity', http://leh.nic.in/VISION_DOCUMENT.PDF.

[21] Interviews with locals in Ladakh.

[22] See Tsewang Namgail et al., 'Pashmina production and socio-economic changes in the Indian Changthang: Implications for natural resource management', *Natural Resources Forum* 34(3) (August 2010): 222–230.

Any efforts to open the LTK region for border trade should consider the opening of Kargil–Skardu–Gilgit axis; else, it will create new political and communal problems within Ladakh. Skardu and Gilgit are part of the Northern Areas administered by Pakistan. Islamabad has always been reluctant to open the Northern Areas to outsiders and has been treating this region as its colony.[23]

The Road Ahead

Given the inherent problems associated with the LTK region, trade in goods may not be beneficial to Ladakh. Even if it does, it will be one sided. While it may still make economic sense, the security establishment in India will be extremely wary of such a lopsided trade.

However, trade in services may be a better idea worth exploring in terms of tourism and gas pipelines. In particular, the opening of the Kailash Mansarovar route for pilgrim tourism (as mentioned in Chapter 8 as well) is the most popular expectation from the people of Ladakh, especially in the Leh district. Leh is the primary (and the only) airport in Ladakh serving the civilian population, though there are a few military airstrips as well.[24] The government has recently announced activating the airstrips in Fukche (in the Nyoma sector, near Demchok) and has made a new airstrip in Daulat Beg Oldi (DBO) near the Karakoram, both are for military purposes. Besides, there is a well-attended airstrip in Thoise in the Nubra sector, which is used by the military on a regular basis. Neither is there a popular demand for converting these airstrips for civilian use, nor will this help the local population, because there are hardly any human settlements in the regions. If there are, they are mostly nomads (in the Nyoma sector) of Changthang, who can hardly afford to fly.

[23] See Stobdan and Suba Chandran, *Gilgit-Baltistan: The Last Colony* (New Delhi: India Research Press, 2008).

[24] Besides Leh, there is a small airport in Kargil, which is not regularly operated. It is opened seasonally if there is an emergency (due to snow/landslide) or political pressure. However, everyone in Kargil town is in favour of opening a permanent airport here; the local population believes opening a Kargil airport will not only help improve connectivity but also attract tourists, thereby boosting the local economy.

However, there have been proposals and demands to create new satellite towns around Leh to improve tourist inflow.[25] The tourist industry in particular is keen on converting the Fukche airstrip into a full-blown civilian airport; the primary expectation is that Fukche can become the basic jumping point for pilgrim tourists from India and abroad. The local opinion on this issue, however, is divided. A section favouring the opening of Fukche Airport for civilian traffic believes that this will help the region prosper. The entire Nyoma sector and Changthang region is underdeveloped and sparsely populated. Most of the local population has migrated to Leh, for there is no local economic activity except minor agriculture. Animal husbandry by nomads is the only major economic activity; even this is declining rapidly for two specific reasons. First, youths prefer to move to Leh to engage in the tourism industry, and second, an overemphasis on environment (as mentioned earlier) is beginning to affect their livelihoods.[26] Another section believes that creating Fukche as the primary exit for the Kailash Mansarovar pilgrimage will divert tourism.[27]

Whatever may be the differences, the entire Leh district is unanimous that the Leh–Mansarovar route should be opened for pilgrim tourism. Since both India and China, in principle, do not bear any disagreements in allowing pilgrim tourism to Kailash Mansarovar, the local population questions the inordinate delay in opening this route. Though both countries have an agreement to allow pilgrim tourism to Kailash Mansarovar, it is mainly through Himachal Pradesh and Nepal. Both countries have an agreed border along Himachal; hence, both countries do not have a problem in opening this axis. However, the Leh–Demchok–Kailash Mansarovar axis cuts across the Line of Actual Control (LAC) between the two countries, which is yet to be finalized after the 1962 war. Since India has reached an understanding with Pakistan across the LoC in Kashmir and Jammu regions, where the border is yet to be settled, and China has reached an understanding with Pakistan in Gilgit-Baltistan, which is a part of the disputed territory, the local population holds that there is no logic in not opening the LAC across Demchok in Ladakh.

---

[25] See D. Suba Chandran, 'Rebuilding Ladakh', *Daily Excelsior*, August 2010.
[26] Interviews with Changpas.
[27] Interviews with tourist operators and others engaged in the tourism industry.

Currently, growing at a 40 per cent increase annually, the tourist inflow into Ladakh has become the mainstay of the local economy. Given the limitations that nature has imposed on Ladakh (it is opened for tourism for only six months in a year), the local population is anxious to make the most out of these six months.[28]

Besides pilgrim tourism, India and China could also consider opening this route for international tourism, by which both countries could tap into their respective tourists. Tourists could enter Leh and exit through Lhasa and vice versa. Linking the two sub-regions that share a common history and heritage will attract and multiply tourist inflow into both sub-regions.

Opening the Kailash Mansarovar route will help Ladakh largely by contributing to its local economy. In return, India and China could consider allowing the movement of certain goods from Tibet into Ladakh, so that the local economy across the border in Tibet also benefits out of this transaction.

---

[28] By October end, the hotels in Leh start closing and open in May–June. With the closure of hotels, those allied activities of tourism, for example, the local markets selling goods, transport industry, restaurants, bakeries and Internet kiosks, come to a close. Even the beggars and snake charmers leave Ladakh during this period!

3

Nathu La and the Opportunities for Sino-Indian Economic Rapprochement

Teiborlang T. Kharsyntiew

Introduction

Borders under the influence of colonial regimes have been constantly shaped and reshaped according to geopolitical exigencies. Even today, in Asia and elsewhere, borders as a consequence of colonial construction represent varied characteristics. In most cases, the demarcation of border remains disputed and often emerges as a theatre for major conflicts. The cases of India–Pakistan, India–China and India–Myanmar represent few of the many such cases where colonial construction of boundaries has invariably resulted in disorienting the culture, economy and societal fabric of this once contiguous region.

Delineation of borders or boundaries among modern nation states became a reason for conflict during most of the 20th century, resulting in immense human insecurities. However, today the understanding of a 'border' goes beyond the traditional discourse of conflict-ridden dividers. Borders are now seen as a window of opportunity rather than impediment in interstate relations, which can often be realized through cross-border linkages. In fact, in an era informed by globalization, cross-border linkages can lead to the revival of old connections in cultural, religious and trade spheres, which would have existed for centuries but were otherwise suspended due to colonial mapping of disparate frontiers.

Borders, once considered as 'frontier areas' or 'zones' that fuse or dilute a contiguous geographical space, are today conceptualized as 'border regions' which 'encompass areas immediately beside a state's external border, or straddling it, and also administrative regions abutting a border whose centres are physically and socially distant from that border'.[1] In Europe, especially after the end of the Cold War, integration of national economic, social, environmental policies, to name a few, within the framework of European integration gained traction with boundary lines of the former East European countries becoming redundant as the project of a single market and eastward enlargement of the European Union (EU) evolved.

Since the beginning of the 21st century, a change in international system from bipolarity to complex interdependence has been perceptible, which leaves an undeniable impact on the character and functioning of borders. Today, free movement applies not only to goods and services within the EU but also to free movement of people across cultures and civilizations. It is the experience of the European model of regional integration that has drawn attention, both within the academia and policymaking, in re-examining the concept of borderless world from the 1970s onwards. Lately, substantial studies have been done which pay greater attention to the impact of globalization on the concept of territorial borders.[2]

As far as the Indian subcontinent is concerned, boundaries between India and its immediate neighbours for most of the second half of the 20th century resulted in conflicts, mostly hostage to the power politics of the Cold War. But the inevitability of interdependence could be seen in the many rounds of dialogue between India and China, India and Bangladesh and India and Pakistan that sought to link bilateral trade and attempted confidence-building measures (CBM) soon after. These efforts resulted in the revival and increase of border trade between adjacent communities of

---

[1] James Anderson and Liam O'Dowd, 'Borders, Border Regions and Territoriality: Contradictory Meanings, Changing Significance', *Regional Studies*, 33(7), 1999, p. 595.

[2] See Kenichi Ohmae, 'The Rise of the Region State', *Foreign Affairs* 72(2) (Spring 1993), 78–87; also see Kenichi Ohmae, *The End of the Nation-State: The Rise of Regional Economies* (New York: Simon and Schuster Inc., 1995).

India and the Tibet Autonomous Region (TAR); establishment of border *hatt*s (traditional market) between India and Bangladesh; and the revival of bus services between India and Pakistan and India and Bangladesh, to name a few instances. It also signifies that there was and remains a mounting enthusiasm to

1. re-examine 'border' as a mutually beneficial concept and
2. rediscover old ties across communities and civilizations that once drove the entire economy of this region.

History of Sikkim's Trade with Tibet

On the northeastern fringes of India's border is the state of Sikkim that borders Bhutan in the east, Nepal in the west and China in the south. Historically, Sikkim's relations with its neighbours were maintained through matrimonial alliances, religious affinity and political alliances, such as in the case of Tibet. Prior to the advent of the British, the boundary of Sikkim included the eastern section (Ilam district) of Nepal, the Chumbi Valley of the present-day TAR and the Ha Valley of Bhutan. Its southern frontiers reached the plains of India in the Dooars, including the present-day Kalimpong and Darjeeling district of West Bengal.[3] However, much of these territories were lost during the frequent raids and attacks from Nepal and Bhutan between 1788 and 1789, and in 1835, Darjeeling was presented to the Governor of East India Company, Lord William Bentinck.[4]

The first contact with the British came during the reign of the seventh king of Sikkim, Tsugphud Namgyal, when in 1814, faced with the invasion of the Gurkhas, the king invited the British to his aid to recover his territories, including those lost during the Nepalese invasion of 1780.[5] Following this request, the company seized the opportunity and defeated Nepal in the Anglo-Nepal war of 1814 which ended with the signing of the Treaty of Sugauli

[3] Pradyumna P. Karan and William M. Jenkins Jr, *The Himalayan Kingdoms: Bhutan, Sikkim and Nepal* (Toronto: D. Van Nostrand Company Inc., 1963), 58.

[4] Ibid.

[5] B.S.K. Grover, *Sikkim and India: Storm and Consolidation* (New Delhi: Jain Brothers, 1974), 16.

on 2 December 1815. This treaty for the first time highlighted the indispensable part that Sikkim would play in British commercial and political interest towards Tibet and Central Asia.[6]

The Treaty of Titalia between the company and Sikkim was signed in 1817, which, besides restoring the territories recovered during the Anglo-Nepal war to Sikkim, also gave the company trade privileges and the right to trade up to Tibetan frontiers.[7] Besides these two treaties, the Anglo-Sikkimese Treaty of Tumlong, 1861, consolidated their position in Sikkim. The treaty stipulated the abolition of all restrictions on travelling and monopolies in trade; unrestricted access through Sikkim for trading purpose; abolition of duties on trade between British territories and Sikkim; right of Sikkim to levy a custom duty on products entering into or out of Tibet, Bhutan and Nepal; and no interference in construction of roads between Sikkim and Tibet through Jelep La.[8]

With the signing of the Sino-British Chefoo Convention of 1876, the British gained the rights to send an exploratory mission to Tibet and thus the opportunities of commercial linkages with Tibet became more prominent. To this effect, a mission was again 'pressed on the Government of Bengal in the general interests of British trade in the East (and) promoting commercial intercourse with Tibet'.[9] Thus, with these treaties, Sikkim for the first time came under direct British influence, and towns such as Kalimpong, Gangtok, Phari, Yakthung and Chumbi became centres of strategic commercial and military interest to British's Central Asian Policy.[10]

The prospect of trade between British India and Tibet via Sikkim opening up for commercial interest was advocated not only by the British government but also by the merchants and traders of London. Ruth Marie Lepcha pointed out that in 1873 the merchants in London lobbied and presented a memorandum to the Secretary of State for India, the Duke of Argyll, with regard to

---

[6] Ibid., p. 15.

[7] Ibid., p. 16.

[8] Anglo-Sikkimese Treaty of Tumlong, 1861, in A.C. Sinha, *Sikkim: Feudal and Democratic* (New Delhi: Indus Publishing Co, 2008), 320–326.

[9] H.H. Risley, *The Gazetteer of Sikkim: Relations of Sikkim and Tibet* (Delhi: Low Price Edition, 2010 Reprint), vi.

[10] Pradyumna P. Karan and William M. Jenkins Jr, *The Himalayan Kingdoms: Bhutan, Sikkim and Nepal*, n. 3, 58.

trade with Tibet.[11] Similarly, the Society for the Encouragement of Arts, Manufactures and Commerce in their memorandum of April 1873 made a number of suggestions that include the early completion of the Calcutta–Darjeeling railway, the establishment of a frontier mart on the Sikkim–Tibet frontier, opening of consular agencies in Lhasa and Shigatse and the need for permission to trade along the whole of Tibet frontier should be pursued by the British minister at Peking.[12] It is in this importance of Sikkim to British Tibet's policy that the Bengal government recommended that the East Bengal Railways should be allowed to extend their line from Kustia to the Teesta Valley for promoting commerce between India and the trans-Himalayan countries.[13]

The growing interest in Sikkim and its neighbourhood was followed by the mission of John W. Edgar, the Deputy Commissioner of Darjeeling, to Sikkim–Tibet frontier in 1873 to 'enquire into the condition and prospects of trade with Tibet, and the advisability of making a road through Sikkim to the Tibetan frontier'.[14] Edgar visited all the passes of the Chola range and met the officials and officers of the Tibetan district of Phari and noted that the idea of opening up channel for trade via Sikkim was not well received by the Tibetan, but at the same time submitted a report and made a number of recommendations upon his return.[15] The report, similar to that of the Society for the Encouragement of Arts, Manufactures and Commerce, called for an intervention by the British minister at Peking to obtain from the Chinese foreign office a promise that no Indian traders entering Tibet would face an obstacle, an undertaking from the Chinese emperor of an edict against Chinese representative at Lhasa to abstain from any interference towards Indian traders, establishing friendly relations with Tibetan officials and opening of trade mart on the Sikkim–Tibet frontier.[16] From then on the British government's Tibet

[11] Ruth Marie Lepcha, *Sikkim Political Agency and the Development of British Policy in the Eastern Himalaya – 1889-1944*, PhD Thesis (Shillong: North Eastern Hill University, 2008), 17.

[12] Ibid.

[13] Bot Jahar Sen, 'India's Trade with Central Asia via Nepal', Available at Himalaya.socanth.cam.ac.uk/collections/journals/.../bot_08_02_03.pdf.

[14] H.H. Risley, *The Gazetteer of Sikkim: Relations of Sikkim and Tibet*, n. 9, v.

[15] Ruth Marie Lepcha, *Sikkim Political Agency and the Development of British Policy in the Eastern Himalaya – 1889-1944*, n. 11, 17.

[16] Ibid.

policy was routed through Sikkim's administrative and political machinery as in the case of the appointment of a Resident Political Officer primarily first as a British observer on the Tibet frontier and eventually as a British representative for Bhutan and Tibet soon after the Anglo-Tibetan War of 1888.[17] This political necessity was further consolidated by the Anglo-Chinese Convention of 1890, to which Tibet was not a party. It laid down the following:

(i)   Recognized Sikkim as a British Protectorate by which all its (Sikkim) internal and foreign relations would be directly under the exclusive control of the British government.

(ii) Trade opportunity across Sikkim–Tibet frontier would be explored at the earliest.[18]

And with the proclamation of the trade regulation in 1893, British foothold in trade with Tibet was established. By this regulation, a trade mart was established at Yatung on the Tibetan side and a British trade officer was stationed there. Trade that was conducted through this route was inclusive of all products and items (except arms and ammunition), and a duty exemption on products was promulgated for the period of five years.[19] Thus, with the conclusion of the treaty of 1890 and the trade regulation of 1893, the British control over Sikkim's political and administrative affairs was completed, and with the Younghusband mission of 1904, trade and commerce between Sikkim and Tibet was established fully.

With the advance of Russia towards Central Asia, an urgency to open up a direct communication with China gathered momentum by the beginning of the 1900s. However, any attempt to create a channel of communication through the Tibetan authourity proved futile. This was partly because in both the conventions of 1890 and 1893, Tibet was not a party to the conventions signed between China and Britain and thus refused to recognize the

---

[17] B.S.K. Grover, *Sikkim and India: Storm and Consolidation*, n. 5, 24.

[18] 'Convention Between Great Britain and China Relating to Sikkim and Tibet (1890)'in Francis Younghusband, *India and Tibet* (Delhi: Low Price Edition, 1994 Reprint), 439.

[19] 'Regulation regarding Trade, Communication, and Pasturage to be appended to the Sikkim-Tibet Convention of 1890' in Francis Younghusband, *India and Tibet*, n. 18, 440.

legality of these conventions.[20] As early as 1899, Lord Curzon's attempt to open a direct communication with the Dalai Lama to address issues of trading rights as per the regulation of 1893 remained usuccessful. Under such an urgency of opening a direct route to China and Central Asia, the Younghusband mission to Lhasa was commissioned.[21]

Young husband's mission to Lhasa in 1904 can be considered as a first template of modern trade between India and China. The mission resulted in the signing of the convention between Great Britain and Tibet on 7 September 1904. The terms of the treaty stipulated that the

> Tibetan Government undertakes to levy no dues of any kind other than those provided for in the tariff to be mutually agreed upon; establishment of a trade mart at Yatung, Gyangtse, and Gartok; the Chumbi Valley to be under the British government; Britain to have overall power over Tibetan territory with regards to internal and foreign affairs.[22]

Within no time, Kalimpong was transformed from being a small town for local trade with Bhutan and Tibet into a major centre for activities. Its proximity to the gentle and year-round accessible pass of Jelep La made it more relevant and attractive to a host of trading communities such as the Marwari money-lenders, elite Tibetan politicians, Newar merchants and Tibetan Muslim muleteers who preferred this town for providing easy and shorter route to Lhasa as compared to the Katmandu–Lhasa trade route which was longer.[23]

By the mid-20th century, Kalimpong had emerged as such a vibrant centre that Tina Harris observed that it:

> ... had become one of the most important towns in the region for the exchange of commodities; in particular, it was the main center for the sorting and processing of Tibetan wool. The wool was

---

[20] B.S.K. Grover, *Sikkim and India: Storm and Consolidation*, n. 5, p. 26.

[21] A. McKay, 'The Establishment of the British Trade Agencies in Tibet: A Survey', *JRAS*, Series 3 (2–3) (1992), 401.

[22] 'Convention between Great Britain and Tibet, Signed at Lhasa on the 7 September 1904; Regulation regarding Trade, Communication, and Pasturage to be appended to the Sikkim-Tibet Convention of 1890 in Francis Younghusband', *India and Tibet*, n. 18, 441.

[23] Ibid., 205–207.

brought to Lhasa from Ngari or Changthang by nomads or middlemen, where it would then be baled for transport and loaded on mule caravans (led almost exclusively by Tibetan or Newar men). The caravans would make the month-long journey in stages, stopping in Gyantse, Phari, and Yatung, traversing Jelep-la, and eventually ending up in Kalimpong, where the wool would be weighed, sorted, and stored in large godowns (warehouses) for transport to the port of Calcutta. The mules would return to Lhasa laden with Indian grains, household implements, cotton garments, and even Rolex watches. The Tibetan Mirror newspaper (*Yulphyogs so so'igsar 'gyur me long*), published in Kalimpong and distributed along the trade route to Tibet, featured numerous articles on trade, including regular price listings for wool, matches, and black and white yak tails. Due to growing international demand, wool prices were at their peak in the 1940s. During the period from April 1, 1946 to March 31, 1947, the export of wool from Tibet to Kalimpong amounted to 106,615 maunds (approximately 8,742,430 pounds), at 55 rupees per maund. At this time, the three largest trading families in Tibet—Pangdatsang, Sadhutsang, and Reting—held a monopoly over the wool trade, while some smaller-scale traders did not fare as well. According to one man who lived in Lhasa during the 1940s and early 1950s, the economic connections between Kalimpong and Tibet were so important to the local geographical imagination that many Tibetans would use the word 'Kalimpong' to refer to India as a whole.[24]

During the same period, the adjacent pass of Nathu La and its main town of Gangtok became another centre for trade. Trade from this pass could be easily conducted during the dry seasons, and the presence of British political office in Gangtok also enabled it to receive its share of significance. For example, before 1962, 200 mules each carrying about 80 kg of load were used to ferry goods from Gangtok to Lhasa that include pens, watches, cereals, cotton cloth, edible oil, soaps, building materials, unassembled scooters and four wheelers which were exported to Tibet through the pass on mule back.[25]

[24] Tina Harris, 'Silk Roads and Wool Routes: Contemporary Geographies of Trade between Lhasa and Kalimpong', n. 27, 207–208.

[25] Field Interview; also see Tshering Doma Kaleon, *India China Border Trade Through Nathula: Challenges and Opportunities*, M.A. Dissertation (Gangtok: Sikkim University, 2010); A. McKay, 'The Establishment of the British Trade Agencies in Tibet: A Survey', n. 21, 399–421; Tina Harris, 'Silk Roads and Wool Routes: Contemporary Geographies of Trade Between Lhasa and Kalimpong', n. 27, 200–222;

Kalyan Chaudhuri noted that:

Old documents in the Kalimpong sub-divisional office show that trade ties between India and Tibet were so close that three Kalimpong-based private banks—Kuber Bank, Das Bank and a third bank that belonged to Rai Bahadur Ramchandra Mintry—operated in Tibet till the early 1950s.[26]

But with the dawn of the Sino-India war of 1962, trade through these passes was stopped overnight, borders between the two countries were closed and traders from both sides closed their business and returned to their respective countries without any time to wrap up or cash in their transaction (for they were given an ultimatum to leave the country within 24 hours). The war effectively ended the trade between Lhasa with Kalimpong and Gangtok, and most of the traders began to shift their business to Kathmandu and rerouting their trade linkages with Tibet through the long Kathmandu–Lhasa route.[27]

Reopening of the Nathu La Pass: Expectations and Realities

The end of the Cold War brought about a drastic change in India and China's domestic and foreign economic policies. The early 1990s also witnessed congruence between India's Look East Policy (LEP) and China's Southwest policy. In both cases, domestic economic policies aimed at developing the country's peripheries as a major portion of their economic reforms, and

---

Ambar Singh Roy, 'Nathula Passport to better trade prospects with China', *The Hindu-Business Line*, 25 November 2003, Available at http://www.thehindu-businessline.in/2003/11/25/stories/2003112502160200.htm; Sikkim University, 'Oral History Project Archives' (Gangtok: Sikkim University, 2010); 'Nathu La Pass: The India China Border Trade', Available at http://resources.alibaba.com/topic/283037/Nathu_La_Pass_The_India_China_Trade_Border.htm.

[26] Kalyan Chaudhuri, 'Routes of Promise', *Frontline*, 20(14), 05–18 July 2003. Available at http://www.frontlineonnet.com/fl2014/stories/20030718005201800.htm.

[27] Tina Harris, 'Silk Roads and Wool Routes: Contemporary Geographies of Trade Between Lhasa and Kalimpong', n. 27, 208.

such policies were envisaged not only for exclusive domestic diagnosis but also for integrating local economies with their immediate neighbours.

For India, the integration of its northeast region's economy with the provinces of Southwest China and Southeast Asia became an imperative under the LEP. The Eastern Himalayas became an important gateway to China's Southwest. The first initiative towards this end was undertaken with the signing of a 'Memorandum between the Government of the Republic of India and the Government of the People's Republic of China on Resumption of Border Trade' in 1991 during Chinese premier Li Peng's visit to India.

Within this framework, Sikkim gained prominence as it became a focal point for India's China policy. It is, thus, no surprise that besides the Lipulekh Pass in Uttaranchal and Shipki La in Himachal Pradesh that were functional since 1992 and 1994, respectively, China pushed for the opening up of Nathu La for border trade. To meet this pressing need, the prime minister of India and the premier of the State Council of China declared open the border trade through Nathu La at their 2003 summit. What also helped in its speedy functioning was the recognition of Sikkim as an integral part of India in 2004 by China.

Nathu La was declared open in 2006 with Sherathang as the location for trading on the Indian side and Renqingang on the Tibetan side. The reopening of the border served a twofold purpose: First, Sikkim rediscovered its importance as a point of interaction and confluence of trade, commerce and culture. Second, it signified an attempt at identifying border trade as a CBM and a bridge towards improving bilateral relations between the two Asian neighbours.

Nathu La (translated as 'listening ears' in Tibetan) is 54 km east of Gangtok and at a distance of 525 km from Lhasa. The pass situated at 14,140 ft above sea level is considered more treacherous than the Jelep La ('easy pass' in Tibetan), which at 14,000 ft is easily accessible all through the year. However, Nathu La as an entry point to Lhasa is more convenient via the main town of Gangtok. The distance between Lhasa and the main commercial town of Siliguri in West Bengal through this pass is approximately about 638 km, thus a more viable route as compared to the Kathmandu–Lhasa route spanning 1,100 km.

The reopening of the Nathu La for border trade facilitates an attempt to directly re-engage India's northeastern region with southwestern China which historically existed even during the early times.[28] The south-western part of China comprising Sichuan, Guizhou, Yunnan, the two autonomous regions of Tibet and Guangxi and the municipality of Chongqing has, for centuries, maintained close relations with the Eastern Himalayan region, including northeastern parts of India, Bhutan and Nepal. Trade through this route largely consisted of items such as ivory, silk, cinnamon, rock salt, iron implements, China silver and wooden ware, rice, lac, buffalo horns, corals and pearls, conducted by the Tibetan and Assam merchants who came down annually to a mart of Chouna on the border of Assam.[29] Thus, it can be rightly observed that in the whole region from western Tibet in the west to Yunnan in the east and central Tibet in the north and Sikkim and northeast India in the south, there exists a vibrant trade route.[30] With the reopening of Nathu La there exists an opportunity to rediscover this old connections between the two civilizations. Besides, Nathu La can also emerge as a strategic front for both these civilizations to situate themselves in the era informed by economic interdependence and globalization.

In analyzing the potentials of the reopening of Nathu La for border trade, the Nathu La Study in 2005[31] formed an important pre-emptive investigation which projected two ambitious future scenarios. The first scenario anticipated that given a healthy environment, the trade flow from Nathu La will increase to US$48 million (₹2.6 billion) by 2007, US$527 million (₹22.66 billion) by 2010 and US$2.84 billion (₹122.03 billion) by 2015.[32] The second scenario projects that even in a worst-case situation, the volume of

---

[28] Tshering Doma Kaleon, *India China Border Trade Through Nathula: Challenges and Opportunities*, n. 32, 30.

[29] A. Mackenzie, *The North East Frontier of India* (Delhi: Spectrum Publication, 2003 Reprint); also see Gurudas Das and R.K. Purkayastha, eds., *Border Trade: North-East India and Neighbouring Countries*, n. 28, 7.

[30] Gurudas Das and R.K. Purkayastha, eds., *Border Trade: North-East India and Neighbouring Countries*, n. 28, 4.

[31] A group was constituted by the Government of Sikkim headed by Prof. Mahendra P. Lama to study the prospects of border trade through Nathu La and its impact on the State of Sikkim and the entire region.

[32] Government of Sikkim, 'Sikkim-Tibet Trade via Nathu La: A Policy Study on Prospect, Opportunities and Requisite Preparedness', A report by Nathu La Trade Study Group (Gangtok: Government of Sikkim, 2005), 162.

trade from Nathu La will be US$70 million (₹3.53 billion) in 2010, US$89 million (₹4.5 billion) in 2015 and US$109 million (₹5.47 billion) in 2020.[33]

These projections by the Nathu La group were based on ground research and historical considerations of not only the Jelep La and Nathu La trade but also other cross-border trading arrangements between India–Myanmar border and China-Nepal border, among others. In its findings, the study group concluded that the nature of trade in these border areas had been extremely dynamic and without much restrictions on items or product of trade historically. For example, the study group listed a number of items that can be traded through this route. This includes construction materials, machinery food items, pharmaceutical and medicine, flowers and orchids, to name a few. This conclusion was quite similar to the idea that the British India government had proposed in the trade regulations of 1893. The study group also recommended that the inherent dynamism of the trade cold engulf and eventually change the economy of the whole Eastern Himalayan region if given proper direction and attention and need not be restricted to Sikkim alone. Nonetheless, the report did envisage Sikkim as a major dry port, along with Siliguri, a town in West Bengal, as a major trading centre which could be connected to the port of Kolkata and also to the rest of northeast India and beyond.

But when the trade was finally opened up, only a limited number of rather obsolete items were allowed to be traded. A total of 29 items were allowed to be exported from India to China and a total of only 15 items were included in the import list from China (Tables 3.1 and 3.2). The restriction of trade to limited items meant that the volume of trade could never cross beyond ₹20 million or US$0.4 million (Table 3.3). This miniscule volume of trade which represented only a fraction of the total India–China bilateral trade diminished the importance of Nathu La, rendering it as a mere symbolic gesture of confidence-building among the two countries. By limiting the Nathu La trade, the potential of border trade to act as a fulcrum of sub-regional interdependence and a binding factor for future India–China bilateral relations and conflict resolution became mislaid.

---

[33] Ibid., also see p. 162; G. Srinivasan, 'Nathula Pass: A springboard for India-China trade ties', *The Hindu Business Line*, 06 July 2006, Available at http://www.thehindubusinessline.in/bline/2006/07/06/stories/2006070602020700.htm.

Table 3.1
Original list of export items from India to China

1. Agricultural implements	11. Dry fruit	21. Utensils
2. Blankets	12. Dry and fresh vegetables	22. Wheat
3. Copper products	13. Vegetable oil	23. Liquor
4. Cloth	14. *Gur* and *misri*	24. Milk-processed products
5. Cycles	15. Tobacco	25. Canned food
6. Coffee	16. Snuff	26. Cigarettes
7. Tea	17. Spices	27. Local herb
8. Barley	18. Shoes	28. Palm oil.
9. Rice	19. Kerosene	29. Hardware
10. Flour	20. Stationary	

Source: Government of Sikkim, Department of Information and Public Relations.

Table 3.2
Original list of import items from China to India

1. Goat skin	6. Yak hair	11. Goat Kashmiri
2. Sheep skin	7. China clay	12. Common salt
3. Wool	8. Borax	13. Horse
4. Raw silk	9. Seabelyipe	14. Goat
5. Yak tail	10. Butter	15. Sheep

Source: Government of Sikkim, Department of Information and Public Relations.

Informal Trade: The Bane of Trade Restrictions

The limitations placed on the items of trade prior to the revision of the tradable lists led to a spurt of informal trade. A field visit to the trade mart revealed that most major items that were not included in the trading lists are today (and have been previously) illegally exported and imported in bulk through Nathu La. Food products such as Dalda (hydrogenated oil), rice, biscuit and sugar are major products of export through Nathu La as they are in much demand by the Chinese traders (based on personal interviews). For instance, around 500 units of Dalda were being loaded on a single day as

Table 3.3
Details of trade (2006-2011) (₹ million)

	2006	*2007*	*2008*	*2009*	*2010*	*2011*
Export from India to TAR	0.887	2.787	9.5	13.5	40	20 crore (approx.)*
Import from TAR to India	1.083	0.688	0.135	0.296 lakhs	NIL	NIL
Visit of Indian traders to trade mart at Renquingang	696	2,117	1,034	587	NA	NA
Visit of Chinese traders to trade mark at Sherathang	1,253	3,701	3,948	1,879	NA	NA

Sources: Data compiled from various sources.
Notes: 1. Government of Sikkim, Department of Commerce and Industries,[34]
2. Office of the Inspector General of Police, Check Post Branch, Gangtok,
3. Tshering Doma Kaleon, *India China Border Trade Through Nathula: Challenges and Opportunities*, M.A Dissertation (Gangtok: Sikkim University, 2010), p. 38.
4. GOI,
5. Indian customs and
6. News reports.
* Data for the month of June, July and November are not available.

observed during the field visit. At Kupup, which is about 15 km away from the Sherathang Trade Mart, more towards Rongli and Jelep La, a female trader divulged that she could sell about 100 jars of 15 kg each of Vanaspati/Dalda every day (the value of each jar is approximately ₹750). The profitability of this product/trade had in fact enabled her to buy a new mini truck for the purpose of transporting her tradable items (based on personal interviews).

Major products of import in this informal trade include ready-made garments, glassware crockery, blankets, bed sheets, pillows, pillow covers, sweets, finished carpets, footwear and decorative items. Even among these, the major items of demand are ready-made garments and blankets, followed by footwear, crockery items and so on. The field visit revealed that 100–150 blankets were sold in a single day at an average of ₹500 per blanket. These are the statistics for the Sherathang Trade Mart alone. No data of trade in these informal items could be traced for the trade mart at Renqingang on the Chinese side (Table 3.4). However,

[34] Available at http://sikkimindustries.gov.in/report%20on%20nathula%20trade.pdf

Table 3.4
Major informal export items traded at Sherathang up to 2011

Items
Rice
Sugar
Vegetable oil
Dalda
Tea leaves
Biscuit (Parle G brand)
Incense stick
Dalay — local chillies

Source: Field study.
Note: The value of all these items cannot be estimated as these items are sold in bulk and traders are reluctant to divulge details.

most traders acknowledge that as most of the items on the current trading lists are obsolete, it is these items that are imported in bulk from the Chinese side, thereby earning a huge profit for the Indian traders. This is also evident in the large-scale presence of these items in the market at Gangtok, where a blanket of ₹600 acquired at Sherathang is sold for a price of ₹1,500–1,700 (based on personal interviews).

Thus, a huge volume of informal trade continues to flourish along this border trade. Considering the increase in the number of Chinese traders visiting Sherathang (Table 3.5) and based on personal interviews conducted with many Indian traders, the author believes that the total value of informal trade could be much more than that of the formal trade, which is currently around ₹1.50 crore. For instance, if by a very conservative estimate about 50 units of 15-kg jar of Dalda with a maximum retail price (MRP) of ₹750 per unit are sold every day, this would translate to ₹37,500 of Dalda being sold in the market every day. Even if one considers that the trade is open for 50 days in one season, the value would amount to ₹1.875 million for Dalda alone.

To put a check on the informal trade along Nathu La, the government revised the lists in May 2012, and new products have been included for both export and import. These include ready-made garments, shoes, quilts/blankets, carpets and local herbal medicines as major products of import from the Chinese side, while

Table 3.5
Major informal import items traded at Sherathang up to 2011

	Items sold in a day (estimated units)	Approximate price sold in a day (₹)
Blanket, bed Sheet, pillow, pillow covers	100–150	1 lakh
Ready-made garments (jackets, sports-wear, socks, women and children dress)	200	1 lakh
Footwear	50	7,500
Crockery (glassware)	50	25,000
Carpet	50	30,000
Electronic items — mixer juicer grinder, electric water flask	15	10,500

Source: Field survey.

items such as processed foods, flowers, fruits, spices, religious products such as beads, prayer wheels, incense sticks and butter oil lamp, ready-made garments, handicraft and handloom products and local herbs materials have been included as major products that can be exported to China from Nathu La.[35] The Government of India (GOI) has also increased the Indian currency value limit from ₹25,000 to ₹0.1 million per day per trader (2007–2008).[36]

Another impediment that was identified for the slow take-off of the Nathu La trade during the early years of opening up was the stipulation that the border market would remain open only for a certain period of the year. This seemed very impractical given the fact that the route to Nathu La could be operated throughout the year, yet for alleged security reasons, the market was opened only from 1 June to 30 September, and later on, from May to November only. Moreover, the market was to remain open only for a few days in a week, that is, Monday to Thursday only, from 7.30 am to 3.30 pm. This limited duration of a few months a year, a few days in a week and certain timing rendered the

[35] Directorate General of Foreign Trade (DGFT), Ministry of Commerce and Industries, Public Notice No.110/2009–2014 (RE-2010) The 7 May 2012, Online Web URL: http://www.eepcindia.org/circulars/dgft/DGF-PN-110-2010.pdf.

[36] *The Hindu Business Line,* 20 July 2012, 'Duty-free import of Chinese garments, shoes via 3 more border points', Available at http://www.thehindubusinessline. com/industry-and-economy/dutyfree-import-of-chinese-garments-shoes-via-3-more-border-points/article3662315.ece?css=print.

trade virtually impossible to take off. Other problems associated with this trade were that this trade was restricted to Sikkim only, and only permanent residents of Sikkim were issued a trading pass. Even the revised amount of transaction for one day, that is, ₹100,000, seems too meagre as it makes the trade unattractive to big businessmen or older traders.

It is such restrictions that can be held responsible for the slow pace of change in the nature of border trade despite the huge expectations of the study group. Despite the quantum jump in China–India bilateral trade over the last few years, such growth has not translated at the micro-level of border trade as estimated by the Nathu La study group. Nathu La along with Jelep La, which once constituted 80 per cent of India's border trade with China today, records a dismal contribution of less than 0.1 per cent of the overall bilateral India–China trade (see Table 3.6).

Table 3.6
India-China trade (2001-2011) (US$ billion)

Year	Indian imports	Indian exports	Trade balance	Trade volume
2004	5.92	7.67	+1,746.94	13.59
Growth 2005	77.15%	80.41%		78.99%
	8.93	9.76	+834	18.70
Growth 2006	50.5%	27.2%		37.4%
	14.58	10.46	−41.18	25.05
Growth 2007	63.23%	7.05%	−93.77	33.87%
	24.03	14.65		38.69
Growth 2008	64.7%	40.02%		54.42%
	31.50	20.30	−11.20	51.8
	31%	39%		34%
Growth 2009	−6.17%	−32.63%	−15.87	−16.55%
	29.57	13.70		43.28
Growth 2010	38.25%	52.19%	−20.02	42.66%
	40.88	20.86		61.74
Growth 2011	23.50%	12.26%	50.49%	19.71%
	50.49	23.41	−27.08	73.90

Source: Confederation of Indian Industry.[37]

[37] Online Web URL: http://www.indiachina.org/trade_statistics.htm; Government of India, http://www.indianembassy.org.cn/DynamicContent. aspx?MenuId=3&SubMenuId=0.

Yet, a need for further revision of the list is still felt. The number of items on the lists needs to be increased much more than what exist today. Local products should be included in the list, such as sugar, beer and other alcoholic beverages, medicines and construction materials such as steel and cements, and even rice and raw silk which have been discontinued should also be allowed again.[38]

However, it must be borne in mind that increasing the number of tradable items in the lists will not be of much benefit if border trade continues to be bogged down by structural problems of infrastructure development and geographical limitations around certain areas and traders within Sikkim alone. It is saddening to note that the region which constituted almost 80 per cent of bilateral trade between India and China in the earlier days does not expand beyond the town of Gangtok now.[39] This trade can be revived beyond its present state only when the two governments recognize the need for transforming it into trade across borders instead of the traditional conceptualization of border trade and recognize its increasing role in the overall bilateral trade between the two countries.

It is to be further noted that trade through both the Jelep La and the Nathu La was never restricted to the immediate communities along border even in the earlier days, rather it was spread across the length and breadth of the Eastern Himalayas and up to the Kolkata port and beyond. It is therefore imperative that a mechanism for transforming border trade to a full-fledged bilateral trade at border be established at the earliest. Converting this border trade into a full status of trade in goods and services across international border is even more significant if one has to take advantage of the potential of this sub-region. This also calls for harmonization of policies at both the domestic and bilateral levels if trade through the Nathu La is to be expanded into international trade across the border.

As per the World Trade Organization (WTO) norms, there is a need to improve three specific articles of the General Agreement on Tariffs and Trade (GATT) relating to the transit of goods, fees

---

[38] Field interview; also see Tshering Doma Kaleon, *India China Border Trade Through Nathula: Challenges and Opportunities*, n. 32, 34.

[39] Gareth Price, 'China and India: Cooperation and Competition', Chatham House, *Asia Programme Briefing Paper*, ASP BP 07, 2007, 6, Available at http://www.chathamhouse.org/publications/papers/view/108488.

and formalities (documentation and procedures) and the transparency of laws and regulations in order to ease border procedures and to facilitate the movement, release and clearance of goods across international border.[40] This can be done only when the negotiating parties/governments

1. apply and conduct border controls more efficiently
2. allow traders to move their goods across borders more quickly and easily
3. reduce transaction costs and hence reduce prices for consumers and producers
4. reduce transit costs in landlocked countries
5. reduce bureaucracy and corruption
6. facilitate trade for small- and medium-sized businesses burdened with excessive bureaucracy and red tape
7. add to members' gross domestic product (GDP) by making trade less costly
8. improve coordination among border agencies
9. enhance transparency in customs rulings and administrative procedures.[41]

In short, such policies, if adopted, will reduce the cost of cross-border trade to the benefit of exporters, importers and consumers. This harmonization of policies is still lacking in border trade today. Though according to the agreement on border, tradable items are rendered free from custom duties, yet instances of both India and China levying custom duties on products have been found.[42] Besides, financial banking system to promote trade and payment and insurance for cross-border trade are yet to take off.

---

[40] WTO, 'Trade facilitation', Available at http://www.wto.org/english/tratop_e/tradfa_e/tradfa_e.htm; UNCTAD, 'UNCTAD Technical Assistance in Trade Facilitation', Available at http://www.wto.org/english/tratop_e/tradfa_e/wkshop_2001/gurunorthlieb.doc; The GATT (GATT 1947), Part II-Article V, Article VIII; UN ESCWA, 'Key factors in establishing single windows for handling import/export procedures and formalities: Trade facilitation and the single window' (New York: United Nations, 2011), Available at http://www.wto.org/english/tratop_e/tradfa_e/symp_nov11_e/escwa_e.pdf.

[41] Ibid.

[42] *The Assam Tribune*, 'China imposes tax on Indian goods at Nathu la', 22 May 2012, Available at http://www.assamtribune.com/scripts/detailsnew.asp?id=may2311/oth06.

Infrastructure Development: Nathu La as a Gateway to the TAR

Developing infrastructure to support the trade momentum has been one of the most challenging features to any cross-border trade, and even more so in case of the Himalayan region bordering China. The mountain ranges of the Eastern Himalayas are highly fragile. The Eastern Himalayas receive heavy rainfall in the monsoons and extreme snowfall in the winters, making it difficult to conduct smooth trading activities between the two adjacent regions. The earthquake of September 2011 in Sikkim is one such instance where infrastructure development or lack of quality infrastructure proved to be a major stumbling block for border trade.

The main passage that connects Nathu La with the nearest city of Siliguri runs along the national highways (NHs) 31 and 31A and is maintained by the Border Road Organization (BRO) and the State Public Work Department (PWD). Soon after the opening of the Nathu La trade, and considering the larger strategic interest of developing border regions, a new approach by the GOI on development of border regions and its infrastructure began to take shape. Widening and improving the conditions of NH was taken as primary task. The aim of this new approach was to (i) upgrade NH connecting State capitals to 2/4 lane, (ii) improve roads of strategic importance in border area and (iii) improve connectivity to neighbouring countries.[43]

With the opening of Nathu La, Sikkim that shares its border with China, Nepal and close to Bangladesh began to attract greater attention in this infrastructural development. In Sikkim, various departments and ministries of state and central government are involved in this development project. Most notable in this are the roads being funded under the Special Accelerated Road Development Programme in North East (SARDP-NE) under the Ministry of Road Transport and Highways (Tables 3.7–3.10).[44] As per Phase A of this scheme, besides improving road quality,

---

[43] GOI, Ministry of Development of North Eastern Region, 'SARDP-NE', Available at http://www.mdoner.gov.in/content/sardp-ne#map.

[44] GOI, Ministry of Development of North Eastern Region, 'SARDP-NE', Available at http://www.mdoner.gov.in/sites/default/files/silo3_content/railways/List_of_Roads.pdf.

Table 3.7
Details of roads originally approved under Phase 'A' of SARDP-NE (double laning of existing single-lane border road from Gangtok to Nathu La — 89.56 km)

Scope of work	Category of road and implementing agency	Length (in km)
Double laning of Gangtok–Nathu La road from km 24.250 to 51.385	BRO	27.25
Double laning of Gangtok–Nathu La road from km 0.00 to 6.80	BRO	9.93
Widening of existing single-lane road to double lane from km 47/0 to 51/0 (km 0.00 to 5.666 corresponding to km 51.385 on new double-lane road, net length = 5.67 km) of GS road from Gangtok to Nathu La	BRO	5.67
Improvement of Gangtok–Nathu La road from km 0.0 (existing km 6.8) to 19.35 to double-lane standards	BRO	19.35
Improvement of Gangtok–Nathu La road from km 19.35 to 24.25 to double-lane standards	BRO	4.36
Construction of double-lane Gangtok bypass under SARDP-NE Phase 'A'	Sikkim PWD	23
Total		89.56

Source: GOI, Ministry of Development of North Eastern Region, 'SARDP-NE'.[45]

Table 3.8
Details of roads originally approved under Phase 'A' of SARDP-NE (improvement of NH 31A from Sevoke to Ranipool to two-lane standards — 79.87 km)

Scope of work	Category of road and implementing agency	Length (in km)
Construction of 80.0-m cut and cover structure at Bardang slide area at km 60.75 of NH 31A (Sevoke–Gangtok road) under Phase 'A' of SARDP-NE	BRO	–
Improvement of some of the critical portions to double lane from km 0.0 to 14.32 and 16.75 to 20.00 (8 locations) of NH 31A	BRO	1.33

(Table 3.8 Continued)

[45] Available at http://www.mdoner.gov.in/sites/default/files/silo3_content/railways/List_of_Roads.pdf.

(Table 3.8 Continued)

Scope of work	Category of road and implementing agency	Length (in km)
Improvement of some of the critical locations to double lane from km 22.650 to 22.800 and 29.500 to 52.100 of NH 31A (33 locations)	BRO	2.26
Improvement of existing NH 31A to double lane (Sevoke–Gangtok road) at critical locations between km 52.10 to 81.10 in Sikkim under Phase 'A' of SARDP-NE	BRO	3.28
Widening and Strengthening of NH 31A from km 54.00 to 80.60 (length = 20.80 km) to double-lane standards in Sikkim	PWD Sikkim	21
Construction of double-lane bypass at ninth mile of NH 31A in Sikkim	BRO	6
Construction of double-lane NH for realignment stretch between km 20.00 and 27.700 on NH 31A in the State of West Bengal	BRO	16
Improvement of NH 31A from Sevoke to Ranipool to double-lane standards (balance length)	BRO	30
Total		79.87

Source: GOI, Ministry of Development of North Eastern Region, 'SARDP-NE'.[46]

Table 3.9
Proposed alternative route under Phase 'A' of SARDP-NE

Scope of work	Category of road and implementing agency	Length (in km)	
Sikkim/West Bengal	Alternative highway to Gangtok (via Chalsa, Khonya, Moreh, Lhaldhaka, Tode, Rachella, Aritar, Rangpo to Ranipool along with link to Menla, Sikkim). New road alignment. Survey in progress by BRO	New NH	242

Source: GOI, Ministry of Development of North Eastern Region, 'SARDP-NE'.[47]

[46] Online URL: http://www.mdoner.gov.in/sites/default/files/silo3_content/railways/List_of_Roads.pdf.

[47] Available at http://www.mdoner.gov.in/sites/default/files/silo3_content/railways/List_of_Roads.pdf.

Table 3.10
List of roads under Phase 'A' of SARDP-NE (state roads)

S. no.	Category of road	Scope/section of road	State	Tentative length (km)
State roads				
1	State road	Double laning of Melli–Manpur–Namchi road	Sikkim	33
2	State road	Double laning of Legship–Naya Bazar road	Sikkim	26
	Total			59

Source: GOI, Ministry of Development of North Eastern Region, 'SARDP-NE'.[48]

converting the existing single to double lane of the 169-km NHs 31 and 31A between Sevoke in West Bengal and Nathu La in Sikkim is currently undertaken. Similarly, state roads and general staff roads are also covered under both Phases A and B of this scheme (Tables 3.10–3.12) that connects district and NH.[49]

Similarly, the Department of Border Management entrusted with the mandate for development of border roads in northeastern region undertakes road infrastructure development in Sikkim through two border organization, that is, the Indo-Tibetan Border Police (ITBP) and the BRO.[50] While ITBP is engaging in the construction of three border roads of the total length of 103 km, the BRO is constructing two roads of a total length of 47.28 km.[51] Other schemes from Non-lapsable Central Pool of Resource (NLCPR) (Roads and Bridges Sector),[52] North Eastern Council (NEC),[53] and Prime Minister Gram Sadak Yojana (PMGSY) are similar road infrastructural projects that connect NH, border, state and district roads.

[48] Available at http://www.mdoner.gov.in/sites/default/files/silo3_content/railways/List_of_Roads.pdf.

[49] Ibid.

[50] GOI, Ministry of Development of North Eastern Region, 'Border Roads', Available at http://www.mdoner.gov.in/content/border-roads.

[51] Ibid.

[52] GOI, Ministry of Development of North Eastern Region, 'Roads from NLCPR', Available at http://www.mdoner.gov.in/content/roads-nlcpr.

[53] GOI, Ministry of Development of North Eastern Region, 'Roads from NEC', Available at http://www.mdoner.gov.in/sites/default/files/silo3_content/roads/road-from-nec/State-Wise.pdf; GOI, Ministry of Development of North Eastern Region, 'Roads from NEC', Available at http://www.mdoner.gov.in/sites/default/files/silo3_content/roads/road-from-nec/Plan-Wise.pdf.

Table 3.11
*List of roads under modified Phase 'B' and transferred to Phase 'A' of SARDP-NE
(state roads)*

Category of road	Scope/section of road	Tentative length (km)
State road	Double laning of Tarku–Namchi road	32
State road	Double laning of Gyalshing–Singtam road	85
Total		117

Source: GOI, Ministry of Development of North Eastern Region, 'SARDP-NE'.[54]

Table 3.12
List of roads under Phase 'B' of SARDP-NE (general staff road)

Category of road	Scope/section of road	Tentative length (km)
General staff road	Double laning of Gangtok–Mangan road	68

Source: GOI, Ministry of Development of North Eastern Region, 'SARDP-NE'.[55]

To facilitate uninterrupted movement towards Nathu La, an alternative route has also been proposed by the government of Sikkim and the BRO. According to the preliminary study by BRO, an alternative link connecting Gangtok with Siliguri via Chulsa can be explored. This route can also be extended towards Nathu La by aligning the road that begins at Khunia nearer to Chulsa, touching Jaldhaka, Tode, Tangta and Rachela on the Bengal side and ends at Kumrek via Aritar in Sikkim. According to the survey, the same road from Aritar can be diverted to Gangtok through Rangpo or Pakyong, and another can be extended by another 53 km from Aritar to Menla, near the Nathu La border, via Rongli, thus facilitating an alternative road to reach the India–China border (see Table 3.9).[56]

It is, however, imperative that while there is an impending need to speed up the process of construction of both the existing

---

[54] Available at http://www.mdoner.gov.in/sites/default/files/silo3_content/ railways/List_of_Roads.pdf.

[55] Available at http://www.mdoner.gov.in/sites/default/files/silo3_content/ railways/List_of_Roads.pdf.

[56] GOI, Ministry of Development of North Eastern Region, 'SARDP-NE', Available at http://www.mdoner.gov.in/sites/default/files/silo3_content/ railways/List_of_Roads.pdf; also see 20 August 2010, 'Route to reduce lone-road dependence', Available at http://www.telegraphindia.com/1100820/jsp/ siliguri/story_12831490.jsp.

highways and alternate ones, what is most crucial is improving the quality of their construction to provide longevity to the roads. The unpredictability of weather, natural disasters such as the major earthquake of September 2011 and upcoming rampant unplanned developments around the town of Gangtok and poor quality of housing construction has compromised the widening of road network on this route. For example, it takes about three hours to cover a distance between Nathu La and Gangtok, which is merely at a distance of about 54 km. Likewise, it takes another three to four hours to cover the distance between Gangtok and Sevoke at Coronation Bridge, which in a good condition can be travelled in about two hours (see Tables 3.13–3.15).

At certain places, even the existing plain gradient road between Siliguri and Sevoke and Teesta Bridge, which is the starting road towards Nathu La, is of very poor quality and can be washed away by monsoon rain within a year or two of blacktopping. Another challenge in terms of developing roadways and infrastructure in this region is the lack of skilled labourers. This is more in the case of Sikkim, where besides the difficulties of working in extreme weather and high altitude, hiring of labourers from outside the state is prohibited or has to undergo through strict screening rules.[57]

Table 3.13
Siliguri to Nathu La: Point-to-point distance and travel time

From	To	Time (minutes)
Sevoke	Teesta	30
Teesta	Malli	10
Malli	Rangpo	20
Rangpo	Ranipool	30
Ranipool	Gangtok	20
Gangtok	Changu	45
Changu	Nathu La	35
Total		190

Source: Government of Sikkim, 'Sikkim-Tibet Trade via Nathu La: A Policy Study on Prospect, Opportunities and Requisite Preparedness', A report by Nathu La Trade Study Group, p. 225.

[57] Tshering Doma Kaleon, *India China Border Trade through Nathula: Challenges and Opportunities*, n. 32, 36.

Table 3.14
Siliguri-Nathu La road

Road	Formation width (m)	Carriageway width (m)	Gradient
Sevoke (Coronation Bridge—Teesta)	8.00	5.50	Gentle
Teesta–Malli	8.00	5.50	Gentle
Malli–Rangpo	8.00	5.50	Gentle
Rangpo–Ranipool	8.00	5.50	Gentle
Ranipool–Gangtok	8.00	5.50	Steep
Gangtok–Changu	6.10	3.66	Gentle gradient with intermittent steep gradient
Changu–Sherathang	6.10	3.66	-do-
Sherathang–Nathu La	5.00	3.00	Steep

Source: Government of Sikkim, 'Sikkim-Tibet Trade via Nathu La: A Policy Study on Prospect, Opportunities and Requisite Preparedness', A report by Nathu La Trade Study Group, p. 215.

Table 3.15
Landslide-prone zone

A	*Sevoke to Gangtok*	
	Between 2 km and 2.5 km	Sinking zone. Approx 2 m Sinking occurs during monsoon every year
	8.00–8.50 km	Slide zone
	At 12 km (Berrick)	Slide zone
	At 26.00 km (Lukhbir)	Major slide zone
	52.10 km (Mining)	Slide point
	60.80 km (Barding)	Slide point (not active)
	Between 77 and 78 km	Sliding zone
B	*Gangtok to Nathu La*	
	Between 0 and 1 km	Moderate
	9–10 km	Slide area
	11–12 km	Sinking zone
	12–14 km	Slide area
	15–16 km	Slide area

Source: Government of Sikkim, 'Sikkim-Tibet Trade via Nathu La: A Policy Study on Prospect, Opportunities and Requisite Preparedness', A report by Nathu La Trade Study Group, p. 225.

Sikkim, with a population of a little more than half a million, faces numerous problems in attracting skilled and manual labourers for building roads or housing constructions. With the introduction of rural employment schemes such as those of the Mahatma Gandhi National Rural Employment Generation scheme, more and more migrant workers from outside the state (or even those from within the state) prefer to work closer to home than in extreme climatic conditions.[58] Moreover, the absence of proper amenities such as housing, nutritional food, shelter, clothes and medical facilities makes it difficult to retain them at work in these difficult terrains.[59]

The lacunae are even more evident when compared to the infrastructure on the Chinese side. Indian traders who frequented Renqinggang remarked that in comparison to the Indian roads, the road infrastructure leading to the Renqinggang trade mart is of high quality on the Chinese side, where cars can easily travel at a speed of 100 km per hour (based on personal interviews). Chinese prowess in road and rail networks in the border region is unsurpassable by the Indian standards. For example, China realized that the distance of 8,000 km between its coastal production centres and the TAR could be shortened to take further benefit of the 1,000-km stretch from Kolkata port to Lhasa. This reduction in travel distance will thus greatly lower the cost of transportation as well as speed up the process of its south-west development strategy.[60]

Most of the Chinese consignments towards the TAR and Xinjiang region are routed overland from Shanghai and Hong Kong port. Another route which can be used effectively is through the Karachi port, facilitating movement of goods through the Karakoram highway (KKH). But for China, it is more viable to access its products through the Kolkata port, which

---

[58] Tshering Doma Kaleon, *India China Border Trade through Nathula: Challenges and Opportunities*, n. 32, 36.

[59] Ibid.

[60] John W. Garver, 'Development of China's Overland Transportation Links with Central, Southwest and South Asia', *The China Quarterly* 185 (2006): 14; Zhang Yunling, ed., 'Development of China's Transportation Infrastructure and International Connectivity', *ERIA Research Project Report* 7(5) (2009): 74, Available at http://www.eria.org/publications/research_project_reports/images/pdf/y2009/no7-5/all_files.pdf.

reduces both the time and cost of consignments as compared to the Karachi port. The Nathu La study group also mentions that 'making use of ports in West Bengal and other neighbouring countries like Bangladesh, Bhutan and even Nepal can give quicker and economical access to mainland China'. Further it would also be much more attractive for Bangladesh, eastern Nepal and southern Bhutan to trade with Lhasa through the Nathu La Pass than through traditional sea ports in Kolkata or through the Kathmandu–Kodari highway.[61]

The Qinghai–Tibet railway, which began in 2001, was completed in 2006 and linked Golmud on the southern edge of the Qinghai province with Lhasa in the TAR.[62] It is anticipated that this line will again connect the southern fringes of the TAR in Shigatse, passing Yadong County with the Nathu La border,[63] thereby linking China's rail network with that of India's rail network at the proposed junction at Rangpo and Siliguri. By linking such rail and road networks, China's strategy would be to get an access to the Kolkata port not only for development of its south-western region but also to give a direct access for Chinese products and help Tibet to become a new frontier of economic communication with South Asia.[64] With the possible extension of the Qinghai–Tibet railway, it is expected that land transportation between the Chinese mainland and Nepal would also be greatly reduced through the Zhangmu port in the TAR with Nepal. Thus, the Lhasa–Shigatse–Nielamu railways will also link railways in Nepal and India and eventually help to form better China–South Asia corridor and promote China–South Asia regional cooperation.[65]

Thus, to emphasize the Nathu La study group's argument, Nathu La 'could trigger off a range of activities thereby leading

[61] See Government of Sikkim, 'Sikkim-Tibet Trade via Nathu La: A Policy Study on Prospect, Opportunities and Requisite Preparedness', A report by Nathu La Trade Study Group, n. 40, 149–163.

[62] John W. Garver, 'Development of China's Overland Transportation Links with Central, Southwest and South Asia', n. 58, 14.

[63] Zhang Yunling, ed., 'Development of China's Transportation Infrastructure and International Connectivity', *ERIA Research Project Report* 7(5) (2009): 74. Available at http://www.eria.org/publications/research_project_reports/images/pdf/y2009/no7-5/all_files.pdf.

[64] Ibid., 75.

[65] Ibid.

to wholesome gains for the partner countries both at the local and national levels'.[66] This trade route has the potential to serve as a major supplier of immediate products from India for Chinese manufacturing units in the TAR region. Furthermore, with increase in the volume of trade, there is bound to be an impact on the transport economy through collection of toll taxes, license fee and so forth. Besides, the government and private transport providers will also emerge as direct beneficiaries from these arrangements. However, for this vision to be realized, there is an urgent need to speed up and improve transport infrastructure and amenities between Siliguri and Nathu La.

The transformation of 'border trade' into 'trade across border' would require much larger infrastructure development and a greater willingness from the governments to collate their needs with the fragile environment in these regions. In the case of transport, winding roads and fragile environment posit a huge challenge for navigability of container trucks. According to the GOI's plans to develop the borders of the northeast region, improvement of connectivity through infrastructure, including road, air and rail networks would be of high priority. The Ministry of Railways has proposed a ₹1,340-crore railway line from North Bengal in 2009 which will extend up to the border town of Rangpo in Sikkim.[67]

The presence of a railway line at Rangpo will facilitate fast movement of products and, at the same time, will also cut the cost of transportation from Nathu La to Siliguri. This railway line could further be supplemented by utilizing the proposed alternative route to Nathu La which will bypass Gangtok. With the alternative route, expansion of roads from single to double and four lanes will be facilitated, further enhancing the viability of container trucks for easy, fast and cost-effective movement of goods. This alternative route will also provide uninterrupted flow for government or private transportation trucks of medium

---

[66] See Government of Sikkim, 'Sikkim-Tibet Trade via Nathu La: A Policy Study on Prospect, Opportunities and Requisite Preparedness', A report by Nathu La Trade Study Group, n. 40, 148.

[67] Railway Technology, Railway-technology.com, 'North Bengal-Sikkim Railway Link, India', http://www.railway-technology.com/projects/northbengal-sikkimrai/.

size to carry goods. Respondents during field interviews, who are engaged in transport business, are of the view that containerization of transport will deprive the locals of their fair share of benefits, as the investment in this economy will be dominated by big players with which the locals will not be able to compete, while investments in medium-range transport will provide an equitable playing field for the local players and generate employment at the same time (based on personal interviews). Moreover, medium-range transport would also be much more suitable to the fragile ecosystem (based on personal interviews).

Looking Ahead

India's LEP and China's preferential investment policies for its south-western provinces are two respective policies that sought to address their domestic peripheral economic development by linking the periphery to the larger transnational network. In this scheme of things, northeast India, Southwest China and Southeast Asia became an integral part of the sub-regional cooperation. The Kunming Initiative, Bangladesh–China–India–Myanmar Forum for Regional Cooperation (BCIM) and other sub-regional cooperation mechanisms reflect the strategic outlook of the South Asian countries to link their border economies. What provides a binding factor is the shared cultural milieu and similar experiences along similar geographies endowed with vast natural resources on the one hand and environmental challenges on the other hand.

Yet, these regions have remained underdeveloped for a long time due to colonial demarcation of boundary lines which led to isolation and indifference of the two sides towards each other and thereafter conflict and securitization of the respective borders. It is only of late that there is a general understanding that borders as product of colonial construction and source of conflict need to be relooked at and collectively tap the untapped resources such as oil and petroleum, hydro power, forest products, horticulture and floriculture and tourism of this sub-region. According to Biswa N. Bhattacharya and Prabir De, the combined advantage of developing trade and infrastructure along northeast India and Southwest China can be summed up as follows[68]:

1. A market of 400 million people is emerging, including neighbouring countries such as Bangladesh, Bhutan, China, Myanmar and Nepal which can be tapped.
2. The region has the potential of developing into India's powerhouse; the area is a vibrant source of energy, rich in oil, natural gas, coal and limestone, and India's largest perennial water system—the river Brahmaputra and its tributaries—can be tapped for energy, irrigation and transportation purposes.
3. The fertile soil around the Brahmaputra Valley is a storehouse of horticultural products, plantation crops, vegetables, spices, rare herbs and medicinal plants, which can be utilized.
4. Unlimited tourist potential exists in this region, considering the rare flora and fauna, natural scenic beauty, unique performing arts, varied cuisine and the textiles.
5. Locational advantages make this region attractive to foreign investment; it has unique proximity to other countries in South and Southeast Asia regions.

Therefore, this region can emerge as a strategic base for foreign/domestic investors to tap the world's largest market evident in regional groupings such as the South Asian Association for Regional Cooperation (SAARC), Bay of Bengal Initiative for Multi-Sectoral Technical and Economic Cooperation (BIMSTEC) and the Association of Southeast Nations (ASEAN).[69] Opening of the border and initiatives such as border trade will be a much welcome step towards this direction.

These observations are even more relevant in the case of northeast India which shares 98 per cent of its boundary with

[68] Biswa N. Bhattacharya and Prabir De, 'Promotion of Trade and Investments between China and India: The Case of Southwest China and East and Northeast India', *CESIFO Working Paper* 1508(7) (2005): 16. Available at http://www.ifo.de/pls/guestci/download/CESifo%20Working%20Papers%202005/CESifo%20Working%20Papers%20July%202005/cesifo1_wp1508.pdf.

[69] Biswa N. Bhattacharya and Prabir De, 'Promotion of Trade and Investments Between China and India: The Case of Southwest China and East and Northeast India', n. 66, 16.

the neighbouring countries and only 2 per cent with India. Its border with Bangladesh covers 2,500 km; with Bhutan, it shares 650 km; with China, it covers about 1,000 km; with Myanmar, it shares 1,450 km; and with Nepal, 177 km (while just 92 km with West Bengal and 85 km with Sikkim). It is therefore natural that India's northeast economies should be integrated more with its neighbouring countries, and that the success of India's LEP will depend on how much the region can act as a gateway. However, as a gateway to the east and south-western part of China, this region demands major intervention in the form of infrastructure, technology and human resources investment.

Infrastructure development as discussed earlier remains critical to connecting the borders. If one is to take into consideration the future dynamics of trade across the border, quality roads and connectivity are critical, especially as the region is seismologically sensitive and bears fragile natural environmental. Here the role of technology becomes vital in addressing infrastructure development which can make drastic contributions by applying both traditional and modern forms of knowledge in infrastructure development.

Over the past few years, Sikkim has become one of the most sought-after tourist destinations.[70] Between 1980–1981 and 2006–2007, the average contribution of tourism and allied industries (transport and communication, trade, hotels and restaurant, banking and insurance) accounted for 11.4 per cent of the Gross State Domestic Product (GSDP)[71] of which trade, hotels and restaurants were the highest contributors with 6 per cent weightage, transport and communication had 2.9 per cent share and while banking and insurance had 2.3 per cent share.[72] Today, the number of tourist arrivals in Sikkim is among the highest in northeast India (see Tables 3.16–3.18). It is also argued that the opening of Nathu La for tourism besides trade will enhance the regional economy of both the countries.

Such a view is also perceptible among the Chinese government officials and policy groups. Speaking to a reporter on the

---

[70] Government of Sikkim: Tourism Department, Sikkim Tourism Policy 2010, Available at www.sikkimtourism.travel/.../pdf/Sikkim_Tourism_Policy_10.pdf.

[71] Anjan Chakrabarti, 'Tourism in Sikkim: Quest for A Self-Reliant Economy', *The NEHU Journal* 7(1) (2009): 96.

[72] Ibid.

Table 3.16
Domestic tourist arrival in Sikkim (included the unrecorded 25%)

	2005	2006	2007	2008	2009	2010	2011	2012
January	14,245	17,887	22,286	24,035	30,395	40,160	42,314	30,258
February	16,100	18,550	23,465	26,098	35,883	48,420	50,652	29,642
March	26,100	41,593	47,465	51,018	55,965	60,560	62,438	33,421
April	43,702	61,084	70,684	76,539	85,669	87,172	89,238	50,698
May	70,744	80,052	86,448	99,625	108,778	116,641	124,323	NA
June	30,480	32,912	34,025	35,172	63,905	68,236	69,784	NA
July	13,760	17,268	19,462	22,010	26,992	27,021	29,540	NA
August	14,382	20,628	21,428	22,628	35,826	37,180	38,964	NA
September	22,738	25,028	25,295	26,910	41,285	53,624	13,943	NA
October	35,396	39,834	43,218	49,456	44,865	59,582	9,682	NA
November	33,480	35,899	38,215	43,018	43,720	48,764	8,326	NA
December	26,523	31,208	33,213	35,864	42,345	52,651	13,249	NA
Total	347,650	421,943	465,204	512,373	615,628	700,011	552,453	144,019

Source: Government of Sikkim, Tourism and Civil Aviation Department, Statistics of Tourist Arrival in the State of Sikkim.[73]

[73] http://www.sikkimtourism.travel/Webforms/General/DepartmentStakeholders/TouristArrivalStats.aspx.

Table 3.17
Foreign tourist arrival in Sikkim

	2005	2006	2007	2008	2009	2010	2011	2012
January	721	789	866	910	696	984	1,436	1,904
February	1,082	1,262	1,286	1,106	1,053	1,320	1,065	2,406
March	2,280	1,981	2,225	2,406	2,184	2,605	2,423	3,199
April	2,198	3,124	2,386	2,411	2,544	3,036	2,615	3,939
May	1,351	1,445	1,058	1,857	1,335	1,593	2,875	NA
June	611	488	631	393	429	830	643	NA
July	372	471	549	453	646	680	553	NA
August	625	741	811	864	846	979	873	NA
September	991	1,372	1,230	1,330	1,275	1,678	1,415	NA
October	3,053	2,961	3,106	3,386	2,925	2,780	4,286	NA
November	2,313	2,198	2,471	2,867	2,406	2,410	3,323	NA
December	921	1,217	1,218	1,171	1,391	1,862	2,438	NA
Total	16,518	18,049	17,837	19,154	17,730	20,757	23,945	11,448

Source: Government of Sikkim, Tourism and Civil Aviation Department, Statistics of Tourist Arrival in the State of Sikkim.[74]

reopening of the Nathu La border in 2006, the then Chinese ambassador to India, Sun Yuxi, remarked that China expects the border will soon open for tourists and that a bus service from Gangtok to Lhasa will be started in due course of time.[75] It is thus evident that while on the Chinese side, there is not much reservation in exploring the option of opening of the border for tourism, it is for the GOI to respond to this initiative with a viable policy framework, safeguarding its own interest at the same time. Bus services akin to those of Amritsar–Lahore, Srinagar–Muzaffarabad, Agartala–Dhaka and Kolkata–Dhaka could be operated between Gangtok and Lhasa.

It has also been proposed that the concept of circuit tourism could be experimented in these regions. Circuit tourism of

[74] http://www.sikkimtourism.travel/Webforms/General/DepartmentStakeholders/TouristArrivalStats.aspx.

[75] *People's Daily*, 7 July 2006, 'Round up: "Silk Road" rejoins at Nathu La Pass after 44 years', http://english.people.com.cn/200607/07/eng20060707_280785.html.

Table 3.18
Number of tourists who visited Nathu La (2006-2010)

Months	2006	2007	2008	2009	2010
January	1,380	2,217	1,410	685	2,525
February	1,342	698	249	1,688	2,735
March	1,247	2,521	1,536	2,069	2,918
April	3,453	6,657	5,179	2,059	1,056
May	5,045	8,490	10,523	8,641	NA
June	4,910	7,757	3,710	8,759	NA
July	2,614	1,743	723	2,266	NA
August	1,431	573	589	NIL	NA
September	3,106	1,330	1,794	5,082	NA
October	5,390	7,295	7,305	6,040	NA
November	3,627	7,835	4,830	3,822	NA
December	3,972	5,622	3,950	3,700	NA
Total	37,517	52,738	41,798	44,811	12,234

Source: Office of the Inspector General of Police, Check Post Branch, Gangtok; Kaleon, *India China Border Trade through Nathula: Challenges and Opportunities*, MA Dissertation, Sikkim University, 2010, p. 42.

pilgrimage has major potential in the Eastern Himalayas. By opening up the border for tourism, Sikkim, Darjeeling, Bodh Gaya, Bhutan and Tibet could enable enhancement of people-to-people contacts in the region. The Nathu La study group in its assessment of tourism potential remarked that, in comparison to any other existing route from India, namely, Pulan Port at Taklakot (Uttar Pradesh), Nathu La 'would be logistically more economic, historical and culturally a better port of entry for potential outbound Indian tourist coming into Tibet'.[76]

The route to Mansarovar Lake from Gangtok–Nathu La–Lhasa, which is a distance of about 1,500 km, has been one of the traditional route which the pilgrims and traders took during the earlier centuries. These linkages can be explored by easing restriction of movement of people not only across the border but also within

[76] See Government of Sikkim, 'Sikkim-Tibet Trade via Nathu La: A Policy Study on Prospect, Opportunities and Requisite Preparedness', A report by Nathu La Trade Study Group, n. 40, 206.

Sikkim itself. Therefore, a review and subsequent removal of the Restricted Area Permission (RAP) regime could be a relevant move towards achievement of the above-stated ideal. Easing the movement of people within and across the border will bring positive changes for the local economy of the regions where development of infrastructure and trade will become inevitable through mushrooming of structures such as hotels, guest houses and markets on both sides of the border. Improvement of tourist infrastructure within Sikkim also remains critical to this vision.

Human resource development would then become both a means and an end for these linkages. The region possesses a high literacy rate and better sex ratio than the rest of India but lacks credible institutions for higher education, professional and technical training as well as research. It is only when these issues are addressed adequately that the potential of the region can be fully realized.[77] The role of institutions in generating employability will be meaningful if such institution(s) focuses on the existing strengths of the region like reviving the carpet industry. In Sikkim, the department of capacity building for employment generation is one such department which is imparting training on weaving, arts and handicrafts. These measures can be, however, beneficial only in the short term, but if trade through Nathu La is to be internationalized, then a long-term investment and road map are required.

Anticipating increased volume of trade in the future, areas for conservation and livestock management would also be required. Thus, the need for a transboundary conservation programme between India and China will provide local employment and income generation. Cross-breeding programmes between the Tibetan sheep and yaks with that of the Indian stock will help to generate a better and wider gene pool of high-quality sheep and yaks and thus benefit production of high-quality wool and dairy products.

To contextualize the Nathu La border trade and its relevance, it is essential to draw upon P. Banerjee and X. Chen's argument that boundaries 'are perhaps the most palpable political geographic phenomena' because they mutate and evolve based on

[77] Biswa N. Bhattacharya and Prabir De, 'Promotion of Trade and Investments Between China and India: The Case of Southwest China and East and Northeast India', n. 66, 29.

their history and natural and political resources'.[78] According to them, the impact of globalization on borders cannot be ignored for globalization has caused borders to push and pull, as a result, over a period of time, borderlands that are affected by globalization develop their own distinctive regional and local characters through mutation.[79]

It is within this push and pull of the forces of globalization that borders and peripheries of India and China that were previously guarded by national boundaries are now being seen as economic opportunities. However, it has also been pointed out that any attempt at integrating the local economy with the global economy depends on how well the local economy on both the sides of the border is connected to other localities through some sort of regional centres.[80] If the region fails to integrate with the global economy, the result would be over-localization of economic ties. Such localization will itself mitigate the integrating effect of globalization on borderlands, thus contributing to a local territorial confinement of social and economic transactions.[81] The Nathu La border trade, which was initially conceived with a view to not only reviving and transforming India–China bilateral ties but also developing the sub-region, is today, alas, over-localized with no prospect of integrating its border trade with the global economy, thus depriving both the underdeveloped regions of India and China from mutually benefiting from this process of integration.

Integrating this trade with the regional economy requires an imaginative and sustainable policy. In this age informed by interdependence, integrating the economy of Nepal, Bhutan, Bangladesh and part of Bihar, West Bengal, Odisha and north-eastern region of India with that of south-western China becomes

---

[78] P. Banerjee and X. Chen, 'Living in in-between spaces: A structure-agency analysis of the India–China and India–Bangladesh borderlands', *J. Cities* (2012): 1. Available at http://dx.doi.org/10.1016/j.cities.2012.06.011; J. Minghi, 'Boundary studies in political geography', *Annals of the Association of American Geographers* (1963): 407.

[79] Ibid.

[80] P. Banerjee and X. Chen, 'Living in in-between spaces: A structure-agency analysis of the India–China and India–Bangladesh borderlands', n. 76, 1. Available at http://dx.doi.org/10.1016/j.cities.2012.06.011.

[81] P. Banerjee and X. Chen, 'Living in in-between spaces: A structure-agency analysis of the India–China and India–Bangladesh borderlands', *J. Cities* (2012): 1. Available at http://dx.doi.org/10.1016/j.cities.2012.06.011.

inevitable, more so, in order to expand economic activities along the various existing border trade routes. Movement of people and goods in the form of people-to-people contacts such as cultural and religious tourism, expansion of the status of border trade into a bilateral trade will, to a large extent, provide a momentum to India's LEP.

At present, the figures of trade seem miniscule, but the scale and volume of trade from Nathu La cannot be over-ambitious in the immediate term. With relatively new approaches towards border region, specially as a zone of strategic importance in terms of trade and connections, and along with sustainable policies, trade routes can be transformed into devices for CBM and mutual gains for both India and China along with assimilating their immediate underdeveloped regions and provinces.

Suggested Readings

Official Sources

Government of India, Tourism Department, Sikkim Tourism Policy 2010, available at www.sikkimtourism.travel/.../pdf/Sikkim_Tourism_Policy_10.pdf.
World Trade Organization, The General Agreement on Tariffs and Trade (GATT 1947) (Geneva: WTO), available at www.wto.org/english/docs_e/legal_e/gatt47_e.pdf.

Books/Articles

Alvarez, R. Jr., (1995), 'The Mexican–US Border: The Making of Anthropology of Borderlands', *Annual Review of Anthropology* 24: 447–470.
Chen, X.M. (2000), 'Both Glue and Lubricant: Transnational Ethnic Social Capital as a Source of Asia-Pacific Subregionalism', *Policy Sciences* 33: 269–287.
——— (2005). *As Borders bend: Transnational Spaces on the Pacific Rim* (Lanham, MD: Rowman & Littlefield).
——— (2009), 'Pacific Rim'. In R. Kitchin, & N. Thrift (eds), *International Encyclopedia of Human Geography* (Oxford: Elsevier), 66–71.
Coleman, M. (2007), 'A Geopolitics of Engagement: Neoliberalism, the War on Terrorism, and the Reconfiguration of US Immigration Enforcement', *Geopolitics* 12: 607–634.
Kloos, P. (2000), 'The Dialectics of Globalization and Localization'. In D. Kalb, M. van der Land, R. Staring, & B. van Steenbergen (eds), *The Ends of Globalization:*

Bringing Society Back In (Lanham, MD: Rowman & Littlefield Publishers), 281–297.

Mackenzie, A. (2003 Reprint), *The North East Frontier of India* (Delhi: Spectrum Publication).

Newman, D. (2000), 'Into the Millennium: The Study of International Boundaries in an Era of Global and Technological Change', *Boundary and Security Bulletin* 7(4): 63–72.

———— (2003), 'On Borders and Power: A Theoretical Framework', *Journal of Borderland Studies* 18(1): 13–25.

———— (2006), 'The Lines That Continue to Separate Us: Borders in Our 'Border-less' World', *Progress in Human Geography* 30(2): 1–19.

Paasi, A. (1999), 'Boundaries as Social Processes: Territoriality in the World of Flows'. In D. Newman (ed.), *Boundaries, Territory and Postmodernity* (London: Frank Cass).

Ray, Sunanda & K. Datta. (2006), 'Nathu La: It's More Than Revival of a Trade Route', Available at http://www.phayul.com/news/article. aspx?id=13200&t=1&c=1, 10 July 2006.

Sikkim Now, 30 November 2012, 'Despite Unfavorable Environment, Border Trade Crosses 7 Crore Mark', available at sikkimnow.blogspot.in/2012/11/despite-unfavorable-environment-border.html?m=1#!/2012/11/despite-unfavorable-environment-border.html.

4

Reviving Old Routes: Sino-Indian Border Trade via Himachal Pradesh

Uttam Lal

Introduction

Remote mountainous areas have always enjoyed relations across the Himalayas. From time immemorial, people have wandered across these regions in search of better resources or to secure survival amid harsh environmental conditions typical of higher altitudinal regions and even in search of better fortune. Rugged topography and severe climatic conditions not only limited the access to natural resources but also instilled a fear of the unforeseen, which led to the prominence of religious factors among these Himalayan communities. Yet, limited natural resources forced people to move across the mountainous wilderness on a regular basis. For centuries, caravans moved across the Himalayan range transporting holy men, traders and mules along with several tradable items.

Himachal Pradesh, a western Himalayan state of India, shares boundary with the Tibet Autonomous Region (TAR) of China. This natural boundary comprises numerous peaks, mostly towering above 6,000 m. Bordering communities in this region enjoyed free flow of men and materials to the other side (TAR in China) till the movement was suddenly disturbed by the Sino-Indian border conflict in the 1960s. The link remained severed for the next three decades, where after the respective governments realized the criticality of border trade for the development of these regions. Thus, a joint decision was taken by both New Delhi and Beijing to formally open Shipki La for cross-border trade. Protocols were signed in 1992 and 1993, following which the trade route was officially opened.

The rationale for this study is to assess the current position of interactions across the Sino-Indian border and to arrive at a real picture of the state of trade in the Himachal sector. Keeping this in mind, traders, shepherds and porters who ventured across into Tibet and subsequently returned have been interviewed (to generate primary data). As the area under study is hindered by not only environmental limitations but also seasonal and bureaucratic hurdles, direct observations on the trade were not possible. Therefore, some officials from the custom department, district administration and Indo-Tibet Border Police (ITBP) as well as military have been interviewed. The fact that there was no proper existing marketplace for border trade in this region has further hindered the chances of direct observation. In order to gauge the nature of trails and understand the intricacies of trade, a trek to Shipki La was undertaken. Besides, some other not so renowned routes, through which men, material and monks have traversed to Tibet and back during their quest for trade and pilgrimage to holy shrines, have been trekked within the permissible official limits (as per directions of the defence personnel).

The study relies on both qualitative and quantitative techniques; the latter includes processing and analysis of both secondary and primary data. Primary data was gathered through questionnaire-based interviews. As there were not many regular trekkers along the trails to trade their goods across the borders in recent times, snowball sampling method has been employed to generate primary data. In the first stage of the study, relevant information was accumulated from the available literature and government documents. Interviews of various government officials were conducted. In the second stage, traders, shepherds, porters and monks were interviewed in the months of May and June 2010 and 2011.

Besides, the relevant trails/tracks were also traversed in both the first and second stages. A total of 78 people who were interviewed claimed to have crossed the border at different times for trade purposes. Out of these, only 13 claimed to have made it to Tibet with proper trade permits, while others went across without a valid document. Most of these people went across when the cross-border movement was not so restrictive. The other respondents were shepherds, pilgrims and monks. Besides, focused group discussions were also conducted to understand the practices and preferences of the people. Such groups also included individuals who had never been to Tibet but were living close to the border areas.

Several constraints were also witnessed to the study. Direct observation was hindered as the period of formal trade is only between 1 June and the end of November, when traders, porters, shepherds and monks are most busy with their respective activities and can spare little or no time for questionnaire-based interviews. While on the one hand, the time period between June and October usually presents fair weather conditions ideal for crossing over the high Himalayan pastures and passes and negotiate inhospitable heights, on the other hand, the same period is also the time of hectic sociocultural and economic activities as it coincides with the harvest season and almost every inhabitant has their share of chores chalked out to be performed before the rain or snow takes them by surprise.

Extremely low number of traders crossing the Shipki La is another limitation. The year 2009 registered about 46 willing inhabitants buying the 'trade permit' forms from the Subdivisional Magistrate Office (SDMO). However, only 17 persons came back and submitted their permit forms and were subsequently issued the trade permits. It is still not clear whether all the 17 persons crossed the border last year. Such confirmation would have been possible only with the 'record books' of ITBP and custom department, which were not accessible. Of the inhabitants who were issued trade permits in 2011, only 13 could be traced and interviewed. Out of these 13, 11 confirmed to have gone across the border. Moreover, not everyone who is issued trade permits is actively engaged in the trade.

As most of the traders are engaged in trading items which are not listed on the permissible trade list, they are reluctant to divulge the details of their trade. Therefore, questionnaire-based interviews had to be changed into informal dialogues frequently. The study was constrained not only by the harsh environmental conditions but also by virtually non-existent infrastructure. The lack of a common marketplace coupled by the age-old mode of transportation, use of pony, and the not so welcoming attitude[1] of military/paramilitary as well as custom personnel, were sufficient to keep the Tibetans traders away from venturing into the Indian side of the border for trade. So far, no traders from the TAR have ventured onto the Indian side. Therefore, interviews with traders from across the border could not be conducted.

Historical Overview

Trade has been one of the most fundamental activities among human societies living across border. The limited carrying capacity of the land coupled with short growing seasons force people to establish trade relations with their geographically adjacent societies. Thus, trade across the Himalayas in the Himachal sector has had a long history.

It is alleged that some portion of the present Himachal Pradesh came under Tibetan rule during the regime of King Srong-Tsan-Gampo during the 7th century AD.[2] With the invasion of Tibetan king Srong-Tsan-Gampo's army (AD 620–649), the region underwent a process of Tibetanization. This resulted in intermingling and influx of the Tibetan blood among the local populace.[3] The most significant development in the history of Himachal took place however during the 17th century AD with the rise of Raja Kheri Singh of Bushair State. He was a powerful chief in the western Himalayas. During the war between Tibet and Ladakh in 1681–1683, he sided with Tibet due to which he was granted some portions of the present Kinnaur district and free trade licenses were given to traders of Bushair State for using market centres of western Tibet.[4]

Hordes of ponies, goats and sheep loaded with merchandized goods freely crossed over to the other side, though the

[1] Based on personal interviews.

[2] Rahul Sanskritayan (1948), *Kinner Desh Mein*, 2nd edition (Hindi) (Allahabad: Kitab Mahal Publication, 2006), 149.

[3] Giuseppe Tucci, *Tibet: Land of Snow*, translated by J.E. Stapleton Driver (London: P. Elek, 1973), 23–28.

[4] Ramnath Singh Fonia (1991), *Socio-Economic and Cultural Study of Western Himalayas during Early Medieval and Medieval Times*, Unpublished PhD Thesis, Centre for Historical Studies, Jawaharlal Nehru University, New Delhi, 27.

local *Chakpa* robbers remained a huge disturbance to the trade.[5] In order to codify the trade agreement, Rampur Bushahr and the Tibetan side agreed to conduct trade fairs at Rampur and Gartok, the main towns of Rudokh province and Tibet, respectively. At Gartok, where one of the biggest regional markets was held every year in August and September, traders from Lahaul, Spiti and Rampur Bushahr congregated after travelling up the Sutlej Valley and over the Shipki La and various other routes through the Rupsu plateau of south-eastern Ladakh.[6] Traders from Kullu arrived at both Gartok and Rudok to buy wool.[7] Gartok emerged as a vibrant wool mart in Tibet; the seasonal trade congregation at Gartok drew about 10,000–20,000 people. Besides, the inhabitants of Spiti traded with their neighbours on the other side of the Himalaya; the exports mainly consisted of wool, borax, salt and blankets, and other imports articles from the plains and a great deal of iron.

The old Hindustan–Tibet Road was also visualized as alternate route for acquiring pashmina wool from Tibet for the shawl industry in Punjab.[8] But very few foreign travellers took this route during the latter half of the 19th century. Yet the logbooks of forest and PWD rest houses give interesting entries of famous visitors such as Francke, Sven Hedin, Marco Pallis, Giuseppe Tucci and so forth who were headed to Gartok, indicating trade relations with Tibet. Also prominent among them were Gerard, Jacquemont and Hutton as they gave extensive account of their visit. Moorcraft was of the view that the East India Company's agents should procure pashm themselves via the valley of the Sutlej from Tibet for the shawl industry in Punjab. To this end, a company's factory was established as early as the beginning of 19th century at Kotgarh in Shimla district[9] which was not very successful. However, the to and fro movement of traders across Himalayas up till Rampur became well established by the 1830s.

---

[5] Gazetteer of Kangra District (1899), 74.

[6] Janet Rizvi, *Trans-Himalayan Caravans* (New Delhi: Oxford University Press, 1997), 37.

[7] Ibid. (1899 Report by Captain R.L. Kennion).

[8] Deepak Sanan and Swati Dhanu, *Exploring Kinnaur and Spiti in the Trans-Himalaya* (New Delhi: Indus Publishing Company, 1998), 175.

[9] Janet Rizvi, *Trans-Himalayan Caravans* (New Delhi: Oxford University Press, 2007), 61.

Table 4.1
Movement of merchandized goods from Chini and Yarkand

	Imports (₹)			Export (₹)		
Year	Chini (Kalpa)	Yarkand	Total	Chini (Kalpa)	Yarkand	Total
1879–1880*	339,744	6,150	345,894	16,774	5,358	22,132
1880–1881*	201,147	4,800	205,947	13,311	5,647	18,958
1882–1883**			202,276			39,972
1902–1903**			177,106			15,296

Source: *Gazetteer of Kangra District, Vol. II, 1883–1884.
**Imperial Gazetteer Provincial Series (Punjab), 1908–1909.

For remote mountainous societies like these, with harsh environmental conditions and simple technological skills at their disposal, it was imperative to take on trading expeditions guided by subsistence and search for fortune. But in due course of time, the need for subsistence was supplemented by the desire to accrue extra as well. Therefore, apart from the goods for subsistence, traders frequently begin to negotiate the high altitudes of wilderness primarily for profit-generating items such as pashm, wool and borax. As there was a flourishing European market for these products, return from these trails were promising. Table 4.1 shows that Kalpa became a prominent place for both import and export of these items by 1879–1880. The table also shows that trade volume progressively decreased over the years primarily because of the decrease in demand of pashm and borax as the European markets began to squeeze on account of indigenous synthetic production and borax production in Europe itself.

However, this trade was able to preserve many of its original nuances till as late as the 1960s when Indo-Chinese border conflict broke out leading to restrictions on flow of men and materials.

Trade Routes

Peripheral societies of the Himalaya have always moved across high pastures and passes encompassing various river valleys and ridges. In the Himachal sector, the two main established routes of

Figure 4.1
Kongma La Valley

Source: Author.

transborder trade of pre-1960 are Kaurik and Shipki La/Kongma La trails (Figure 4.1).

Note that the circle in Figure 4.2 denotes Chuppan, where a custom booth is located. Close to it is the site for yet to be established Indira Market. The curved line in the figure denotes trail to Kongma La, while the grey serpentine trail leads to Shipki La.

Ridge in the foreground has Shipki La; Tibetan territory lies beyond this ridge (Figure 4.3).

The crest line of three mountain ranges encompassing higher Himachal, namely, the Zanskar Range, the Great Himalayan Range and the Dhauladhar Range, is generally covered with permanent snow. Peaks mostly rise between 5,180 m and 6,850 m. The crests are interspersed by many passes with varied altitude between 3,700 m and about 5,600 m. There are about seven passes on the eastern boundary with Tibet. These passes were once frequented by traders and shepherds who used to travel to Tibet and vice versa. Shipki La is the lowermost pass which

Figure 4.2
Kongma La and Shipki La trails

Source: Author.

Figure 4.3
Ridge in the foreground of Shipki La pass

Source: Author.

connects Kinnaur with Tibet. It lies close to the point where the Sutlej River enters into India. Lukma La (4,800 m) lies just south of Shipki La and is alternatively known as Kongma La or Gogma La. Many times, it was preferred over Shipki La for trade. That is because though Lukma La is higher, it was frequented because the ancient trail to Tibet through Shipki La involved negotiating a dangerous cliff near Namgia Village. Raniso is another pass on the border which connects to the habitable part of Kinnaur via Ganthang Pass and Hojlis Gad. South of Raniso Pass is Keobarang Pass which connects Nesang/Gyamthing Valley with Tibet. Other passes also connect essential trade routes (Table 4.2).[10]

Shorter but more difficult routes are strewn across between prominent trails which experienced frequent movement of trade caravans. They primarily served the needs of local communities and small traders. Kaurik has been a prominent getaway to Tibet for the people of Spiti and some villages of upper Hangarang Valley of Kinnaur. Lahuala traders frequented these difficult but prominent routes to Tibet. It required traders to negotiate almost seven passes along these routes and took about 20–25 days for one-way journey. Though all these passes used to record seasonal nomadic beats of men, material and mules or other pack animals such as goats and sheep because almost all the highland society were directly or indirectly involved with this trans-Himalayan trade, but now only people from upper Kinnaur use this trail for trade.

Present Status and Organizational Capacities

The deputy commissioner of Kinnaur district at Reckong Peo has been designated as a trade authority by the Government of Himachal Pradesh to account for all formal and check informal trade in the region. The Director of Industries, Himachal Pradesh, has been has been appointed as the state-level coordinator.

[10] Shimdang Pass connects Tirung Valley to Tibet via Kunu Village and Shola pasture ground. Khimokul Pass also known as Gumrang Pass connects Tirung Valley via Charang Village. Mule track to Tibet for people of Baspa Valley primarily passed through Yamrang Pass. Yamrang is the southernmost pass on Kinnaur–Tibet border.

Table 4.2
Cross-border trade trail of Himachal sector

River valleys	Trading trails	Connects	Journey days (one way)	Difficulty level
Tirung Valley	1. Kuno–Kota–Shimding La 2. Charang–Baratikhad–Khimokul La	Thangi/Charang to	3–5	Moderate to difficult
Baspa Valley	1. Chitkul–Nagasthi–Yumrang La–Tango–Bekhar–Dumbora	Connects Baspa Valley to Tango/Bekhar/Dumbora in Tibet	15	Difficult
Sutlej Valley	1. Namgia–Chhuppan–Shipki La/Kongma La–Shipki La 2. Tashigang–Somang–Kholodombo–Puri	Namgia to Shipki in Tibet	1	Easy
Hojilis Valley	1. Dubling–Rishidogri–Gantang La–Zungchan–Raniso/Keobarang La–Baikhar	Pooh/Dubling to Baikhar in Tibet	4–5	Very difficult
Hangarang Valley	1. Hurling–Sumdo–Kaurik–Lapcha–Shurup 2. Chango/Shalkhar–Changarang lamo/Thongba la–Simsim–Kaurik–Lapcha–Shurup	Sumra, Shalkhar, Chango, Hurling and Kaurik to Shurup, Sumgil and Naksun in Tibet	2	Easy
Gyamthing Valley	1. Nesang–Bhupa–Jungchun–Raniso La/Keobrang La	Moorang/Nesang to Baikhar in Tibet	5–6	Moderate to difficult
Lahaul Valley	1. Kyelong–Jispa–Patseo–Jinjibar–Sarchu–Baracha La–Longlachha la–Kyagsu–Chogar	Kullu and Lahaul Valleys via Rupshu plateau to Rudoh, Rubang and Gartok in Tibet	20–25	Difficult

Source: Field interviews.

Table 4.3
Administrative infrastructure and its present status

S. no.	Administrative infrastructure	Status
1	Police check post	Exists at Namgia
2	Custom office	Exists at Namgia
3	Shopping complex	Does not exist
4	Post office	Exists at Namgia
5	Bank	Does not exist
6	Health post	Exists Ayurvedic dispensary at Namgia
7	Guest house/hotel	Does not exist; only PWD rest house at Namgia

Travel/trade passes between India and China are to be issued by an officer not below the rank of executive magistrate of first class. At present, the tehsildar, Pooh subdivision (SD) of Kinnaur, is performing the functions of this designation (Table 4.3).[11]

Informal Trade

The inadequate ceiling on the value of tradable goods as well as restrictions on various desired commodities across the border has led to informal trade. Field observations suggest that informal trade takes place not only through Shipki La but also through other passes. As food products have maximum demand across the border, they are more frequently traded. However, informal import basket consists of blankets, cutleries, footwear, ready-made garments, fancy items and so on.

Quantifying informal trade is not possible because of the unwillingness of the traders to share details about their trade and absence of vigil due to multiple entry and exit points. Many such informal traders avoid interviews also because they travel for trade purposes without relevant documents thereby being scared of legal reprehension. It is suspected by several segments of the society that informal trade is still being carried on, with

[11] General Manager, District Industries Centre, Reckong Peo, Kinnaur Brief Background: Note on setting up of China-Border Trade Post via Shipki La, District Kinnaur (HP).

implicit knowledge of the military and intelligence personnel. This proposition is difficult to establish, but it has undoubtedly added to the trust deficit between the two countries (India and China) which is not favourable to future trade and flow of men and materials via this sector. It is interesting to note that even legal traders indulge in informal trade. They carry goods much beyond the list of items permitted as these items have high appeal due to profitability.

Formal Trade

After remaining closed for trade for almost three decades, the Shipki La Pass was reopened in 1992 with a lot of enthusiasm on both the sides. This formal trade route remains open from 1 June till the end of November every year. For the rest of the year, the pass remains closed for trade on account of being snow-laden.

Indian traders wanting to trade across the border are required to procure the trade permit form against a payment of ₹50 from the tehsildar at the office of subdivisional officer, Pooh. The first trade permit was issued in the year 1994. Figure 4.4 shows the number of people plying across the border every year; almost 90 Indian traders crossed over to TAR. Figure 4.4 also indicates that there has been a steady decline in the number of traders taking the trail to Shipki La. There was considerable rise in the amount of traders going to TAR in 2000 followed by an immediate decline, which can be explained on account of disruption of economic activities due to the devastating flood. The general nature of the formal trade is still 'subsistence type', which is not promising enough for the new generations of Kinnauras, Spitians and Lahaulas. Earlier, people used to carry their horticultural produce to the cities and towns of the lower hills and plains, and some headed to the TAR, but the contemporary generations are much more prosperous and disinclined to travel far for trade. Therefore, there has been a continuous decrease in traders going to the TAR.

In the year 2009, only 17 traders went across the border. It is to be noted that not all the valid permit holders cross the border for trade.[12] There has been a marginal increase in the numbers

---

[12] Interview with local traders.

Figure 4.4
Number of traders who travelled to TAR between 1994 and 2011

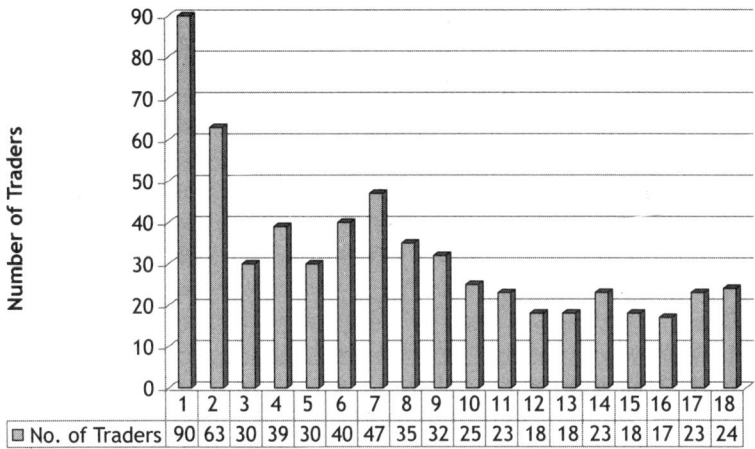

	1	2	3	4	5	6	7	8	9	10	11	12	13	14	15	16	17	18
No. of Traders	90	63	30	39	30	40	47	35	32	25	23	18	18	23	18	17	23	24

Source: SDMO, Pooh, Kinnaur.
Note: 1 to 18 is the consecutive years starting from 1994 to 2011. Figures are for official trade routed through Shipki La.

of traders who went across in 2012 and 2011 which resulted in a minor increase in the volume of trade. This was driven by the failure of the main cash crop of the area, apples, which did not do that well these two years; therefore, the small farmers of upper Kinnaur had to venture across the border to compensate for their profit margins. This does not indicate that cross-border trade had actually become attractive enough in these years.

Table 4.4 gives the list of items exported and imported without taxation through Shipki La. Other commodities either attract custom duties or are simply prohibited. Majority of the items of Table 4.4 are the ones either needed by peripheral mountain communities for subsistence or are for small-scale trade benefits.

Among the items of export, there is considerable demand for toffees, noodles, sauces, similar packaged food and ready-made apparels. These commodities are said to drive in smaller profits, while items such as transistors, Swiss watches, saffron, copra and dried apricot are said to drive in handsome profit (Table 4.5).[13]

[13] Interview.

Table 4.4
List of items imported without taxation through Shipki La

1	Goat skin	11	Yak hair
2	Sheep skin	12	China clay
3	Horses	13	Borax
4	Goats	14	Szaibelyte Szzinelyite
5	Sheep	15	Goat cashmere
6	Wool		
7	Butter		
8	Common salt		
9	Raw silk*		
10	Yak tail		

*Taxable commodities.

Table 4.5
List of items exported without taxation through Shipki La

1	Agricultural implements	11	Flour	21	Local herbs
2	Blankets	12	Dry fruits	22	Dyes
3	Copper products	13	Dry and fresh vegetables	23	Spices
4	Clothes	14	Vegetable oil	24	Watches
5	Textiles	15	Gur and misri	25	Shoes
6	Cycles	16	Tobacco	26	Kerosene oil
7	Coffee	17	Snuff	27	Stationery
8	Tea	18	Cigarettes	28	Utensils
9	Barley	19	Canned food	29	Wheat (Ua and Buck)
10	Rice	20	Agrochemical		

As Figure 4.5 suggests that the balance of trade is lopsided. This is because presently only Indian traders dare to venture across the order, as no trader from the TAR side ventures into India. Unless there will be an inflow of traders from across the border, including mainland China, Figure 4.5 is set to maintain this characteristic. According to Indian traders, People of the TAR region are more interested in entering India for pilgrimage. For trade purposes, the mainland Chinese traders need to be attracted to the potentials of

Figure 4.5
Volume of trade through Shipki La between 1994 and 2011

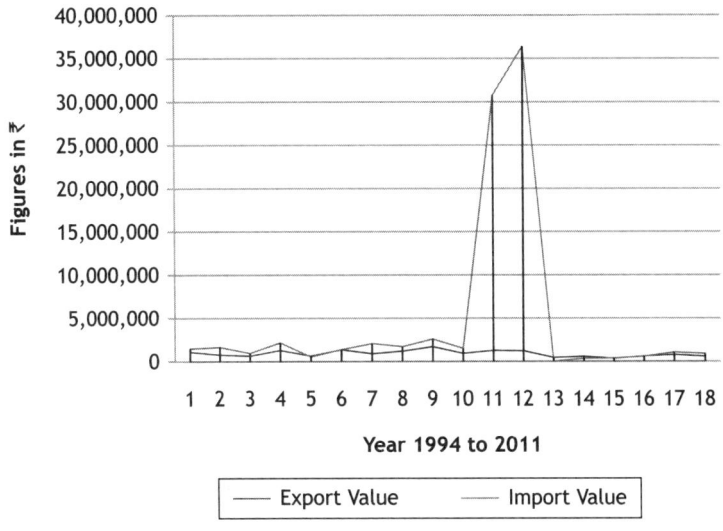

Export Value   Import Value

this trail, which is hindered by lack of proper paperwork across the border. It is also to be noted that religious artefacts also have considerable demand in the TAR. These commodities are said to be manufactured primarily by Tibetan communities residing in India. Table 4.4 gives the list of items with considerable export potentials. The state of Himachal being one of the hubs of pharmaceutical companies in India is strategically located to export medicines to TAR and even mainland China. On account of being a surplus state for hydroelectric power, Himachal is well placed to export electricity to TAR as well.

Cross-border Sociocultural Interactions

Journey across the Himalayan wilderness has always been strenuous but an ecological compulsion. During the course of annual nomadic movement, people have identified many places as sacred and picked up some of their local deities from territories which now lie across the border on both sides. Many lakes, mountain peaks, forest grooves and so forth have become symbols of divinity and are still revered. Thus, pilgrimage is common phenomenon among remote Himalayan communities on both sides of the border. Local deities of Kinnaur and Spiti such as Yulsa, Dabla, Ormig, Purgeol and so forth have their origins in the neighbouring Tibetan regions. Besides, few peaks such as Shurangbal of Timchhe group of mountains above the Moorang–Nesang villages in Kinnaur figured in the religious psyche of not only some villages of Kinnaur but also the Tibetans.

Likewise, the holiest peak and lake for a multitude of Indians lie in Tibet, which are Mount Kailash and Mansarovar, respectively. Similarly, the hot water springs of Sumdo near Kaurik and Spiti and the hot water spring site near Shipki La in Kinnaur used to be frequented by the people on both sides for both religious and health purposes. Rewalsar and the sacred trail of Somang have attracted many Tibetans to Himachal side for pilgrimage. Instances such as these are spread all along the Himalayas from Leh–Ladakh to Arunachal Pradesh. Trails to numerous pastures and different economic nodal stations on both sides of the border are strewn with places of religious significance. There have also been affinities between the border communities based on dialects and, at times, incidences of cross-border marriages as well. Before the current border restrictions were put in place, people of these remote areas moved across the border on regular basis to visit various *Gompa*[14] and other places of religious importance. Thus, religion along with better opportunity for trade has been the core factor behind people's movement across borders.

Hindrances to Trade

The GOI has so far allowed only traditional items to be traded across Shipki La. Cheese, butter, yak tails, pashm, wool, sheep and goat skins and so forth were some items of trade which were sought after as these used to be dirt cheap in Tibet, and there was no internal from within Tibet. However, now there is a huge demand from the mainstream Chinese towns owing to establishment of world-class roads and rail communication linkages and overall development of the nation, due to which such items command

---

[14] 'Gompa' is the Tibetan word for a Buddhist Monastery.

handsome price in Tibet itself. But these items of trade have lingered on in the official lists permitted by the government. It needs to recognize that with time, societies have changed and so have the requirements and demands of the people. Thus, the nature of trade also has to change.

There is an urgent need to revisit the list of items allowed to be traded across the border and make it contemporary so that the profit accruing to the traders are not only economically sustainable but also appealing in the long term. Slim profit margins for small traders are forcing them to keep away from it, even though they would like to continue trading and meeting people across the border. In 1991, when border trade was formally opened, goods worth of ₹25,000 were exempted from custom duty. But inflation has grown manifolds since then, but the ceiling of ₹25,000 still remains. The bar of ₹25,000 needs to be raised so that transborder trade remains economically viable and attractive.

As per the instruction of the Deputy Inspector General of Police (DIG) Intelligence ITBP, New Delhi, vide his letter No.VII-12011/06/Chinese Movement/Int./2011-/541 dated 29 July 2011, the Indian traders visiting China for trade are required to report back to India within three days from the date of their visit to China. This clause has become a hindrance in trade across the borders. As there is no proper trade mart on either side of the border as in the case of trade across Nathu La Pass, there is no set marketplace where Tibetan/Chinese can congregate with required amount of tradable goods. According to the Indian traders arranging for commodities of their choice by the Tibetan traders in required quantity takes time. At times, even the People's Liberation Army of China takes time to give clearance to traders. Therefore, they are compelled to come to India either without import goods or with little amount, even though some of them are willing to pay taxes for such items exceeding the ₹25,000 ceiling.

Common Perceptions on Trade

Movement of men, mules and materials across the Himalayan heights were not only ecological and monetary necessity but also been a part of our shared heritage. However, cross-border trade has become unattractive to people involved because of the following facts:

1. Lack of marketplace and related infrastructure on either side of the border.
2. Trading and travel passes being issued only to the inhabitant of Kinnaur.
3. Dialect itself is a major hindrance. The trade has been personalized and acquaintance based in the absence of marketing infrastructure. So, owing to similar dialect and some acquaintances, mostly it is traders from upper Kinnaur who venture out.
4. Government policies and the attitude of the ITBP personnel itself is quite unfavourable for the trade. An archaic restrictive list of items that can be imported and a ₹25,000 ceiling for tax purposes for the traders has been a great put-off among the traders. They have been demanding an upgradation of the list of items and relaxation of tax ceiling from ₹25,000 to ₹100,000.
5. Intimidating attitude of the Indian officials is perceived to be the reason why no Tibetan traders have crossed over to the Indian side ever since Shipki La was formally opened for border trade. Some respondents even believed the Chinese officials to be much more cooperative than the Indian officials.

The Way Forward

At present, small vehicles ply the Indian roads till Shipki La, while the Chinese have already constructed road arteries till Shipki village. With the opening of market places on the Indian side, this route can be opened for thriving mainstream trade and cross-border tourism. In order to make this trade more promising, construction of shops, warehouses, guest houses, along with simpler paperwork for incoming traders and friendly attitude of the government agency personnel, are required on priority basis. Besides, goods-laden vehicles should also be allowed till the Indira Market from the TAR and from Himachal to at least till Shipki village; the first village in TAR. The already commenced markets need to be completed; for instance, the market near Chuppan is yet to take shape. Though the area has been earmarked for market and is known as 'Indira Market', it is just a patch of wild-land fenced by barbed wires.

Table 4.6 enlists the potential export items compiled on the basis of field interview.

There is an impending need for policy and perception change within the Indian government. In Shipki La and many such border passes, the prospect of governing border areas with better initiatives like 'Know Your Borders' and Army/ITBP-regulated domestic tourists can be explored. Such initiatives will not only bring remote border areas psychologically closer to the so-called mainland India but also help in escalating the amount of infrastructure build-up right till our border posts. For long, the geography of our borders has remained equally alien to us as it is to our neighbours. Thus, common heritage and mutual existence can pave way for future cooperation in these regions.

Cultural heritage can be kept alive by allowing at least annual regulated traffic of tourists and trekkers under schemes such as 'Know Your Army, Border, Neighbour and Heritage' before such trails become fully worn down by decades of disuse and completely relegated to legendary accounts. Such initiatives will keep the local economy vibrant, the border more humane and

Table 4.6
Potential items of export through Shipki La to TAR

S. no.	Sectors	Commodities
1	Food products	Pulses, sugar, juices, etc
2	Agricultural and horticultural products	Seeds of various crops, temperate and tropical fruits, including apples and herbs
3	Cultural/religious items	Thanka, beads, prayer wheels, incense, silk cloths, etc. produced at Dharamshala and Bangalore
4	Construction materials	Steel, cement, building stones, including marbles, etc.
5	Energy	Export of HEP energy
6	Manufactured goods	Bicycles, automobiles and other hardware
7	Pharmaceutical products	Medicines

Source: Compiled after field interviews.

easier to patrol even when there are no activities for large part of the year.

Border trade or trade through borders is an issue which has gained much less attention than it deserves in the policy circles as of now. At best, the opening up of Shipki La has been a half-hearted measure towards Sino-Indian greater cross-border inter-actions or confidence-building measures (CBM). It has been a mere diplomatic exercise towards minimizing border disputes. So far, the trade across this pass has remained rather cosmetic. Perceptions have now moved beyond the concept of keeping the borders merely militarily guarded to governing the border areas to managing the border areas as the engines of growth, windows of opportunity as well as regions of integrating geog-raphies through out-of-box initiatives. The border of Himachal is no exception. Stereotypical barb-wired borders should give way to better communication channels and routes with ever increasing flow of (regulated) people and trade commodity.

Suggested Readings

Francke, A.H. (1914), *Antiquities of Indian Tibet. Vol. 1* (Calcutta: Superintendent Government Printing, Reprint 1999; Delhi: Low Price Publication).

Gerard, A. (1840), *Journey from Caunpoor to the Boorendo Pass in the Himalaya Moun-tains. Vol. II* (London: J. Madden & Co.)

——— (1841), *Account of Koonawar in Himalayas, etc. etc. etc.* (London: J. Madden & Co., Reprint 1993; New Delhi: Indus Publishing Co.).

Harcourt, A.F.P (1993), *The Himalayan District of Koolu, Lahoul and Spiti* (Delhi: Vivek Publishing House, First Published in 1871).

Hedin, S. (1909), *Trans-Himalaya; Discoveries and Adventures in Tibet. Vol. III* (London: Macmillan and Co. Limited).

Lal, U. (2009), *Environmental Constraints and Developmental Processes in a Mountain Ecosystem of Trans-Himalaya: A Case Study of Kinnaur*, Unpublished PhD Thesis, Center for Study of Regional Development, Jawaharlal Nehru University, New Delhi.

Thomson, T. (1852), *Western Himalaya & Tibet; A Narrative of a Journey through the Mountains of Northern India, during the Years 1847–48* (London: Reeve and Co.).

Wilson, A. (1882), *The Abode of Snow: Observations on a Journey from Chinese Tibet to the Indian Caucasus, through the Upper Valleys of the Himalaya* (Edinburg and London: William Blackwood and Sons).

5

Manipur and Arunachal Pradesh: India's Gateway to Southeast Asia

N. Vijaylakshmi Brara

Introduction

On 29 May 2012, the official daily of Myanmar, *New Light of Myanmar*, hailed the visit of the then Indian prime minister Manmohan Singh to Myanmar in the following words: 'India needs Myanmar, and Myanmar also needs India, and that is the common ground'. Its significance can be gauged by the fact that though various Indian officials have visited Myanmar in recent years, the prime minister's visit to the country after 25 years symbolized the only high-level visit in a long time, the last being that of Rajiv Gandhi. Much has changed in intervening years, the military rulers in the South East Asian nations have opened the path of reforms in their countries, allowing leaders such as Aung San Suu Kyi to visit abroad, and conducted general elections considered by and large as free and fair. Besides, Myanmar has emerged as a strategic country linking South Asia to Southeast Asia and as a major connecting point and transportation bridge for the region.

Sceptics have raised doubts that India's stint with Myanmar will not be smooth as it will face stiff competition from players such as China. At present, the bilateral trade between India and Myanmar stands at US$1.2 billion, while that between Myanmar and China stands at about US$4.4 billion. China is far ahead of

India in developing joint projects in Myanmar. But, that imbalance can only be corrected with more vigorous cooperation between the two countries, rather than perceiving the issue from a zero-sum game framework. Healthier competition can be encouraged and India and China can cooperate with each other in developing trilateral joint projects in the country. The Chinese foreign ministry has sought to dispel such suspicions through statements 'China is glad to see India and Myanmar develop friendly cooperative relations, and hopes that the development of their relations is conducive to the peace, stability and prosperity of the two countries as well as the region'[1] as Liu Weimin, the spokesperson, was quoted in the official newspaper — *China Daily*.

Meanwhile, the two Asian neighbours have sought to keep the conflict at bay. In *The Hindu*, dated 12 February 2012, Ananth Krishnan quoted a Chinese official statement which read as 'Refrain from taking action that could complicate border dispute: China'. The Chinese foreign ministry 'asked India to work with China to maintain peace and stability in border areas', in another statement issued by the official Xinhua News Agency. The statement was a response to news reports of Indian officials 'participating in activities organized by the so-called Arunachal Pradesh region', *Xinhua* said. China, which holds claims on the State, refers to the region as 'southern Tibet'. (China first began to strongly stress its claims and refer to the region as 'southern Tibet' in the late 1980s, coinciding with the declaration of its statehood by India.) However, the Foreign Ministry spokesperson Hong Lei reiterated China's position on border issues as well as the dispute over the eastern section of the border as being 'consistent and clear-cut'. 'China advocates seeking a fair and rational solution through equal and friendly negotiations,' he said, adding that India needed 'to refrain from taking any action that could complicate the issue'.

While these statements did not directly mention A.K. Antony's visit, his attendance at the 20 February celebrations in Itanagar, marking the 25th anniversary of Statehood Day, seems to be the apparent trigger. It, however, remains unclear why the Foreign Ministry waited five days to issue the statement. Speaking at the celebrations, Antony described border security as the 'topmost

---

[1] Arobinda Devidutta Mahapatra, 'Russia and India Report', cited on 1 June 2012, *China Daily*.

priority' and said that New Delhi would give serious considerations to proposals made by the state government to boost infrastructure in border areas, according to media reports. He did not, however, directly refer to either China or the border dispute in his remarks. Chinese analysts viewed this move as an attempt by India to enforce its 'territorial claims'.[2]

The above two quotations have been brought to focus to highlight the India–China bilateral relations along with regional implications for countries such as Myanmar. These would reflect on the trade scenario in relation to Myanmar and China. While one can see the 'opening of the eastern doors' (*Nongpok Thong Hangba*) as per the local Manipuri adage towards Myanmar, the opportunities of open trade ties with China through Arunachal or border trade continue to be subverted by the shadows of territorial claims.

This chapter is a result of vigorous fieldwork in the border towns of Manipur and Arunachal Pradesh to understand the scope of expansion of economic activities through borders. Intensive interaction with the local populace with open-ended but structured questionnaires, informal conversations as well as interactive sessions with the officials of the state machinery at both the capitals in Imphal and Itanagar as well in the borders have been undertaken. The primary questions which were examined are stated below in the footnote.[3]

---

[2] Ananth Krishnan, 25 February 2012, *The Hindu* (e-edition).

[3] Primary Questions:

1. Since how long has trade been going on in this region? What is the history? Are the traditional trade routes still used? What were the goods traded then and what are the goods traded now?
2. Do you have any remnants of Silk Route? (local organizations)
3. Do both the communities belong to the same religion? Would you also like if the pilgrims get a free access to the areas of pilgrimage in both the countries?
4. Do the goods usually come from Nepal or Bhutan or directly from China?
5. Are there any restrictions on goods traded — governmental or non-governmental? How do you suggest it should be done away with?
6. How is your relation with the people on the other side of the border?
7. Do you have good roads and transport system to transport your items?
8. Are you more dependent on the goods from the other side or are they more dependent on you?

Although this was the structural framework around which queries were asked, there were certain add-ons as per the situation required or even avoided due to sensitivity. Few of the research questions did not hold water in the fieldwork situation. The border dispute in Arunachal Pradesh and the security concerns in Moreh have led to a 'flyover' situation about the people of this region whereby the deliberations on policy and big investments exclude the indigenous people and make their opinion irrelevant.

Obstacles to Field Research

Manipur is one of the northeastern states of India sharing its border with Myanmar along the three districts of Ukhrul, Chandel and a small portion of Churachandpur. An erstwhile princely state formally acceded to the Union of India in the year 1949, it was one of the theatres of fiercely fought battles between the Japanese and the allied forces during the World War II which proved to be major turning points. Imphal is its capital.

The state largely consists of hilly terrain covering about 90 per cent of its 22,347 sq km (8,628 sq miles) which surrounds a fertile

---

9. (Question to key leaders) Are the relations between India and Bhutan or Nepal and India and China affecting the trade relations between the border towns? What can be done to improve the relation with India? Will it enable to expand the trade between the two countries?
10. How much is the volume of formal trade and how much is the volume of informal trade? List the items for formal trade and also that of informal trade.
11. (Question to the organizations and institutions) How can informal trade be formalized?
12. (Question to the organizations) Do you think opening of the trade and expansion will lead to territorial issues and conflict? How?
13. Would you like that the trade should be expanded?
14. The ethnic composition of the border town. The local issues and the historical background of the region. Nationalist movements or other such uprisings. Their view of the government at the state as well as the centre.
15. Region's topography and population—the demographic composition.
16. Role of organizations/institutions/local communities in economic activities of the region.
17. List out the economic activities of the region.

valley in the centre. The hills are inhabited by numerous tribes belonging to Naga and Kuki-Chin groups who mostly profess Christianity. The valley is mainly inhabited by Meiteis who are predominantly Hindus with a small percentage of Muslims locally known by the term 'Meitei-Pangals'. About 70 per cent of the population lives in the valley, while the rest lives in the hills. Racially, Manipuri people are similar to Southeast Asians and the languages spoken belong to the Tibeto-Burman group which explains their sense of commonality along the border region.

Moreh town in the Chandel district of Manipur has been the traditional link between Burma, now Myanmar, and the erstwhile kingdom of Manipur. In the present times, it has been enlisted as one of the four most important border trade centres of India. The word 'Moreh' is derived from the Burmese word 'Mo-Leh' which literally means 'tiredness'. It is said the Burmese on their journey towards Manipur had to undertake a long steep inclined journey and used Moreh as a resting joint. From it the word 'Moleh' and thus 'Moreh' came to be used to name this place. The specificity of Moreh is not the physical obstacles but the man-made ones. This place is an extremely sensitive zone when it comes to intercommunity relations. Conflicts lead to indefinite bandhs and increase in state vigilance, making it very difficult to reach, stay and talk to the local populace.

On the other hand, Arunachal Pradesh, earlier known as the NEFA, was governed indirectly by the centre till it attained its statehood in 1987. It is situated in the northeastern part of India with an area of 83,743 sq km and has a long international border with Bhutan to the west (160 km), China to the north and northeast (1,080 km) and Myanmar to the east (440 km). It stretches from snow-capped mountains in the north of the Himalayas to the plains of Brahmaputra Valley in the south. Though Arunachal is the largest state in the northeast region, yet it is the least populated. Itanagar, its capital located at an altitude of 530 m above, is named after Ita Fort, meaning fort of bricks built sometime in 14th century AD.

For the purpose of this study, the area of Bomdila, also called Bumla in Tawang subdivision (SD) of West Kameng district, was taken into consideration. This area borders Tibet and is the district headquarters of West Kameng. Bomdila is 160 km from Tezpur (headquarters of the district with the same name in Assam bordering Arunachal Pradesh), and it takes about seven hours to reach there. Tawang is 345 km from Tezpur, and it takes about 13 hours to reach Tawang. In this case also, because of difficult geographical terrain and climatic conditions, border roads are open only for about five to six months in a year, that is, from July to October and closed from November to May.

The fieldwork revealed that the geopolitical situation is such in Arunachal Pradesh that because of the difficult geographical terrain and climatic conditions, border roads are open only for five to six months in a year that is from July to October and closed from November to May. In most of the border areas along China, Bhutan and Myanmar, traditional exchange has existed from a very long period of time. The government is now planning to build formal structures in these areas to facilitate trade.

The most common obstacles faced during the field visit were bandhs (the closure of all establishments to protest anything they find relevant) which led to delays in the field or more specifically the need to ease off the situation. Whenever there was any rumour of increase in extortions by the underground elements, the army went on a frisking spree, escalating the situation by increasing extortion in direct proportion to the frequency of frisking.

The Myanmarese army kept a close watch on the observers/researchers. An ID card was a must-have; no camera and no phones were allowed. The departments were not forth coming with sharing of information. Road conditions were very bad. In Moreh especially, the strong presence of insurgent outfits led to less level of enquiries for research. At the same time, there was a discomforting presence of the army across the border.

Topographical hardships gave limited time for field visits accentuated by discomforting weather and incessant rainfall. Any non-resident of the state has to acquire an Inner Line Permit (ILP) which gives access only for seven days. In Arunachal Pradesh, most of the government officials are non-locals; hence, they prefer to restrain to comment on border trade issues. Many officials were constantly on leave and offices were being shifted at the time of the field visit. So, the ability to access official records was affected. Another mater of grievous concern was that bordering villages within Arunachal Pradesh had been depopulated as the army had taken over those areas. Villagers seemed fed up of queries on border trade as many researchers and journalists asked the same issues with no tenable results. In Arunachal specifically, it was observed that the local populace was not very interested in trade expansion and economic activities of the government.

Thus, while the obstructions in visiting Moreh were mostly man-made, such as bandhs due to conflict and violence, the obstructions in Tawang were more due to its geographical location and unfriendly terrain, though bad roads and poor infrastructure are common to both the regions. A detailed study is given below as two sections on the areas under consideration.

Part I: Manipur

Moreh and the Corridors to Myanmar

The boundary line between India and Myanmar stretches up to a length of 1,643 km. Apart from Manipur, other two northeastern states, Mizoram as well as Nagaland, also share boundary with Myanmar. Of the total length of 398-km boundary line that Manipur shares with Myanmar, only 52 km are manned by the security personnel. The shortest route that reaches India from Myanmar emerges from Mandalay which is split northwards at Tamu–Manipur border, and the national highway number 39 (NH 39) also known as the Indo-Myanmar Road acting as a springboard to Imphal, then to Nagaland, from where it traverses to Assam and finally reaches Kolkata and other parts of India.

The other direct routes that reach Myanmar emerge from Noklak and Tobu situated in the eastern areas of Nagaland bordering Myanmar. These are the most preferred options of the illegal traffickers. (Unfortunately, all the above-mentioned northeastern states of India have been identified by the United Nations Drug Control Programme [UNDCP] and International Narcotics Control Board [INCB] as a transit point for illegal drug trafficking originating from the Golden Triangle.) Apart from these two well-known routes, there are also two other trade routes which have been used since ancient times. The first is the one that reaches Somrah tract of Myanmar from the Chingai SD of Ukhrul district and the other one too reaches Somrah tract of Myanmar from the Kamjong SD of Ukhrul district.

Early Settlements and Trade

Meiteis, the largest ethnic population in Manipur, mostly Hindus, first began settling in Moreh around 1949. Before 1949, some Meitei traders used to carry on trading activities by venturing into the Tamu territory of Myanmar. Ravages due to the World War II created acute shortages and scarcity of essential commodities in Myanmar, more so in the frontier areas, which were transported from Manipur through Moreh.

Daily consumable items such as mustard oil, kerosene, towel, vests, cigarettes and other tobacco products and milk powder and other milk products brought from India had been in great demand from the Myanmarese military officials as well as general public. But trade did not take off well as the Meitei traders were bullied by the Myanmarese military junta. Thus, on the intervention of the then chief minister M.K. Priyobrata, the Meiteis were given certain amount of land within Moreh to carry on their trade without entering Tamu.

Simultaneously, the 1950s saw a sudden rise in the Kuki population (one of the major tribes, the other being the Nagas) in Moreh due to prolonged ethnic clashes between them and the Naga tribes which were followed by another major influx during 1992–2000. Functionaries of the Meitei Council of Moreh (MCM) contend that as per the land *pattas* issued in the latter half of the 1940s, it is evident that Meiteis and Koms (one of the smaller tribes in Manipur with their traditional settlements in the foothills of Manipur) were the earliest settlers of Moreh. On the other hand, Kukis also contend that they were the first settlers of Moreh. These debates on the earliest 'origins of settlements' are one of the reasons for local internal conflict for domination in Moreh. Confrontations of all kinds are given an ethnic twist, with the result that even small issues such as controversy over parking space get ethnically coloured and become extremely volatile. These ethnic tensions majorly affect smooth functioning of border trade in this region (Table 5.1).

At present, Moreh is a hub of border trade with a strong presence of informal as well as illegal trade, ranging from consumer items, drugs to arms. It is now a home to three major communities, the Meiteis, the Nagas and the Kukis. In addition, there is a strong and traditional presence of Tamils and a very small number of Punjabis who had migrated from Burma (the south

Table 5.1
Distribution of ethnic population in Moreh town

Wards	Total HH	Population	Kukis	Meteis	Nagas	Others Tamil, Marwari, Punjabi, etc.
1	375	2,149	1,501	–	–	648
2	312	1,770	1,414	356	–	–
3	213	1,141	430	–	–	711 (Tamils)
4	312	925	49	236	–	650 (Tamils)
5	384	2,129	09			2,120 (Metei-Pangals, Nepali, Punjabi)
6	128	604	07	80	–	517 (Punjabis, Marwari)
7	597	3,211	801	2,410	–	–
8	359	1,871	1,326	545	–	–

Source: 2001 census.
Note: There was a total Naga exodus from the Moreh town in spite of the fact that its Chandel district traditionally had a balanced population of both the Nagas and the Kukis.

Indians claim that their ancestors travelled to Burma during the Chola dynasty through the sea route). There is an uneasy relationship between the Hill Tribe Council (HTC) (mainly controlled by the Kukis) and the MCM due to local politics of community dominance. The Tamil Sangam maintains neutrality on this case, as though traditionally they had been dominating the trade through a large network of fellow ethnic Tamil traders in India, Myanmar and other South East Asian countries and multilingual skills, but at present, the population and influence of Tamils are on the decline. The Kukis, though they constitute the majority of the population, are still not in competition for trade or business. Most of them are marginal workers and petty vendors.

Therefore, at present, the original settlers are very few, and there is constant migration into and out of the area, and many armed outfits are said to have their presence openly or secretly, perhaps to control the trade. The inflow of drugs as well as small arms has made this border a core centre for the various insurgent outfits as these two items bring in cash as well as armaments. Then, they also find safe havens across the borders easily. Myanmar's government too has its own anti-state groups to grapple with, who often try to find safe places on the Indian side.

With its multiracial population, Moreh has assumed a cosmopolitan character. On the basis of the electoral roll issued for the recent Ninth Assembly Election of Manipur, Moreh has a total number of 14,584 registered voters. But due to differences among the various communities, elections for the small town committees have not been held for quite some time. The nomenclature 'small town', legitimizing the rights of all the communities living there, is seen as a threat by the tribal groups, who see it an attempt at usurpation of their customary rights as tribals in the area, and prefer to call it as a tribal town. There is a special enactment for administration of the hill areas in Manipur called the Manipur (Hill Areas) District Councils Act, 1971. However, the development funds sanctioned to the area are being disbursed with an assumption that Moreh is still a small town.

On the contrary, the demand for upgradation of Moreh to the status of a municipal town from a small town has brought in opposition from not only the Kuki conglomerates but also other Naga organizations who are settled in the neighbouring areas of Moreh in Chandel district such as the Chandel Naga People Organizations (CNPO), Naga Students Union Chandel (NSUC) and the Naga Women Union Chandel (NWUC). The only matter on which these two major tribes seem to have a consensus is that 'Chandel being a "tribal region" any development plan, policies, or its implementation in (any part of) the district shall not be against the aspirations and interest of the tribal people'. Recently, the demand for bringing the entire hill area of Chandel district under the Sixth Schedule, including Moreh, has given impetus to the urge to retain this border area as part of the indigenous land of the tribals.

Altogether there are five high schools in Moreh recognized by the Board of Secondary Education Manipur, and only one of these is a government school. Different places of worship belonging to different faith exist, namely, gurdwara, Jain temple, masjid and Hindu temples. A number of churches dot the topography of this area as most of the tribals are Christians. There are about 30 churches, and most of these belong to the Evangelical Baptist denomination. In addition, there are some Kuki brethren who consider themselves as Jews and follow Judaism, though there is also one synagogue at Moreh.

Market Centres in Moreh and Tradable Items

There are four important market centres in Moreh: (i) Prem Nagar (also known as morning market), (ii) Hao Keithel, (iii) Dharmashala and (iv) Meitei Keithel (also known as parking market). Among these, Prem Nagar is the largest. Prem Nagar and Meitei Keithel remain open both in the morning and in the evening. On the other hand, Hao Keithel and Dharmashala remain open only in the morning. In Hao Keithel, the vendors are mostly Kukis. The items of commodities sold include vegetable, rice and grocery items. Most of the rice vendors are from the Tamil community who come from Tamu. In Prem Nagar, Burmese Shans, including men and women, sell ready-made garments, cosmetic products, electronics item and the like. It is also called Lei Gullee (flower lane) as flowers are available for sale in this market.

However, with the coming up of Namphalong trade centre on the Myanmar side of the border after 1998, the once flourishing trade centres in Moreh steeply declined. Despite efforts by the Ministry of Home Affairs, Government of India (GOI), to revive trade by enlisting Moreh as one of the three most important land custom centres of India and providing new infrastructure, most market centres on the Manipur side of the border have shrunk. This was also due to the Free Border Trade Agreement signed in 1995 between India and Myanmar. Import and export activities are currently being carried out at Moreh gate 1 as per an agreement between the two countries. Efforts are being made to extend the trading activities at Moreh gate 2 which also connects with the Namphalong market in Tamu region directly.

Goods exported to Myanmar via Moreh include flour, soya bean, pulses, cumin seed, rose powder, incense stick (agarbatti), gold finger, aniseed, asafoetida, bicycle and spare parts, auto spares, stainless steel utensils, gas cylinders, X-ray papers and pharmaceutical products and so on. Cloths made in traditional loom of Manipur are also exported. Some medicinal drugs are not legally permitted for export, but are openly trafficked to Myanmar with minimal quality control. It is suspected that expired medicines are used in the production (distillation and refinement) of cocaine/heroine which is known locally by the name 'No. 4'. Goods brought in from the other side include betel leaves/nuts, ginger, garlic, turmeric, raisin, reed brown, timber, electronic items and ready-made garments, originating from a Myanmarese town bordering Thailand, Tachileik. Illegal trade items brought in from Myanmar via Moreh include narcotics and abusive substance such as heroine (No. 4), World's Yours (WY) tablets, arms and ammunitions, precious stones and timber and so on. The trade is highly lopsided as the market in Moreh is flooded with the third-grade goods from the neighbouring regions while the goods traded from India are very limited.

In Tamu, most of the traders belong to Nepali, Tedim Chins and Shan origin, of which the Shans are predominant. In addition, Tamil and ethnic Chinese (Burmese citizens) also trade in Tamu. Horticultural edible products are traded illegally through Moreh border. Various community-based organizations such as the HTC, the MCM and the Tamil Sangam play an important role in the trade and business affairs of Moreh.

The rapid development on the Myanmar side is being attributed to assistance from the Chinese government. Seventy per cent of the big businesses are controlled by the Chinese. Another reason is that being under the military junta, the pace of development in Myanmar is comparatively swift unlike in India, where generating consensus makes decision-taking and implementation on developmental works a long-drawn process. The local officials are also concerned about the losing importance of Moreh. According to the Additional District Commissioner, every day, about five to six businessmen and tourists, domestic as well as international, visit Moreh.

Improper marketplace and infrastructure discourage customers from across the border. Also, the market sheds are dull and haphazard, necessitating fresh initiatives in infrastructure. As far as local crime is concerned, the government officials prefer it to be handled by the Border Line Officer (BLO) and that it need not reach the diplomatic channels of both Delhi and Yangon which are located far away (based on personal interview with the Additional District Commissioner). The BLO has already taken initiatives in this regard.

Lack of efficient banking facilities adds to the inconveniences. Moreh does not yet have any proper nationalized bank with ATM, core banking and electronic money exchange facilities, which hampers the emergence of Moreh as a thriving trade centre. There is no bank, no Internet; hence, the communities are not in touch with the outside world. The state newspaper only reaches in the evening and the national dailies the next day (provided there is no bandh or communal tension). There is also a need to develop a formal currency converter to enable the trade to be regularized. Currently, the traders roughly calculate the value of rupees and kyats in comparison to US dollars, and the volume of trade is also calculated based on these measurements.

Besides, integrated check posts (ICPs) need to be developed. These would be expected to perform functions such as land customs, police protection, customs prevention department, check on the forest produce, check on the narcotics, postal services, banking, telecom, animal and plant quarantine, quality certification counter, food testing laboratory, parking and cafeteria. These kinds of ICPs were estimated to help check the quality of the tradable items as well control the illegal and informal trade.

The Land Ports Authority of India has already approved the setting up of ICP at 13 different locations along the border with Bangladesh, Nepal, Pakistan and Myanmar. Towards this end, the government has acquired 45.50 acres of land near Moreh gate 2 with adequate compensation to 405 landowners. It is estimated that the proposed ICP construction at Moreh will cost 130 crores and is being built on the models of Wagah border in Punjab. The main implementation agency for this will be the Rail India Technical and Economic Services.

On an average, trade amounting to the value of around 55 crores is exchanged every day at Moreh alone. The major portion of it is unaccounted and therefore does not contribute much to the state's economy. The informal trade far exceeds the items of that of the formal trade. Items in the range of electronic items, clothing, edible items, toiletries and so on made in China, Taiwan and other products in a small quantity from Myanmar enter from the Tamu side and flood the Manipur market and also other parts of northeast and even go as far as Delhi. Furthermore, dumping of all kinds of consumer items in the state is leading to rapid deindustrialization. There is thus a strong demand to revise the official list of tradable items. Keeping in mind these requests, the government has already increased the variety of goods to be traded in formal trade from 22 in the previous list to 44 items. According to Seithong Kaokip, a school principal and church leader, the Indian side should focus on getting Burma's oil and gas, which can help in replenishing the stocks in India.

There is also an ethnic dimension to the border trade in this region, as is the case with all the other issues in Moreh. Some groups feel that only a particular ethnic community may benefit from the measures being suggested by the government, for instance, those will benefit on whose traditional lands these check posts are coming up, while other communities continue to be neglected. As of now, the economic dependency on Myanmar for daily livelihood is to such an extent that Moreh seems like the extension of Tamu, the border town of Myanmar. In sharp contrast, Tamu has no traces of being influenced by its counterpart on the Indian side.

The lack of frequent transport services between the two regions is another concern for all those involved. Tamil businessmen in Moreh were counting on the regular bus service between Imphal and Mandalay in Myanmar via Moreh, which was to start following a resolution adopted by the Manipur Assembly on 1 August 2003, with a view to boost trade between the two countries. The Tamil Sangam president V. Shekhar said, 'We were eagerly waiting for the bus service. It would have transformed the entire economic scenario of this town'. He further mentioned that the bus service would also help resume ties between the Tamils and Manipuris who are still residing in Mandalay and other parts of Myanmar. However, such initiatives continue to be in a limbo due to bureaucratic obstacles.

There are currently four bridges connecting Moreh to the Myanmerese town of Tamu. While the first two are used by people to visit Namphalong market, the other two (not really proper routes) are mostly used for illegal trade by jumping fences on the border at night. The porters for such goods are usually Biharis and Kukis. Arms and ammunition received by the northeast insurgent groups often come from Thailand via Myanmar. Many of the arms seizures suggest that the arms used by the insurgent groups are of Chinese origin. The second area of concern is the region being the trade route for drugs. India has become both a passage/transit country and a market for drugs produced in the Golden Triangle encompassing Myanmar–Thailand–Laos.

Non-state actors create a huge amount of disturbance for the trade. Sometimes, the traders and transporters have to face more than 20 extortion demands by militants on a single tour across the border and sometimes have to make do with loot of goods. The Tata Sumos (smaller passenger vehicles) have also reduced their services and the owners of these vehicles have diverted their services to other routes. Several women vendors from border villages such as Kwatha, Khudengthabi, Bohang and Pallel also complained of militants trying to collect taxes from them. These women contribute a major portion of exports to Myanmar such as bamboo shoot, bamboo and cane handicrafts, betel nuts, jackfruits, wheat, maize, local fish and red potato. In short, they add to the volume of tradable items to Tamu, yet they are rendered helpless because of frequent transporter strikes and bandhs.

Extortion and intimidation of traders also discourages outside traders from venturing into this area, forcing them to take other routes through the sea or via Kolkata or Chennai. Traders have submitted many memorandums to the government to implement the National Highway Security Act in the interest of the business communities of the state. However, the above arguments are not to suggest that only India is dependent on border trade in this region. Nearly 80 per cent of the people from the border of Myanmar (Tamu) depend on the Indian side for medicines and other medical facilities. Many times, they take the risk of coming to Imphal, the capital of Manipur, which is nearly five to six hours' drive, for treatment at the various hospitals located at Imphal by risking arrest and detention by the authorities.

Thus, major efforts and interventions are needed to encourage formal trade between the two countries. Manipur's relation with Myanmar dates back to several centuries. There was a time in history when Manipur was considered to be much closer to Myanmar, called Awa by the Manipuris, as compared to the rest of India. There are instances of matrimonial alliances between the kings of two countries, as well as fierce fights which led to major bloodsheds. But, nevertheless, there was and remains a strong physical as well as psychological proximity. The traditional exchange pattern was disturbed by the redrawing of political boundaries when it officially joined the Union of India. The creation of international boundaries and political issues and activities of insurgents further complicated the trade relations.

Ironically, some of the main items imported today from Myanmar under formal trade are the ones which are produced abundantly within the state, such as ginger, turmeric garlic and red broom, whereas the goods exported are the ones which are produced in other parts of the country. As a result, the local state economy has not really benefited and has become a captive market of the products produced outside the state as well as the goods imported from Myanmar. It is rather giving impetus to a dependency syndrome in Manipur. There is a need to expand the economic activity in the following ways:

1. The area should be industrialized, giving emphasis on small-scale- and horticulture/agriculture-based industries so as to enable greater volume of exports.
2. Barter system of exchange should be accounted for in all policy decisions.
3. The local people should not be reduced to head load workers. They should be handed over the charge of agro-based industries, such as food processing, horticulture and handlooms.
4. Currently, all the export items are coming from other parts of India. This has retarded the export of local goods considerably. Hence, the manufacturing units of cycle spare parts, herbal medicines, food processing and so forth should be established in this area.
5. Letter of credit facility has been provided between the United Bank of India, Moreh, and the Myanmar Economic Bank, Tamu, and US dollars settlement accounts have been opened at both the sides. However, it has not been operationalized because of US sanctions on Myanmar. One suggestion would be to conduct transactions in Indian rupees, till the time the political imbroglio is not settled.
6. India needs to co-opt those elements which are directly linked to the formulation of its Myanmar policy. Only then India–Myanmar relations will become meaningful to Manipur and consequently play a constructive role in the broader perspective of the Look East Policy (LEP).

Of late, there have been positive indications towards these aims. Recently, a team of ambassadors from all the countries representing Southeast Asian countries (ASEAN, Association of Southeast Asian Nations, countries) visited Manipur to make their first-hand assessment of the situations and facilities and potentials of this area. Among other things, they visited Moreh as well as Tamu. A trade delegation comprising 25 members met around the end of September 2014. They have submitted an 11-point representation to increase the volume of trade through the land customs station (LCS) at Moreh. They also suggested hastening of measures to restore peace in the border areas so that trade can take place without any hindrances. An agreement between India and Myanmar on a market rate of conversion of the rupee into kyat and vice versa and allowing the Indians to access the markets of other ASEAN countries were some other highlights of their presentation. It is only when Manipur no longer remains the 'east' or the 'northeast' but becomes the 'west' for Southeast Asia that trade and business in its true sense can become meaningful for the region.

Part II: Arunachal Pradesh

Tawang and Bomdila

Arunachal is perhaps one of the largest states among the seven northeast states of India and least populated. In spite of having such a vast stretch of international boundary, border trade is still in an incipient form. The majority of the population follows Buddhist religion. Unlike the case in Manipur, Tawang and Bomdila, inhabited by the Monpa tribe, presented a much more amicable environment for research. However, they could not provide many insights as the locals themselves lived in a fairly closed set-up and had been hardly exposed to the outside world and hence their views and mindset on political and economic issues of the state were not tenable.

The most striking element of this region, however, was the assertion on part of the locals of being 'Indian'. The student's movements in the region have time and again tried to ban Chinese goods and take out rallies. These reactions were enlightening, given the fact that this region lies at the core of territorial disputes between the two countries and therefore impacts heavily on the policy formulations of both the countries. Security takes the main stage while trade and economic activities take a back seat. Despite government apathy and Chinese reassertions, the local populace does not want to be associated with China.

While there are not many restrictions on mobility in Tawang, for visiting villages such as Zemithang and Bumla, an official permission from the district collector of Tawang is strictly required. Army checks at the Bumla border post are hectic. Visitors without ID cards are generally detained for questioning, but the army officers are quite reticent to share their views on border trade. At Bumla, the villages seemed depopulated and displaced. Borders are commonly perceived as *lalban*s (forts), and not quite amenable for border trade.

Early Linkages

Most recollections about border trade among common people, elders, shopkeepers and public leaders constitute of memories from the British period and the pre-1962 traditional trade systems with Tibet, Myanmar and Assam. These trade routes continue to be sketched from Upper Assam to Tibet through Kameng Valley via Bomdila, Sela and Tawang; trade routes frequented by Mishmi (one of the indigenous tribes in Arunachal Pradesh) and Tibetan traders which ran through Derai Valley and Tiding Valley.

One can find trade routes along the course of Katze and Phupu rivers, from the Upper Lohit Valley to Tibet and also as open roads from Upper Assam to Myanmar through Patkai Pass. The existence of numerous routes and passes to Tibet, Myanmar and China shows that there was regular cross-country trade that was the bass of subsistence in this region, especially the Monpa tribes. These roads and routes pass through dense forests, mountain passes and rivers, and goods had to be often carried by human beings as roads were not fit for the beasts of burden. Items were traded without any quantification, which mostly comprised musks, rice, chillies and animal hides for salt, wool, woollen cloth, Tibetan dao, resembling a sharp knife, Tibetan religious bell and white shell beads.

The Adis, another tribe of this state, used to go to Tibet in groups of 80–100 as they were not allowed by the Tibetans to enter their villages during night. Hence, the Adis had to camp in the outskirts of the villages on the hill sides. The Apatanis, inhabiting the middle belt of the territory, found themselves handicapped by their geographical location. They were not given permission by the surrounding tribes to venture out. Given this scenario, they found a solution in becoming interpreters with the British officials and buying rubber from the other side.

Summer markets used to be held during the fifth month, autumn markets in the seventh month and winter markets in the tenth month of the year. The other tribes such as Akas, Miris, the Khamptis and the Singphos traded mostly within the territory of India. These trading centres have also been regularized now and an 'all Arunachalee fair' is held to promote goods made by the locals.

Current Trade Routes

In Tawang district, the major ethnic group is constituted of Monpas. Today, their population has become heterogeneous with diverse occupations (Table 5.2). The Monpas claim to be the original inhabitants of the area and constantly demand an autonomous status for their district due to the fear that their identity may be lost.

But it needs to be emphasized that it is not a secessionist or nationalist movement. The Monpas are very much attached to India but also express frustration at the pace of development projects undertaken by the GOI; the decisions are pathetically slow, and the focus is more on security issues than development.

They are emerging as a major trading community in the agricultural and horticultural areas. Many local non-governmental

Table 5.2
Tawang district population

Population	M	F	Religion	Culture	Demand
39,243	22,082	17,161	Buddhism	Monpa	Autonomous district

Source: Census 2001.

organizations (NGOs) as well as NGOs from other parts of Arunachal Pradesh work in these sectors and sell their produce in other states. Indigenous products of the area are being promoted extensively. Orchid's preservation and rearing of sheep, cows and yaks are becoming important activities. Craft centres adept at producing local art, textile and clothes and so on are cropping up everywhere. Apples from Arunachal are also being sent to other states along with organic products, yak milk, orchid products, sheep wool and vegetables products.

Along with the Monpas, a small minority of Tibetans in Tawang also sell Chinese goods imported from Nepal, Bhutan and Myanmar. Chinese restaurants are run by the local people, while non-locals such as Biharis and Marwaris sell Indian goods like grocery, grain and other household items. House construction materials brought in by non-locals are generally marketed by the local people. However, low literacy levels are disabling the development of human resources in the region. There is an urgent need to build educational institutions in these border areas.

Presently, the trade routes to Tibet are completely sealed due to which there is no trade at all. There has been a mass exodus of people in the border villages as the whole area has been overtaken by the army. This has led to reduced desire for trade among people on both sides because of the political situation and army vigil, although traditional trading is still seen on a small scale through barter system, such as exporting rice, lentils, vegetables, chilly, timber, ginseng, in exchange of yak milk product, gold, precious stone, thick woollen clothes, wool for weaving and silk from the Tibetan side. A particular area in the Tawang district grows a typical plant named Yarcha Kampu, which is much in demand by the Chinese because of its nutritious value and usefulness in manufacturing medicine. They often take assistance of the villagers to pluck these plants.

Most individuals and organizations are of the view that until the political imbroglio is not resolved, there is absolutely no use discussing expansion or even the existence of border trade with China, although they do see immense potential in the field. There are altogether 36 NGOs in the Tawang district, but none of them hold the Sino-Indian bilateral trade as an issue in their agendas, with a few exceptions such as Gompa association of

Tawang monastery, the Monpas Welfare Association, Tawang and Indo-Tibet Friendship Association. According to these organizations, first and foremost, the traditional Silk Route[4] should be given prime attention if both countries have to open trade routes. Bomdila, being the district headquarters of West Kameng district, is a transit point for goods coming from Nepal, Bhutan and Siliguri. The Chinese goods therefore make their inroads into the Arunachal market indirectly. Hence, they are costly and limited. The Silk Route can assist this trade because it joins almost seven countries in this trade circuit.

Interviews with local people also revealed that they felt an intense need for managerial skills to be imparted among the communities which would like to indulge in cross-border trade. Lack of these skills has rendered them vulnerable in the modern-day set-up of globalized trade and communication. They also wanted to revive the cultural linkages based on Buddhism. They also insisted on free access to the areas of pilgrimage in both the countries. Lamas in Tawang wanted to visit monasteries in Tibet, such as the Lhaba temple and Potala palace where all their contemporaries are residing. Similarly, the Tibetan monks also wanted to visit the monasteries in Arunachal Pradesh. There are villages on the Chinese side which speak the same language as that of the Indian side, such as Le, Kissa komri Kawangkyo village, Jora, Khanta, Shou village and Tsona. On the Indian side, Jiminthang, Tawang proper, Lumla and Lungar also enjoy these linkages, which were snapped post 1962, but there is a great demand for revival now.

---

[4] The Silk Routes (collectively known as the 'Silk Road') were important paths for cultural, commercial and technological exchange between traders, merchants, pilgrims, missionaries, soldiers, nomads and urban dwellers from Ancient China, Ancient India, Ancient Tibet, Persia and Mediterranean countries for almost 3,000 years. It gets its name from the lucrative Chinese silk trade, which began during the Han dynasty (206 BCE–220 CE). Extending 4,000 miles, the routes enabled people to transport goods, especially luxuries such as slaves, silk, satin and other fine fabrics, musk, other perfumes, spices, medicines, jewels and glassware, as well as serving as a conduit for the spread of knowledge, ideas, cultures and diseases between different parts of the world (Ancient China, Ancient India [Indus Valley, now Pakistan], Asia Minor and the Mediterranean). Trade on the Silk Road was a significant factor in the development of the great civilizations of China, India, Egypt, Persia, Arabia and Rome and, in several respects, helped lay the foundations for the modern world.

Goods and Structure of the Trade

Right now, both the demand and the supply sides in the markets of Tawang area are dominated by Indian goods, unlike in Moreh. Most of these comprise essential items of daily consumption and some luxury goods such as electronic items, while the Chinese goods are only for cosmetic use. But if the border trade opens, there is a general feeling that Chinese goods will flood the market due to their competitive prices. At present, foreign goods enter from Nepal, Bhutan and Myanmar indirectly through Siliguri, and Kalimpong in West Bengal, Dimapur in Nagaland, Imphal and Moreh in Manipur, and hence, the cost of the goods rises tremendously due to transportation costs. There are several other trade routes across India–Bhutan and India–Nepal border, but these are practicably inaccessible due to bad weather conditions or political stalemate on development issues.

Interestingly, even though there is no formalized trade activity in this state, they have a Department of Trade and Commerce which has a vision of building a world trade centre in Itanagar on the lines of Mumbai. The World Trade Center Mumbai (WTCM) has agreed to set up this centre in Itanagar in tune with 'LEP' of the central government. This department is proposing to activate the traditional trade routes between Bhutan, Myanmar and China to formalize the trade between these countries. These sectors include:

India–China sector:
1. Kenzamane (Zemithang) in Tawang district
2. Bumla in Tawang district
3. Gelling (Kepangla Pass) in Upper Siang district
4. Kibithoo in Anjaw district
5. Mechuka (Lolla Pass) in West Siang district
6. Monigong (Dumla Pass) in West Siang district
7. Taksing in Upper Subansiri district

Indo-Myanmar sector:
1. Pangsu Pass (Nampong) in Changlang district

Indo-Bhutan sector:
1. Bleting (Namtsering) in Tawang district
2. Dongshengmang and Bongkhar in Tawang district

This department has also formed a State-level Export Promotion Committee (SLEPC) under the chairmanship of the chief secretary of the state. The committee has started examining, prioritizing and sanctioning the various proposals under the scheme.

This is also the nodal department for issuing trade licenses. All the district commissioners as well as their deputies have been empowered to issue trade licenses up to ₹10 lakhs. Normally, trade licenses are issued to Arunachal Pradesh scheduled tribe entrepreneurs only, but in the case of lack of indigenous traders in exceptional circumstances with the approval of the government, it may also be issued to a non-tribal.

Following are the items exported from the Indian border to China as a part of the traditional trade prior to 1962, with some additions (modern electronic goods such as computer parts):

1. Food grain items
2. Chitramala oil
3. Pulse and tea
4. Seasonal green vegetables
5. Garlic
6. Onion
7. Dehydrated vegetable (radish, turnip, carrot and cauliflower)
8. Mushroom (both moist and dry)
9. Green chillies and capsicum (in fact, the whole of Tibet is fully dependent for chillies imported from Tawang)
10. Spices
11. Fodder for cattle
12. Medicinal plants (herbs and shrub)
13. Raw materials for making incense sticks
14. Clay pottery items
15. Handicrafts items
16. Barbets
17. Wooden furniture
18. Bamboo and bamboo products
19. Woollen carpet
20. Apple
21. Kiwi
22. Wooden mask
23. Thanka painting

24. Mineral salt
25. Computer software

And the following items were imported from China to the border state of Arunachal Pradesh as a part of the traditional trade prior to 1962:

1. Milk and milk products
2. Yak and sheep wool, including pashmina
3. Silk
4. Walnut
5. Gold, silver, precious stones and gems
6. Articles of religious importance
7. Stone utensil
8. Fish
9. China blanket
10. Thermoplastic
11. Electric goods
12. China clay bowl
13. Dry meat

The above-stated items denote a collection of the old trade and new trade items which were a part of both formal and traditional trade. Gunpowder, drugs and ammunitions, mainly imported from Nepal, Bhutan and Myanmar, are some items that formed the corpus of illegal trade. But from India only, some medicines (which need prescription) are exported. Unfortunately, no separate official lists for formal items or informal trade items could be found. The respondents were mostly confused about the distinction between formal and informal tradable lists.

Meanwhile, government officials were of the view that ICPs should be developed, and customs offices and immigration offices too should be constructed at the border gate, so that proper vigil can be kept and proper information can be given on how informal trade can be formalized. While the first step will be to officially announce the opening of border trade with certain guidelines and norms, it would eventually result in greater people-to-people ties.

It is interesting to note that while there is much more relaxed movement at the Moreh border in Manipur and formal trade exists, the balance of trade is tilted towards Myanmar, whereas in Arunachal, where the only trade is the informal or traditional trade and where the borders are sealed and topography so hostile, the balance is tilted in favour of India in terms of the number of goods traded between the two countries. The cost factor then seems to be the key word.

The GOI has already started planning the outlay for the integrated check post to be established on the Moreh–Tamu border. Table 5.3 illustrates the infrastructure facilities that are planned to be available. There is a plan to make cargo sheds, passenger processing area, administration building, waiting halls, currency exchange, Internet facility, laboratory, duty-free shops along with surveillance issues such as closed circuit televisions (CCTVs), security huts, watch tower and isolation bay.

But one can see the laxity as they have already crossed their time line. Table 5.4 will bring it out more clearly.

Figure 5.1 is the detailed ICP as proposed by the Home Ministry.

Another major factor influencing the trade along these borders is bilateral border talks between India and its neighbouring countries. The fourth round of border talks between the liaison officers of India and Myanmar was held on 16 February 2012.

Table 5.3
Facilities: The DPR prepared by RITES provides demand-based capacity plans with unit area-based cost of the proposed elements of ICPs

Cargo	Passenger	General	Surveillance and security
Cargo process	Passenger	Admn. Bldg	DFMD/HHMD
Building	Process Area	Electric Sub-	CCTV/PA System
Cargo Inspection	Waiting halls	station	Boundary Wall
Sheds	Duty Free Shops	Area Lighting	Gates/Barriers
Warehouse/Cold	Passenger utilities	Borewells/	Security huts
storage	Dispensers	Pump house/	Watch Tower
Quarantine	Currency	Watertanks	Isolation Bay
Laboratory	exchange	Water treatment	
Dormitory	Internet facility	plant	
Dispensary		Area drainage/	
Restaurant		Cross drainage	
Clearing agents		Sewerage STP	
Banks			

Table 5.4
Implementation schedule: Raxaul macro level

| | | | | | Implementation schedule | | | |
| | | | | | Fiscal year | | | |
Sl. No.	Stage	Duration in months	Start	End	2008– 09	2009– 10	2010– 11	2011– 12
i)	DER	6	Feb '08	Aug '08	▬			
ii)	BID Process & Award	6	Sept '08	March '09	▬			
iii)	Construction	18	Apr '09	Oct '10			▬▬	
iv)	Commissioning	3	Nov '10	March '11				▬

Figure 5.1
A layout of detailed ICP as proposed by the Home Ministry

Source: Author.

The fifth India-Myanmar Regional Border Committee Meeting was held in Imphal in July 2014. Issues discussed include border fencing between two border posts, medical facilities to Burmese nationals, border smuggling and shipping of drugs. The Indian side has suggested issuing ID cards in English to the VIP tourists moving to Tamu without passing through immigration office.

Conclusion

Many political developments in the recent times indicate progress on the matters under consideration. Myanmar has ushered in democracy. Many of the insurgent groups in Manipur are talking with the GOI. If the political situations are handled correctly, the sociocultural similarities between Myanmar and Manipur will augment very well for economic ties. The GOI has accelerated its work along US$400 million Kaladan multimodal project that will link rivers and highways in the region, especially the upgraded port at Akyab to the state in Mizoram. Goods from Kolkata and other eastern ports as well as Indonesia, Malaysia and Singapore will then start to travel from Akyab to India's northeast.

Around December 2011, the joint secretary, GOI, and additional director general, foreign trade, visited the two border areas of Arunachal Pradesh. There has been a proposal to reopen the Stilwell road to trade with southern China, Bangkok and Singapore. Under this proposal, exotic flora and fauna of Arunachal Pradesh, surplus tea of Assam, cotton yarn, branded food items, automobiles components and fruits could be traded with Southeast Asian countries.

Recently, the present chief minister Nabam Tuki also proposed opening of border trade centres in India–China sector at Bumla and Kenzamane (Zemithang) at Tawang, Gelling (Kepangla Pass) at Upper Siang, Kibithoo at Anjaw, Mechuka (Lolla Pass), Monigong (Dumla Pass) in West Siang and Taksing in Upper Subansiri district, and some sectors along the Indo-Myanmar sector, such as the Pangsu Pass (Nampong) in Changlang and Dongshengmang and Bongkhar and Bleting (Namtsering) in Tawang district, along the Indo-Bhutan sector. However, most of these proposed border trade centres will take time to materialize due to lack of proper land routes.

Border trade holds immense potential, and the two growing economic giants of Asia need to cooperate to benefit from the window of opportunity available at the moment. The proposed ASEAN region, led by India and China, has been referred to as the 'Arc of Advantage' by the then Indian prime minister Mr Manmohan Singh. The ASEAN as a singular economic entity has a 19 per cent share in the total world trade and contributes 21 per cent of global output. At the same time, it houses nearly half of the total world population. The long-standing border dispute, however, can derail the process of economic integration in this region. Hence, there is a need to relook at bilateral relations and solve the situations for the larger benefit of the region. China and India hold the potential to emerge as the two pillars contributing to peace and development through partnership rather than conflict of interest.

6

Indo-Bangladesh Border Trade: Misconceptions and Realities of Regional Cooperation

Muinul Islam

Introduction

Trade along the Indo-Bangladesh border and that between China and Bangladesh can be distinguished between two specific trends: legal and illegal trade. In terms of legal trade, China occupies the first position as the largest source of Bangladesh's recorded legal imports with the value of imports surpassing US$4.5 billion in the financial year 2009–2010,[1] while India remains the second largest source of imports coming into Bangladesh. The value of legal imports from India to Bangladesh was US$3.215 billion in the financial year 2009–2010.[2] However, if both legal and illegal imports are considered, it would be quite difficult to ascertain who contributes more among these two countries. Understandably, the flows of smuggled goods from both China and India into Bangladesh are substantial, and it is widely speculated that the flows of smuggled goods from each of these two countries may not be far behind in value compared to the respective legal trade flows

---

[1] *The Daily Star*, 21 October 2010, B3.
[2] *The Prothom Alo*, 21 October 2010, 15.

from these two countries into Bangladesh. Some economists even claim that the flow of smuggling of goods from India to Bangladesh is larger than that of smuggled Chinese goods into Bangladesh, but there is no way to ascertain the authenticity of such claims.

There is no doubt that these two countries are the biggest sources of illegal imports into Bangladesh, but the modus operandi of smuggling operations and the nature of the flows of smuggled goods from China and India into Bangladesh are quite different. Smuggled Chinese goods mainly come into Bangladesh through sea routes and coastal routes, especially Myanmar[3] and Singapore, act as popular transit routes. Therefore, most of the smuggled Chinese goods are popularly known as 'Burmese goods' in some areas of Bangladesh, and the markets where such goods are easily available in different cities and towns of Bangladesh are popularly called 'Burmese market' or 'Singapore market'.

On the other hand, the entire 4,156-km-long land border of Bangladesh and India is used for smuggling of goods from India into Bangladesh. In addition, the rivers and canals flowing from the upper riparian country, India, into Bangladesh are also popular routes of smuggling, because it is virtually impossible for the law-enforcing agencies of both the countries to monitor the vast network of rivers and canal routes running through the several thousand square kilometres of dense forest areas of the Sundarbans.[4] In Table 6.1, the official figures of the yearly flows of legal imports from India to Bangladesh and the yearly flows of exports from Bangladesh to India in recent years are presented.

In the financial year 2009–2010, Bangladesh imported goods worth US$3.215 billion from India and exported goods valued at only US$304.6 million to India.[5] According to some estimates, Bangladesh's yearly legal import flow from India is more than 10 times the legal export flow to India from Bangladesh on average. Analysts also claim that the flows of smuggling of goods from India to Bangladesh carry almost the same type of imbalance compared to the value of smuggled goods from Bangladesh to

---

[3] Myanmar is the only country other than India which has a land border with Bangladesh.

[4] The Sundarbans covers areas of both India and Bangladesh, and the international border between Bangladesh and India runs right through this common mangrove forest.

[5] *The Prothom Alo*, 21 October 2010, 15.

Table 6.1
Bangladesh-India legal trade flow: From financial year 2002-2003 to 2008-2009

Financial year	Import from India (in million US dollars)	Export to India (in million US dollars)
2002–2003	1,355	84
2003–2004	1,560	89.2
2004–2005	2,007.1	143.6
2005–2006	1,848.7	242.1
2006–2007	2,226	289
2007–2008	3,375.1	358
2008–2009	2,863.6	276.5

Source: Yearbook of Foreign Trade Statistics 2009, Bangladesh Bank, Dhaka, Bangladesh.

India, though the actual values of the two flows cannot be accurately gauged for obvious reasons. Though this hugely lopsided trade balance favouring India creates frequent hue and cry in the political circles of Bangladesh, the issue deserves a more lenient view, because the rationale for trade often ignores one's political likings or prejudices, and surprisingly, there is not much protest against trade with China which is also equally lopsided in favour of the latter.

Any serious analysis of the issue of regional trade among the trading partners of the eastern South Asia sub-region, that is, Bangladesh, the eastern states of India, Nepal, Bhutan and Myanmar, should highlight the fact that in the context of an immensely rational urge for expansion of trade in the region, any policy-induced hindrance erected to restrict legal international trade would inevitably encourage cross-border smuggling in the region. At the same time, smuggling should not be viewed primarily as a law-and-order problem.

It is understandable that the geographical location of Bangladesh irrevocably determines Bangladesh's status as a natural trading partner of the bordering Indian states, as it has got a 4,156-km-long border without any major natural barriers with these states. Similarly, Nepal, Bhutan and Myanmar have also been naturally linked to the trade structures of the region, since both are landlocked countries, which are historically dependent on the port of Kolkata for their access to sea trade. In fact, it can be safely argued that their geographical locations have created a classic 'dominance-dependence syndrome' in interstate politico-economic relationships of these two countries vis-à-vis India. India holds the key to economic development of these two countries, and there is a widely held perception that India skilfully manoeuvres its regional policies to maintain this dominant status vis-à-vis these two smaller neighbours.

Bangladesh-India Border Trade in the 20th and 21st Centuries: Brief Historical Outline

Before the end of the British colonial rule in 1947, the regional economy of the eastern side of the Indian subcontinent was functioning as a reasonably integrated economic entity, where the agricultural- and forestry-oriented economic activities were organized around the concept of transportation through the regional metropolis-cum-port Kolkata and the natural harbour of Chittagong in the south-east corner of the subcontinent. Needless to say, the whole eastern and northeastern regions of colonial India were the economic hinterlands of these two seaports, where both the domestic and international trade flows were targeted to and directed through these two major ports along with the river ports and other urban centres of the area.

Even after the partition of colonial India in 1947, the cross-country transport and communication networks were allowed to function to some extent through treaties and arrangements till 1965, but most of the formal channels of trade were severely restricted or totally closed down after the Indo-Pak War of 1965. This politically imposed disruption of legal trade between the two neighbouring countries created and strengthened illegal trade flows of a number of agricultural and industrial goods across the porous land border as well as through the coastal, river and canal routes of the neighbouring areas of the two countries.

Immediately after the independence of Bangladesh in 1971, Bangladesh legalized border trade for a brief period within a narrow band around the international border. But, the experiment did not prove very beneficial for the war-ravaged country, and the government attracted a lot of criticism from the opposition groups in Bangladesh, especially because of the severe disruption in the Bangladesh economy caused by the liberation war which could not be mitigated through the liberalization of border trade. Rather, smuggling of raw jute, finer varieties of rice, hides and skin, fish, poultry birds and so forth was highlighted by the opposition groups to discredit the post-liberation Awami League government as an Indian stooge.

The political changes of 1975 brought forth political forces to power in Bangladesh, which can be termed as more sympathetic to Pakistan, if not downright anti-Indian. Therefore, at least in political posture, the jingoistic tenor of anti-Indian rhetoric of successive governments in Bangladesh gained in momentum in the late 1970s and the 1980s. But, the uneven pace of economic development of India and Bangladesh was gradually unfolding newer trends of legal and illegal international trade between the two countries, where one could easily notice a rapidly increasing flow and fast-changing pattern of cross-border illegal trade. However, in spite of the diatribes against India coming from Bangladesh's military rulers during the 1975–1990 period and the Bangladesh Nationalist Party (BNP)-led elected government of the 1991–1996 period, the flows of both legal and illegal trade between Bangladesh and India increased steadily every year since 1972 (up to 2010).

Increased momentum to this lopsided and almost one-sided trade flow was provided by the markedly uneven pace of import liberalization policies pursued by the two neighbours starting from the mid-1980s. Bangladesh launched a vigorous drive of import liberalization since the year 1986–1987 as a part of the structural adjustment programme prescribed by the donor organizations such as the International Monetary Fund (IMF) and the World Bank for aid conditionality. From then on, the whole complexion of legal trade as well as smuggling between these two neighbours changed very rapidly, especially in the cases of illegal exports from and imports into Bangladesh.

A seminal study on illegal international trade of Bangladesh by Gafur, Islam and Faiz (1990 and 1991) has analyzed the pattern of those changes in the illegal international trade between Bangladesh and India. The liberalization drive was further accelerated in the early 1990s in Bangladesh. On the other hand, India also quickened the pace of import liberalization since 1991. But the fact remains that the asymmetry of these two liberalization regimes continues to be quite substantial even today. Therefore, in the context of this asymmetry and the resultant price differentials in the two countries for a vast number of items, the incentive structure for smuggling remains very strong alongside the increasing flow of legally traded goods.

The issue of cross-border trade between Bangladesh and the bordering Indian states can appropriately be termed as a matter of choice between legal trade and smuggling for the policymakers of the two countries. It would be grossly erroneous to consider smuggling primarily as a 'law and order problem' to be tackled by strengthening the law-enforcing agencies on both sides of the border or by taking more and more draconian restrictive and/or repressive measures as well as giving more severe deterrent powers to those agencies. The two countries will be better served if their policymakers decide to tackle both legal trading and smuggling issues by considering these as problems at policy level, whereby the rationale for smuggling will be gradually weakened through appropriate policy changes in their legal international trade regimes.

In the light of the introductory statement of the problem presented earlier, the present chapter will have the following objectives aimed at developing a framework for regional cooperation: the chapter will use both primary and secondary data and evidence. It also intends to provide authentic data based on field visits—six of which have been undertaken to the major land ports of Bangladesh to gather field-level information on the current situations of these land ports in order to highlight the bottlenecks, infrastructural inadequacies, procedural complexities and operational problems of the ports. The field reports will also provide very recent primary information collected from stakeholders and knowledgeable quarters, which should be immensely valuable to the readers as well as policymakers of both the countries in identifying the hurdles in the way of expansion of border trade between Bangladesh and India. The field reports will be presented in the section 'Inferences Based on Field Visits to the Land Ports'.

The chapter will primarily depend on review of literature, secondary data and evidence collected and/or compiled from existing sources of published data, research publications as well as unpublished research works and newspaper reports and columns for the section 'Nature of Indo-Bangladesh Illegal Trade: Salient Features, Major Issues and Constraints', the section on smuggling. In the concluding section, some suggestions for removing the bottlenecks and improving the facilities will be presented. The conclusion will also highlight the main issues waiting to be resolved in order to strengthen the pace of developing institutional arrangements for regional cooperation.

Non-tariff Barriers to Indo-Bangladesh Border Trade

A very substantial proportion of Indo-Bangladesh legal trade is carried out as border trade. At present, Bangladesh has 15 official land ports and 92 land customs stations (LCSs) at different points of its international border. The land ports are: Bhomra in Satkhira district, Benapole in Jessore district, Sona Masjid in Chapai Nawabganj district, Hili in Dinajpur district, Burimari in Lalmonirhat district, Haluaghat in Mymensingh district, Tamabil in Sylhet district, Chatlapur in Moulvibazar district, Akhaura in Brahmanbaria district, Bibir Bazar in Comilla district, Muhurighat-Belonia in Feni district, Teknaf in Cox's Bazar district, Banglabandha in Panchagarh district, Birol in Dinajpur district and Darshana in Chuadanga district.

Out of these 15 land ports, only one, Teknaf, is used for Bangladesh–Myanmar trade. Another land port, Burimari, is largely used for Bangladesh's trade with Nepal and Bhutan in addition to Indo-Bangladesh trade. Also, Banglabandha is used for trade with Nepal and Bhutan. All the other land ports and LCSs are solely used for Indo-Bangladesh trade.[6] The growth of border trade through these different land ports mentioned above and also through the LCSs is very high. In fact, Benapole land port has become the second largest port of Bangladesh, surpassing Mangla.

[6] Two other land ports are going to be opened in the near future in consequence of the joint communiqué signed between Bangladesh and India in January 2010 during the visit of the prime minister of Bangladesh. One of these two land ports will be established at Ramgarh in the hill district of Khagrachari and the other will be established at Thegamukh in the hill district of Rangamati.

Even trade through Bhomra, Sona Masjid, Akhaura and Hili land ports is also rising substantially every year, though major proportion of the flow of trade through some of these land ports is deliberately kept unrecorded by the government officials and/or private operators of these land ports in order to deprive the government from tariff and tax revenues in collusion with corrupt personnel of various government agencies.

More importantly, it is believed that the major proportion of the illegal trade between the two countries may actually be cross-border smuggling through both recognized land ports and LCSs as well as through innumerable points on the porous land border and rivers and canals flowing from one country to the other. The fast increasing popularity of border trade can be largely explained by improvements in roads and highways, means of road communication and transport, the ongoing information and communication technology (ICT) revolution and modernization of banking and financial transactions in both the countries as well as the recent positive changes in mindsets of the governments of the two countries about expansion of trade, connectivity and regional cooperation.

However, the status quo between India and Bangladesh remains given the following reasons. The South Asian Free Trade Area (SAFTA) agreement was signed a few years back, but it is hardly operational. There was a proposal from India for signing bilateral free trade agreement with Bangladesh, but there is hardly any progress in this front too. The political bias of the last BNP-Jamaat-led government of Bangladesh during the period 2001–2006 was not favourable towards sincere efforts on any front of economic or political cooperation with India. The thinly veiled military government in the garb of a caretaker government, which ruled Bangladesh for nearly two years thereafter (2006–2008), was rather non-committal on this sensitive issue of augmenting Indo-Bangladesh friendly relationship through expansion of trade, connectivity and investment.

The present Awami League-led coalition government has taken some bold steps to strengthen trade, communication and transport connectivity, regional transit/transhipment of goods and the use of Bangladeshi ports by the other countries of the region since early 2010, which are at various stages of implementation at present. Therefore, it can be said that the groundwork for developing a vastly expanded scenario of cooperation in this sub-region has been inaugurated and is currently under process.

However, there are a host of 'non-tariff barriers' which exist at the actual ground levels in the land border to stymie the attempts of the governments of the two countries for friendly and accommodative transformation of Indo-Bangladesh bilateral ties. Most of these are a result of various vested interests and bureaucratic inertia and/or stubbornness, twists and misinterpretation as well as different prejudices of other decision-making authorities in both countries at different levels. The major non-tariff barriers are as follows:

1. Bangladesh's main export items do not get access to the Indian market because they are included in India's sensitive list of 480 items, which include agricultural and textile products. In spite of repeated assurances of the highest policymakers of India such as the prime minister, the finance minister and the commerce minister, the actual process of reduction of the items included in the sensitive list remains very slow and unsatisfactory. For example, even knitwear garments from Bangladesh have not yet got unhindered access to the Indian market in spite of the fact that such items cannot be barred on grounds of the rules of origin (RoO) of the World Trade Organization (WTO).
2. Non-tariff measures relating to compliance with sanitary and phytosanitary standards are often turned into non-tariff barriers and technical barriers to trade by India.
3. Bangladeshi products are supposed to get 'national treatment' from India, but they do not. National treatment assures that Bangladeshi goods will not be subjected to any obstacle that the Indian goods exported from India to Bangladesh do not face.[7]

---

[7] One exporter of fruit juice from Bangladesh to India claims that the customs authorities of India frequently change their positions about where to print the expiry date of the juice — on the bottom of the bottle or on the label of the bottle. Such changed rules increase the cost of production. He further claims that it takes 40–50 days to get the test results of the products from the Indian authorities. A representative of a battery exporter firm claims that they have to fill up a big questionnaire and submit it to Indian customs department before they get the permission from that office.

4. Poor logistic facilities of most of the Indian land ports, restrictions of commodities that can pass through land ports, cumbersome customs requirements, manual clearance, excessive inspection in the name of security, no customs cooperation or joint inspection, no harmonization of standards, lack of warehouse facilities in most of the Indian land ports, no testing facilities in any Indian land port bordering Bangladesh and so forth are major hurdles in the way of smooth movement of goods exported by Bangladesh to India.

5. Non-tariff barriers in India such as testing and certification, technical standards and banking regulations seriously hamper trade. For example, quality standard certificate from Bangladesh is not accepted by India. Indian customs officials do not accept the certificates issued by the Bangladesh Standards Testing Institution (BSTI). Bangladeshi goods are sent to Indian standards testing laboratories or the Bureau of Indian Standards (BIS) for new certificates on quality.

6. Processed food exporters find it difficult to access the northeastern states of India as the region's customs authorities have set a new rule asking the traders to store the imports in bonded warehouses from 1 June 2010 until the completion of laboratory tests on shipments. The earlier practice was to store the goods in the importers' warehouse. Food products also face new rules such as coding and recipe requirement by Central Food Laboratory (CFL), Guwahati. In the absence of any authorized food laboratory near the land ports in the northeastern states of India, the traders have to wait for three to six weeks to get the test results from the CFL, Guwahati. It has been suggested to accept the certificates of BSTI, Bangladesh. The facilities of BSTI can be upgraded with the help of India, if necessary. The introduction of a new rule to send the test results from CFL, Guwahati, by post instead of by fax has also widened the time period.

7. Businessmen from Bangladesh also complain of visa restrictions that make it difficult to travel to the northeastern states of India.

8. The Directorate General of Foreign Trade (DGFT) of India is not the only authority to impose rules and regulations

regarding exports from Bangladesh to India. Even various state agencies impose different barriers on their own. For example, the state customs departments (tariff agencies) sometimes ban different imports from Bangladesh. The customs authority of West Bengal at Kolkata once banned the import of soap from Bangladesh, while the DGFT claimed complete ignorance of the matter.

9. Some Bangladeshi traders complain that there are anti-Bangalee sentiments among a section of the indigenous communities of Seven Sister States. For example, some Bangladeshi traders are afraid that insurgent groups may perceive Bangladesh's involvement in the border trade and investment activities as 'economic exploitation'.

10. Exporters from Bangladesh stress the need for opening Bangladesh consulate offices at the deputy high commissioner or assistant commissioner levels in Guwahati, Agartala, Shillong and Aijol.

11. Normally, Bangladeshis are not allowed to open bank account in the northeastern states of India, and the export–import number is issued from Kolkata, which is at least 1,680 km from Agartala through Indian transport routes.

12. Recently, the Indian authorities have also circulated a new rule which requires that Bangladeshi jute bags need to have seals saying 'Made in Bangladesh' on the body of each jute bag exported to India. This new rule seems to be rather superfluous and deliberately designed to discourage jute goods from Bangladesh. In fact, it has seriously reduced the legal export of jute goods from Bangladesh to India in recent months, as was evident from the responses of the interviewees at the land ports during the field visits.

Inferences Based on Field Visits to the Land Ports

The vision of an integrated trade and transport corridor in South Asia is still marred by several obstacles. Despite attempts such as the Asian Land Transport Infrastructure Development (ALTID) project endorsed by the UN Economic and Social Commission for Asia and the Pacific (UNESCAP) in 1992, which focuses not only on physical integration of South Asian road and rail transport systems through the development of the Asian Highway (AH) and the Trans-Asian Railway projects, but also on the importance of accession to various international facilitation conventions to ensure efficient movement of goods and people across national boundaries, the implementation remains extremely slow.

During the rule of the BNP-Jamaat coalition government, Bangladesh refused to sign the protocol facilitating the use of the AH portions situated in Bangladesh, on the ground that if Tamabil border point in the eastern border of Bangladesh and the Benapole and Sona Masjid border points on the western border are opened up for cross-country transit traffic, then India will use the route as a corridor between its eastern states and the rest of India. Bangladesh proposed an alternative connection with the AH through Teknaf of Bangladesh and Myanmar. But no other member country of the AH project agreed to this alternative proposal of Bangladesh; even Myanmar did not agree. As a result, Bangladesh has been cut off from the agreed route of the AH for the time being. However, things seem to have set in the right direction since the coming to power of the present government in Bangladesh in January 2009.

As a part of the current research project, six field trips to major land ports of Bangladesh during four months from July to October 2010 were undertaken, which are: Benapole, Hili, Sona Masjid, Akhaura, Muhurighat-Belonia and Bibir Bazar. During the field visits, port officials, customs officers/employees, importers, clearing agents, local intelligentsia and community leaders, local villagers, transport workers and so on were interviewed with a checklist of information required to be furnished. The following are the inferences from the six field reports:

Inferences from Benapole[8]

The flow of imports of Bangladesh from India through Benapole was more than 20 times the flow of exports from Bangladesh to India, according to customs officials. Customs revenue of the port came to about Tk. 13,500 million during the fiscal year 2009–2010.

---

[8] Benapole is the largest land port of Bangladesh on the Indo-Bangladesh border situated in the district of Jessore of Bangladesh. On the Indian side of the border, the Indian land port is Petrapole of the state of West Bengal.

A manager of the local branch of the Grameen Bank confidently claimed that the above-mentioned amount represented only about one-third of the total revenue due, because there is a very strong network of institutionalized corruption in the whole port operation and customs clearing which deprives the Bangladesh government of the other two-thirds of the revenue through connivance of importers, Clearing and Forwarding (C&F) agencies and the customs officials (based on personal interviews).

The major items of import from India to Bangladesh are industrial goods, industrial raw materials, chemicals, yarn, truck chassis, pick-up chassis, iron bars, tractors, onion, garlic, spices, pulses, fruits, dry fruits, machinery, motor tyres, fish, autorickshaws, bicycle parts, corrugated iron sheet hot roles and so on. In fact, the complete list of all items that come in through Benapole will include several hundred items — too many to be enumerated, according to the customs officer interviewed. In comparison, there are only a few items of export from Bangladesh to India. The major items of export through Benapole are jute goods, raw jute, fish (mainly hilsa), blue wet hides and leather, battery, ceramic products, some toiletry items, float glass, fruit juice, some knitwear items and so on.

On an average, about 400–450 Indian trucks enter Benapole with imported items on a day. The trucks need more than a day to unload because of the slow pace of unloading and lack of storage spaces in the port yards. Sometimes, the wait may last for several days if some snags hit the process of customs clearance and other formalities. A properly planned truck terminal with a capacity of parking for at least 500 trucks is the immediate need of the port along with separate roads for entry and exit of the trucks. Massive expansion of warehouse facilities is another acutely felt immediate need of Benapole port, as the flow of imports from India to Bangladesh has been fast increasing.

Compared to the expanding demand for port facilities, the operational efficiency of the port is rather poor. No sophisticated unloading equipment is available. Only a few cranes and only one forklift are found in the port yards. Also, the addition of new warehouses has been negligible in the last five years, according to the interviewees. The border areas in the vicinity of Benapole are also used as smuggling routes for many items. The topography and geographical features of the whole region give special advantages to smugglers of both countries for such operations. Local sources informed that money exchange houses on both sides of the border are engaged in smuggling of currencies (based on personal interviews).

Inferences from Hili[9]

The international border between India and Bangladesh lies right at the end of the Hili railway junction. This railway junction is a very vital link between the districts of northwestern Bangladesh. But, there is no railway connectivity between Bangladesh and India through Hili junction at present. On the contrary, there is an Indian railway line through Balurghat town of the district of West Dinajpur of the Indian state of West Bengal, which is about 22 km away from Hili. Sona Masjid, another neighbouring land port, of the district of Chapai Nawabganj of Bangladesh, has recently been taking away much of the business of Hili land port due to this lack of connectivity.

Hili land port has been leased out to a private firm named 'Panama Trading'. Therefore, the land port is now called 'Panama Hili Port Link Limited' (the lease arrangement is on build–operate–transfer [BOT] basis, and the contract will be valid for 25 years). The port official that we have talked to informs that mainly agricultural items and food items are legally imported through Hili land port. Onion, garlic, oil cake, rice bran (*Bhushi*), fruits such as apples, oranges and grapes, fish, dry fish, maize, tomato, pulses, green chilli, spices such as cumin seed, dry chilli, turmeric, mustard and so on are imported from India. Among the industrial goods, bicycle parts, sewing machines and industrial raw materials and chemicals are also imported, but only rarely. Coal, stone chips, marble slabs and mosaic chips are also imported from India.

About 80–100 trucks on an average are handled daily by the land port. The port can be used six days a week. The narrowness of the road on the Indian side is responsible for the decrease of the traffic

[9] Hili land port is situated in Hakimpur Upazila of the district of Dinajpur of Bangladesh. The major part of the original pre-partition township of Hili fell on the Indian side of the border. Therefore, the present Bangladesh town of Hili, which is about half of the original pre-partition township of Hili, is also locally called Bangla Hili.

flow in recent times, the port official claims. (One interviewee narrates a story that a big banyan tree at some point of the road blocks the movement of large trucks on the Indian side of the road from Indian Hili to Balurghat, but the tree cannot be suitably trimmed or sized down or cut down because of religious belief of the local people.)

Hili and its neighbouring areas are also known for frequent use as routes for smuggling of goods. There are two major routes of smuggling: Gobindaganj–Hili road and Palashbari–Ghoraghat–Hili road. Cattle (mostly cow and buffalo) smuggling from India is rampant. Fruits, spices, fish, raw beef, saris, grey cloth (*Than Kapor*), cosmetics and toiletries, bicycle and bicycle parts, chemical fertilizer, garments items, ladies' apparels, jeans cut pieces and so on are the major items of smuggling from India. Drugs such as phensidyle and heroin are also smuggled in. Small arms are also allegedly brought in through these routes. Raw jute, hides, fertilizers, green chilli, hilsa fish and so on are the major items of smuggling from Bangladesh to India. There are allegations that the routes are leased out on a monthly basis by the law enforcement agencies to the smuggling rackets. A news item in the national daily newspaper issue confirms such allegations.[10]

Inferences from Sona Masjid[11]

Sona Masjid land port has gained in importance since the opening of the Bangabandhu Jamuna Bridge (Bangladesh) in 1996. It has now become the second busiest land port of Bangladesh after Benapole for handling import of Indian goods to Bangladesh. To begin with, it was leased out to a private firm called 'Panama Trading' along with Hili land port, but there have been a number of changes in its ownership which have actually stymied the profitable operation of the port. About 250–300 trucks are normally handled by the land port in a day. Onion, rice bran (*bhushi*), maize, stone chips, fly ash (a raw material used in cement production), dry fish, fruits such as mango, apple, orange and grapes, dry

---

[10] *Prothom Alo*, 8 September 2010, 5.

[11] Sona Masjid land port is situated in Shibganj Upazila of the district of Chapai Nawabganj of Bangladesh. It is the land port of Bangladesh linking the Indian district headquarters of Malda of the state of West Bengal.

chilli, garlic, oil cakes, soybean extract, china clay, rubber sandals, industrial chemicals, pulses, spices and so on are the major items of legal import from India to Bangladesh. Jute, jute goods, ceramic items, hides, green chilli and so on are the legally exported goods from Bangladesh to India.

As the port is situated in a rural area with no township in the neighbourhood, the officials face hardship in performing their daily duties. There is no police station, health centre, school or municipality in the area. The revenue of the port has also been decreasing over the years.[12] The reasons cited for the fall in revenue were: (i) The new customs commissioner of Rajshahi, who has built up a reputation for his honesty, did not give any facility regarding correct weight of different perishable items, as was the practice earlier. His behaviour is not businessmen-friendly. (ii) The topography and geographical features of Sona Masjid land port area do not allow large-scale smuggling of goods through the neighbouring areas as in the case of Benapole and Hili. (iii) Infrastructure of the land port is very poor. (iv) The distance of Sona Masjid from Dhaka discourages users. (v) There is a severe crisis of personnel in the customs office, which is causing delay and harassment in clearing the consignments of imports. There is an immediate need to upgrade the customs office at Sona Masjid to avoid the consequences of the above-mentioned roadblocks. At least, a deputy commissioner should be posted to handle the operations at customs clearance. There are gangs of organized toll collectors and politically powerful quarters engaged in extortion (*chandabazi*) in the land port area as well as on the highway, which need to be done away with.

Inferences from Akhaura[13]

After the construction of the new road from Comilla–Brahmanbaria–Sylhet Highway to Akhaura land port, it has become the largest land port on the eastern border of Bangladesh with northeastern states

---

[12] The actual revenue of the financial year 2009–2010 came down to Tk. 1,583.7 million from the targeted Tk. 2,839.5 million, whereas the actual revenue of the earlier financial year of 2008–2009 was Tk. 2,300.9 million.

[13] Akhaura land port is situated in Akhaura Upazila of the district of Brahmanbaria of Bangladesh. It is now the busiest land port on the eastern borders of Bangladesh and India.

of India handling the major share of export items of Bangladesh going to those states, though the flow of imports from northeastern states of India into Bangladesh through Akhaura land port remains quite negligible. Bangladesh exports mainly fish, cement, stone chips, battery, furniture items, glass sheet, plastic goods, soybean oil, bricks, fruit juice and tiles through this port to the northeastern Indian states. In the financial year 2009–2010, Bangladesh exported 442,955 tons of goods through Akhaura. Cement, stone chips and bricks comprise about three-fourths of Bangladesh's exports to India. In the financial year 2009–2010, Bangladesh imported only 557 tons of goods through Akhaura.

It is being proposed to transport Indian goods through the river routes in the near future, especially through the Ashuganj river port. However, the road connecting the land port and the river port is poorly constructed and very narrow. Only about 100 trucks can be cleared through the port in a day currently; therefore, many trucks have to wait for two to three days for unloading goods. Infrastructure limitations remain the main cause of delay and disruption of trade in the region, resulting in an enlarged illegal economy.

Inferences from Muhurighat-Belonia[14]

After becoming an official land port, Muhurighat-Belonia did not get much patronization from the government of Bangladesh. According to the assistant subinspector of land customs, only about 250 trucks use the land port per week. There is wide variation in the number of trucks using the port per day depending on the number of L/Cs opened and/or consignments cleared, which normally do not maintain any regular pattern (based on personal interviews). There is no notable flow of imports into Bangladesh through the land port. Cement, bricks, stone chips, dry fish and so on are the major goods exported from Bangladesh. There are occasional import consignments of bamboo and garlic from India.

---

[14] Muhurighat-Belonia land port is situated about 22 km to the south-east of Feni town, the headquarters of the district of Feni of Bangladesh. On the other side of the Indo-Bangladesh border at that point lies the Tripura township of Belonia.

Inferences from Bibir Bazar[15]

The easternmost portion of the 8-km road (about 3 km) is in terrible shape with some potholes making the road almost unfit for most types of vehicles. Only trucks can ply through these dilapidated parts of the road, and even they face frequent accidents. However, the customs subinspector at Bibir Bazar informed that Tk. 290 million has recently been allocated for improving and widening the Chowk Bazar–Bibir Bazar road. After completion of the project, the road is expected to be 40 feet wide.

The condition of the port facilities remains highly unsatisfactory. The major items exported from Bangladesh to India through Bibir Bazar land port are cement, stone chips, bricks, tiles, soft drinks and juices of different brands, ceramic items, polythene items, machine parts of farm equipment, fish, brick-crushers, dry fish and so on. The main items of import from India to Bangladesh are raw hides, ginger, potato, bamboo and so on. About 20 trucks from Bangladesh use the port every day on an average, according to respondents.

Nature of Indo-Bangladesh Illegal Trade: Salient Features, Major Issues and Constraints

Salient Features and Major Issues

Bangladesh is a typical example of an underdeveloped economy where the trading sector overwhelmingly attracts the surplus generated in other sectors. The 'dependency syndrome' has been making its economy more and more import dependent. New items are being added every day to the list of importable items. In this scenario, there is a growing demand in the domestic economy for an increasing number of items which can be fulfilled through import, legal or illegal.

---

[15] Bibir Bazar land port is situated on the bank of the river Gomti, which enters Bangladesh territory from the Indian state of Tripura at that point of the international border between India and Bangladesh. It is only 8 km to the east of the Comilla town, the district headquarters of the district of Comilla of Bangladesh.

Bangladesh embarked upon a path of import liberalization as early as 1986–1987, while India started the process only in 1991. But, even in the year 2010, the import liberalization regimes of Bangladesh and India remain very asymmetric. The more rapid pace of import liberalization in Bangladesh has created golden opportunities for it to be used as a conduit for a 'legal import–illegal export to India' trade route in recent years. In addition to the legal market for remittances from Bangladeshi overseas migrants and non-resident Bangladeshis (NRBs), an informal market for illegally imported foreign currencies proliferates all over Bangladesh, which has become a big source of foreign exchange used in illegal trade. These multiple foreign exchange markets of Bangladesh create an incentive structure to funnel foreign exchange available at lower official rate of exchange from legal import circuit to illegal trade circuit, as it provides lucrative opportunities for arbitraging.

Institutional credit for import of plant and machinery for newly sanctioned projects and/or existing industries is believed to be the most popular mechanism of capital flight through over-invoicing technique. Frequently, the items which are chosen for over-invoicing are the ones which traditionally carry relatively lower tariff and tax burden, or have experienced a lowering of tariff and tax rates through traditional budgetary or mid-year policy change of the government. Legal import provides the cover for illegal imports from India in most of the cases. Remittance collected by the 'Hundi' rings operating in the Middle East countries, the UK, Malaysia, Singapore, the USA and other major destinations of Bangladeshi migrants finances such illegal trade.

The economy in Bangladesh cannot create sufficient employment opportunities in the industrial sector for the growing labour force. In this scenario, illegal trade offers brighter prospective wherein petty operators as well as hired porters can earn substantially higher returns or wages in the border areas in illegal trade than in legal pursuits. Even the unemployed educated youth or the school dropouts find illegal trade an attractive proposition. Mostly operators finance illegal trade from the trade centres at Dhaka, Chittagong, Khulna, Jessore, Iswardi, Sylhet, Comilla, Brahmanbaria or Narayanganj.

The industrial sector in Bangladesh has been experiencing a rapid growth of assembly plants for electronics items, popularly known as 'screw-driver' factories. These firms take advantage of the tariff and tax structure, whereby imported consumer durable goods and machine parts in completely knocked down (CKD) or semi-knocked down (SKD) forms are taxed at a much lower rate compared to imported finished products. The value added by these firms is quite negligible, and goes mostly to the illegal trade circuit, as an increasing part of their sale proceeds is used for illegal import from India. Similarly, in the garment industry, high-quality garment materials imported tax-free are leaked out to the domestic market through a number of mechanisms. Gold and foreign currencies are also illegally traded traditionally. Most importantly, it is significant to recognize that the growth in illegal trade is largely due to the constraints in the legal trade. These are being enumerated in the following section.

Constraints

Some of the major constraints faced by legal trade between Bangladesh and India, and which are believed to act as stimulants to illegal trade are, firstly, the average tariff protection remains at a higher level in India than in Bangladesh. India steadfastly denies access to many Bangladeshi items of export on the ground that the meagre proportion of value added by the Bangladeshi exporters of those items does not justify their categorization as genuine Bangladeshi goods. This particular policy stance hinders legal export from Bangladesh to India. Procedural formalities of international trade in India and Bangladesh still remain cumbersome and costly. Secondly, Bangladesh and India are competitors in the international market for the same export items in many cases; jute is a prime example. Thirdly, as a part of Bangladesh's import liberalization programme, the value-added tax (VAT) has gradually replaced the multiple-rate sales tax system on imports. This trend of rapid liberalization has contributed to a great upsurge in import of relatively superfluous consumer items into Bangladesh in recent years.

Further, lack in diversification of export items from Bangladesh is a major constraint in expanding the value and volume of exports from Bangladesh to India. Bangladesh has been constantly demanding a greater access to the Indian market for its garments and knitwear items, but India is adamant not to allow this, on the ground that such a move would greatly erode the protection provided to its garments and knitwear industries. The seven eastern states of India neighbouring Bangladesh — Assam, Meghalaya, Arunachal Pradesh, Manipur, Nagaland, Tripura and Mizoram — are economically disadvantaged because of their landlocked geographical location as well as long and difficult terrain. These states are very rich in natural resources, but most of those remain untapped.

It would not be wrong to claim that in one sense, Bangladesh holds the key to economic development of these Seven Sisters. At present, these seven states account for a very small proportion of the value and volume of legal trade between Bangladesh and India. A more substantive proportion of illegal trade is conducted through the long land borders between Bangladesh and these states. These states are already using the Chittagong port through the services of the smugglers of the two countries. Liberalization of legal trade of Bangladesh with these seven states would be mutually beneficial, but this issue remains entangled in political distensions.

After the signing of the Chittagong Hill Tracts Peace Treaty in 1997, Bangladesh seemed to have achieved a temporary respite in its insurgency situation. But, the continuing troubles in the Indian states are used by the anti-Indian political parties of Bangladesh to frustrate any attempt to expand trade and economic cooperation with these states alleging that India would be using the facilities to use Bangladesh as a corridor for military counter-insurgency operations.

The fact that Indian producer goods as well as consumer goods have successfully penetrated a sizeable section of the domestic market of Bangladesh through both legal trade and smuggling has created the spectre of neocolonial domination and dependency syndrome in the relationship between these two neighbours. The perceived notion of Indian hegemony is vitiating the political scene of Bangladesh, and the economic rationale for economic cooperation is getting sidelined compared to the political realities of the region as well as the internal political divide of Bangladesh. The issue of illegal migration and subsequent settlement of

Bangladeshis in the neighbouring Indian states has also proved to be a highly contentious issue between the two neighbours.

In the light of the outline of the nature of smuggling provided above, a list of the major items of smuggling is provided in Tables 6.2 and 6.3.

Table 6.2
List of major smuggled items from India to Bangladesh

Categories of goods	Items
A. Agricultural goods	
1. Fruits	Orange, apple, grape, papaya, pomegranate, mango and pears
2. Livestock	Cow, buffalo, sheep
3. Spices and pulses	Turmeric, chilli, cumin, cardamom, clove, cinnamon, onion, garlic, black pepper, lentil, other types of pulses
4. Tobacco	'Bidi' leaves, 'bidi'
5. Sugar and molasses	Sugar and molasses
6. Fish	Carp, shrimp fries and catfish
7. Poultry	Chicken and eggs
8. Edible oil	Mustard
9. Others	Rice, maize, potato, tomato, livestock feed, fish feed, poultry feed and timber
B. Yarn and textiles	
1. Yarn	32, 40 and 60 counts of cotton and synthetic yarn
2. Sari	Cotton, silk and synthetic
3. Clothes	Cloth for garments, towel, lungi, punjabi, salwar kameez, bed sheet and cover, shawl, sweater, shirting, suiting and trouser
4. RMGs	All kinds of garments
5. Used garments	Sweaters
C. Industrial goods	
1. Construction materials	All types of fittings, mosaic materials and marble slates
2. Electrical goods	Switch, socket, tube light
3. Crockery	All types

(Table 6.2 Continued)

(Table 6.2 Continued)

Categories of goods	Items
4. Machinery and spares	Many types
5. Fertilizer and pesticides	SSP and insecticides
6. Cosmetics and toiletries	Many Indian brands
7. Electronics items	Many Indian brands
8. Computers	Indian-made components
9. Medicines	Many Indian brands
10. Transport vehicles	Truck and bus chassis, minibus chassis, station wagon, tyres, motorcycles, three wheelers, autorickshaws, bicycles and rickshaw parts
D. Industrial raw materials	
1. Industrial chemicals	Indian-made Chemicals
2. Textile materials	All types

Source: Table 4.1 in Gafur, Islam and Faiz: *Illegal International in Bangladesh: Impact on the Domestic Economy (Phase I)*, Bangladesh Institute of Development Studies, Dhaka, Bangladesh, September, 1990, pp. 53–54 and field interviews.

Table 6.3
List of major smuggled items from Bangladesh to India

Categories of goods	Items
A. Agricultural goods	
1. Fruits	Banana, pineapple, mango, guava and 'satkara'
2. Livestock	Goat and pig
3. Spices	Ginger, turmeric
4. Tobacco	Foreign brands of cigarettes
5. Sugar and molasses	Molasses
6. Fish	Hilsa, prawn, sweet water fish and dry fish
7. Vegetables	Various seasonal varieties
8. Jute	B-Bottom, Tossa
9. Edible oil	Imported soybean and palm oil
10. Others	Betel leaf
B. Yarn and textiles	
1. Yarn	Silk yarn, high-count synthetic yarn

(Table 6.3 Continued)

(Table 6.3 Continued)

Categories of goods	Items
2. Sari	Jamdani and Tangail
3. Clothes	Grey clothes ('Than')
4. RMGs	Fashionable garments
5. Used garments	Imported jeans, trousers, coats, blankets, ladies' dress, overcoats and undergarments
C. Industrial goods	
1. Construction materials	Cement, CI sheet, rods, used sanitary fittings from ship breaking yards, tiles and bricks
2. Electrical goods	Cables and wires
3. Crockery	All types
4. Machinery and spares	Imported electronics parts
5. Fertilizer and pesticides	Urea, TSP, imported fertilizers and pesticides
6. Cigarettes	Smuggled foreign brands
7. Cosmetics and toiletries	All smuggled foreign brands
8. Electronics items	All imported or smuggled foreign brands
9. Computers	All imported brands
10. Medicines	Many imported brands
11. Contraceptives	All imported brands
12. Petroleum products	Petrol, diesel and kerosene
D. Industrial raw materials	
1. Hides and skins	Cow hide, buffalo hide and goat skin
2. Leather	Blue wet leather
3. Industrial chemicals	Imported chemicals
4. Metals	Copper and bell metal from ship breaking yards, scrap metals, gold and silver

Source: Table 4.1 in Gafur, Islam and Faiz: *Illegal International in Bangladesh: Impact on the Domestic Economy (Phase I)*, Bangladesh Institute of Development Studies, Dhaka, Bangladesh, September, 1990, pp. 53–54 and field interviews.

Besides the above-mentioned features, certain other patterns can also be established:

1. Since 1991, several items became unimportant for illegal trade, some were dropped out of the list of smuggled

Table 6.4
Changing pattern of smuggling between Bangladesh and the Bordering Indian states in the 1991-2010 period

Changes	Smuggling from Bangladesh to India	Smuggling from India to Bangladesh
1. Items which have become relatively unimportant	Soybean oil, palm oil, VCR, VCP, jute, fish	Cosmetic items, toiletries and rice
2. Items which changed directions	Shrimp fries	Milk powder, fish and fertilizers
3. Items which have become relatively more important in the 1990s	Computers, diesel and petrol, chemical fertilizers, garments materials, grey cloth, gold, silk yarn, etc.	Fish, egg, all kinds of agricultural products also previously smuggled, forest products, seeds, medicines, phensidyle, etc.

Source: Field interviews.

items and some even changed directions — items previously smuggled out to India from Bangladesh have now been smuggled into Bangladesh from India. Table 6.4 lists some of such items. These changes in the pattern of smuggling reflect the fact that if price differentials across the border are narrowed down or eliminated through policy-induced adjustments and changes in the pace of liberalization of import regimes of the two countries, then illegal trade also responds to such changed incentive structures.

2. There is a trend of criminalization and syndication of smuggling operations in Bangladesh.

3. Illegal trade is still considered mainly as a 'law and order' issue by the respective governments and has minimal impact from regime change.

4. Drugs have emerged as major items of cross-border smuggling in the south-eastern districts of Bangladesh: a link may be established between the infamous 'Golden Triangle' of Myanmar, Thailand and Laos and the smugglers of the Indo-Bangladesh region.

5. Smuggling of arms has also been alleged to have increased alarmingly in recent years. Again, the south-eastern coastline of Bangladesh has emerged as a prime suspect in these operations.

In yet another significant study using the Delphi method to estimate the magnitude of the flow of smuggled goods between the two countries through five centres, Rahman and Razzaque (1998)[16] drew the following inferences:

1. About 70 items are smuggled from India to Bangladesh through the five centres that the study looked at, and only 15 items are smuggled out of Bangladesh to India.
2. Smuggling on a massive scale may be a factor for declining border price differentials. Almost a free trade situation has emerged in the border areas in recent times.
3. The operative tariff rates of smuggled items from Bangladesh are high, and VAT makes them higher. Development surcharge, supplementary duties and advance income tax add to the import cost substantially.
4. Tariff values are unrealistic, and much higher than world prices, and Indian prices in particular.
5. Bangladesh's illegal imports are on the rise, but the reverse flow is declining.
6. Import of intermediate goods from India helps export growth in Bangladesh in the ready-made garment (RMG) sector, knitwear sector and the textile sector.
7. The extent to which protection can be given to domestic industries in Bangladesh is limited by the cost of smuggling.
8. About 72.22 per cent respondents think that illegal import increased through their centres; only 13.33 per cent think otherwise.
9. The law-enforcing agencies on both sides of the border could apprehend and confiscate goods accounting for only about 2 per cent of the total value of smuggled goods.

These inferences show the rampant nature of illegal trade between the border regions of the two countries. While the governments can help in curtailing this trade, yet no substantial action has been taken yet.

---

[16] Rahman, A. and A. Razzaque, *Informal Border Trade between Bangladesh and India: An Empirical Study in Selected Areas* (Dhaka, Bangladesh: Bangladesh Institute of Development Studies, May 1998).

Conclusion

Based on the above inferences, certain main issues can be deduced which hold the keys to expansion of Indo-Bangladesh legal trade and regional cooperation.

1. *Increasing Access to Indian Market.* Bangladesh's continuous complaints regarding India's delay tactics in providing increased market access to its exports to India need to be resolved with an open mind and in the spirit of mutual accommodation. It should be repeated that in SAARC Preferential Trade Arrangement (SAPTA-I), 226 products were offered concessions, of which 100 were in favour of the least developed countries (LDCs) in the South Asian Association for Regional Cooperation (SAARC), which include Bangladesh, but the total package proved to be rather inconsequential in enhancing Bangladesh's access to the Indian market. Under SAPTA-II, as many as 2,013 products were offered concessions, of which 764 were offered exclusively in favour of the LDCs. But, again, the pace of implementation was disappointingly slow. More recently, the talks between India and Bangladesh regarding duty-free access of 25 items of export from Bangladesh and India have been dragged on for more than four years. The formally launched SAFTA agreement also remains dysfunctional since 2006.

2. *Regional or Sub-regional Cooperation Arrangements.* The prospect of SAFTA seems quite bleak in the context of mutual mistrust among the major member states of SAARC. In this scenario, the alternative arrangements such as the SAGQ initiated by four existing members of SAARC, namely, Bangladesh, Bhutan, India and Nepal, or the 'Bangladesh, India, Myanmar, Sri Lanka, and Thailand Economic Co-operation' (BIMSTEC), the name of which has recently been changed as 'Bay of Bengal Initiative of Maritime States for Technical and Economic Cooperation', should be vigorously pursued by Bangladesh, India, Nepal, Bhutan, Thailand and Myanmar. It should be noted that such sub-regional arrangements for cooperation can be forged within the ambit of the SAARC Charter too.

3. *The Issue of Transit or Transhipment.* Due to lack of mutual trust and lack of the spirit of mutual accommodation, India has failed to provide transit corridors for Bangladesh. While Nepal signed a transit agreement with Bangladesh a long time back, which was supposed to operate through Banglabandha land port of Bangladesh, but delay tactics on India's part have made it ineffectual and virtually dysfunctional for more than a decade. Thus, this issue needs to be resolved at the regional level.

4. *Opening up of Chittagong Port for Bordering Indian States.* Chittagong has the capacity to become a regional trading and transport hub (entrepôt) by developing its port for neighbouring eastern Indian states, Nepal, Bhutan and even China, Thailand and Myanmar. There is another very exciting prospect revolving around the issue of building a deep-sea port at Sonadia in Maheshkhali Upazila of the district of Cox's Bazar of Bangladesh for use by all the regional countries. But this can also be achieved only when all regional players agree on basic infrastructure necessities.

5. *'Selective Liberalization and Selective Control' of Import Regimes.* An alternative approach, called 'Selective Liberalization and Selective Control' within the context of the WTO legal system, should be adopted to overcome the hindrances posed by selective or distorted liberalization of the two economies. In this proposed trade regime, in lieu of blanket trade liberalization across the board, the range of items selected for trade restriction will be carefully chosen to provide preparatory breathing time and space for domestic producers. For those goods, which the economy genuinely needs, which are not catered to the needs of the relatively affluent sections of the population and which will not be immediately harmful for domestic producers, liberalization of imports should mean the removal of all kinds of tariff and non-tariff barriers, so that smuggling cannot flourish under the umbrella of legal trade.

Alongside, there is an impending need to institutionalize a mutual consultation process between the two neighbours and the region at large. Nepal and Bhutan are keen to use Bangladeshi seaports as alternative avenues for cost-effective transportation of their export and import items, but India has been less than forthcoming in facilitating transit through its territory. Even China, Thailand and Myanmar have shown interest in forging cooperative arrangements of regional trade, connectivity and cooperation. The existing environment of political mistrust and mutual suspicion hampers the scope of economic cooperation mainly due to domestic political agendas of the concerned parties. Yet, regional cooperative arrangements may be a more prospective mechanism to circumvent the perceived notions and apprehensions and will prove successful in resolving long-standing issues. Some of the issues which deserve immediate attention are listed as follows:

1. A system of coordination and monitoring of each other's fiscal, monetary and commercial policies should be developed under the auspices of SAARC or the proposed Growth Quadrangle or even BIMSTEC (or any new arrangement involving these countries and China). Coordinated changes of tariff rates will be the single most important step in transforming the major share of illegal trade into a robust and increasing flow of legal trade in the region.

2. The issue of providing duty-free access to goods from Bangladesh into the Indian market should be resolved in right earnest and with due sincerity.

3. India has been seen to be deliberately slow in removing/reducing the non-tariff barriers hampering the Bangladeshi exports to India in spite of the official public declarations on the contrary.

4. Development of regional transportation networks is the prime need for promoting trade. New improved networks should be developed with joint financing by all the stakeholders. The incompatibilities of the transportation networks of different countries should be removed on a priority basis.

5. Modernization of the land ports and border entry points and banking and telecommunication facilities should also be taken up on an emergency basis.

6. Regional transit or transhipment agreements should be expedited, along with liberalization and relaxation of visa systems.

7. Development of the Chittagong port and another deep-sea port in Bangladesh for the use of the entire region can be taken up as a joint venture of all the stakeholder countries.

8. Steps should also be taken to resume serious consultations to make the existing SAFTA agreement truly effective and functional under the umbrella of SAARC.

Suggested Readings

Bhagwati, J. and T.N. Srinivasan (1972), 'Smuggling & Trade Policy', *Journal of Public Economics* 2(4) (November): 377–389.

Bhagwati, J. and B. Hansen (1973), 'A Theoretical Analysis of Smuggling', *Quarterly Journal of Economics* LXXXVII(2) (May): 172–387.

Bhagwati, J. (1982), 'Alternative Theories of Illegal Trade: Economic Consequences and Statistical Detection', *Weitwirtschaftliches Archir Bd,* C Bd, C XVII.

Cooper, R.N. (1974), 'Tariffs and Smuggling in Indonesia', in *Illegal Transactions in International Trade,* edited by J. Bhagwati (Amsterdam: North Holland).

Falvey, R.E. (1978), 'A Note on Preferential & Illegal Trade under Quantitative Restrictions', *Quarterly Journal of Economics* XVII(1) (February): 175–178.

Gafur, A., M. Islam and N. Faiz (October 1991), *Illegal International Trade in Bangladesh: Impact on the Domestic Economy (Phase II)* (Dhaka, Bangladesh: Bangladesh Institute of Development Studies).

Islam, M. (February 1997), *Externalities, Market Failures and Policy Failures in Migration: A Study of Bangladeshi Migrants in Singapore,* Research Report Submitted to the Institute of South East Asian Studies, Singapore.

——— (March 1997), *Bangladesh Rashtro, Shamaj O Durnitir Arthaniti (in Bengali)* (Dhaka, Bangladesh: Ahmed Publishing House).

——— (2000), 'Trade Between Bangladesh and the Bordering Indian States: A Choice Between Legal Trade and Smuggling', Paper presented in the Second Dialogue on *Interactions with the Indian Bordering States,* Instituted by the Bangladesh Institute of International and Strategic Studies, Dhaka, and the Maulana Abul Kalam Azad Institute of Asian Studies, Kolkata, India, and held in Kolkata, India, on 16–17 August 2000.

——— (2001), 'Trade and Economic Co-operation Between Bangladesh and the Bordering Indian States: A Victim of Policy Induced Distortions', Paper Presented in the Third Dialogue on *Interactions with the Indian Bordering States* organised by the Bangladesh Institute of International and Strategic Studies in Dhaka, Bangladesh, during 21–23 August 2001.

——— (2003), 'Illegal Trade between India and Bangladesh: A Policy-Induced Phenomenon of the Politics of Suspicion and Conflict', in *Comprehensive Security in South Asia: Economic Dimensions* (Delhi, India: Delhi Policy Group, 2003), 121–166.

Islam, M. and N.C. Nag (February 2010), *Economic Integration in South Asia: Issues and Pathways* (London, UK: Pearson).

Kemp, M.C. (1976), 'Smuggling and Optimal Commercial Policy', *Journal of Public Economics* (April–May 1976).

Lessard, D.R. and J. Williamson (1987), *Capital Flight and Third World Debt* (Washington DC: Institute for International Economics).

Nayak, S.S. (1977), 'Illegal Transactions in External Trade and Payments in India', *Economic and Political Weekly* (Bombay, 12 December).

Pitt, M.M. (1981), 'Smuggling and Price Disparity', *Journal of International Economics*, *Vol. II* (Amsterdam: North Holland).

Rahmatullah, M. (2004a), 'Integrating Transport Systems of South Asia', in Rehman Sobhan (ed.), *Promoting Cooperation in South Asia: An Agenda for the 13th SAARC Summit,* South Asia Centre for Policy Studies (SACEPS) (Dhaka: Centre for Policy Dialogue (CPD) and the University Press Limited), 59–68.

———— (2004b), 'Promoting Transport Cooperation in South Asia' in Rehman Sobhan (ed.), *Regional Cooperation in South Asia: A Review of Bangladesh's Development 2004* (Dhaka: Centre for Policy Dialogue and University Press Limited), 373–396.

Reddaway, W.B. and M.M. Rahman (1975). 'The Scale of Smuggling Out of Bangladesh', *Research Report (New Series),* No. 21 (Dhaka: Bangladesh Institute of Development Studies [BIDS]).

Richter, H.V. (1974), 'Problems of Assessing Unrecorded Trade', in *Illegal Transactions in International Trade,* edited by Jagdish Bhagwati (Amsterdam: North Holland).

Roy, A. (1978), 'Smuggling, Import Objectives, and Optimum Tax Structure', *Quarterly Journal of Economics* (August).

Sheikh, M.A. (1974), 'Smuggling, Production & Welfare', *Journal of International Economics* 4(4) (November): 355–364.

Expanding Connectivity for Greater Cooperation in South Asia

7

Nepal as a Transit State: Scope for Sino-Indian Cooperation

Nishchal N. Pandey

Introduction

Due to its geographical location, Nepal has been historically used as a transit for trade between India and China. Historically, Nepal benefited from its close proximity to what are considered prosperous civilizations at different intervals in history. Kerung, Hetauda, Olangchungola and even Kathmandu reflect the highs and lows of affluence in congruence to its influential neighbours' ups and downs. During the Mughal era in India and the wealthy Tang dynasty in China, Nepal too was known for its abundance of wealth and treasure. Most of the historic marvels in the cities of Bhaktapur and Lalitpur were built due to the stability provided by the thriving Licchavi and Malla regimes acclaimed for the encouragement they gave to traders doing business with Tibet and India.

In fact, the Licchavi king Angsuverma got his daughter Bhrikuti married to the Emperor of Tibet, Srang Tchang Gyampo, who later came to be worshipped as 'Goddess Tara'. Of the main reasons for Nepal waging three wars against Tibet, trade-related issues top the list of explanations. The advent of the Shah era coincided with the solidification of the British Raj in India and the weakening of its traditional hold in manufacturing, complete ruin of exports coupled with obstacles to free trade. To the north, in the early 18th century, the economic status of the Chinese peasants also declined. The government's funds were depleted due to foreign expansion, and around the same time, the British introduced Indian opium in Chinese markets, wanting to gain a larger foothold there. Opium trade resulted in depletion of Chinese silver reserves and gave the British a huge advantage over all the other Chinese trading partners.[1] As a consequence, Nepal's leverage vis-à-vis India and China waned gradually, and it adopted a more inward-oriented approach in its economic policies and isolation from the foreign domain.

After the 1960s, Nepal started to diversify its trade, and several measures were taken in terms of revision of both products and countries with which it would trade. In the modern times, Nepal has been excessively dependent on the Kolkata port for both exports and imports. But due to heavy congestion at the Kolkata port and poor road conditions from Kolkata to Raxaul, imported goods—whether petroleum products or perfumes—have become expensive in Kathmandu. Meanwhile, the 'Northern Himalayan Wall' has proven a big hindrance for trade and connectivity. Though the rail services agreement was signed between India and Nepal on 21 May 2004, work on the construction has been relatively slow. For instance, the construction of the Inland Clearance Depot (ICD) was completed in 2000, yet it took another year for the rail line construction to be completed.

The ICD was established in the Indo-Nepal bordering town of Birgunj which is of vital importance for Nepal, since it is desirous of improving transport services through the introduction of multimodal transport, containerization and unrestricted freight trains. However, from Birgunj onwards, goods still have to face several other bottlenecks within the Nepalese territory. The same holds true for exportable items. On the other side, cheap Chinese goods have made entry into Nepal and are largely smuggled into north India—mostly to Bihar and Uttar Pradesh. Most of the trade with China takes place through the Khasa point in Tibet, adjoining the Nepalese district of Sindhupalchowk, and trucks carry the goods via the Kodari highway either to Kathmandu or (straight) to the Terai border towns.

---

[1] 'Dynasties of Asia', Online web URL: http://www.dynastiesofasia.com/asian-history-references/qing-dynasty-period-in-chinese-history.htm.

Nepal also needs to build a reliable rail infrastructure in the country as the present Janakpur–Jaynagar railway only caters to a very small proportion of the Terai population. The railway has faced a terrible neglect from the authorities and is currently in a shambles. Only after a huge demand from the people of almost 50 Village Development Committees (VDCs) in the area and a directive from the Parliament, has the Ministry of Labour and Transport Management of Nepal formulated a 10-year strategic plan to revive the ailing railway service which comes under the Nepal Railway Company Ltd. The plan visualizes programmes to transform the nation's sole line into a public service-oriented structure and a commercial transport service by transforming this more than seven-decade-old railway into a modern, safe and reliable means of transportation in the country. The strategy focuses on strengthening and better management of the 51-km-long railway line (at the moment, only 29 km is operational) by upgrading its service standards.[2] However, this line alone will not be sufficient if the country is to brace for the transit trade between India and China and optimally utilize the opportunities provided therein. The new line must also cater to the commercial cargo along with human traffic.

In January 2010, the prime minister of Bangladesh, Sheikh Hasina, reached an understanding with India that Bangladesh would allow the use of its territory for transit to the northeastern states if India would also permit Nepal and Bhutan to use the land custom station at Banglabandha on the Bangladesh side. The Bangladeshi foreign minister Dipu Moni said that no protocol would likely be required for India to launch the routes with Nepal and Bhutan. A mere exchange of letters between Dhaka and New Delhi would be sufficient to accomplish the formalities and enable the two landlocked countries to use Bangladesh's port facilities.[3] This is an important and promising development for connectivity and would help the three countries (Nepal, Bangladesh and India) to benefit from the opportunities.

[2] Prabhakar Ghimire, 'Janakpur-Jayanagar Railway line to get facelift', Online web URL: http://www.myrepublica.com/portal/index.php?action=news_details&news_id=9335, accessed on 28 September 2010.
[3] 'India to get access to land-locked NE States through Bangladesh', http://news.rediff.com/report/2010/aug/08/indias-landlocked-n-e-states-are-no-more-isolated.htm, accessed on 1 November 2010. 'No New Deal on Transit Now', *The Daily Star*, 5 September 2011.

China would also benefit from this trilateral arrangement as it would bring Tibet closer to Bangladesh. Goods from Tibet could then reach Bangladesh through the Kodari–Sindhuli–Raxaul–Bangladesh route and Bangladesh could avail this opportunity to send its goods in the opposite direction. However, the Indian side will be required to be more flexible to make this a successful economic enterprise given that Nepal and Bangladesh had already signed the transit deal as early as April 1976, but it had remained non-functional devoid of ground modalities.

Trade and Connectivity with India

As a landlocked and lesser developed country, it is in the fundamental national interests of Nepal to open up as many border points as possible for trade with both its neighbours and also try and get access to Bangladesh. Nepal and Bangladesh are separated only by a tiny section of Indian territory. As with the other neighbours such as Bhutan and Pakistan, trade and connectivity issues require a lot more political bargaining than presently acquiesced to. Only after the entire South Asian region is better connected through improved infrastructure and easing of visa restrictions and other bottlenecks, can there be meaningful trade through land between Nepal and these countries.

Transport costs have affected export competitiveness to the extent that there is scarcity of raw materials, and this has led to a smaller export basket for Nepal. It is imperative that the transport sector plays a lead role to facilitate exports and contribute to the economic transformation of the country. There are 15 entry/exit points in Nepal mutually agreed for the purpose of use by Indian traders. However, only seven points are operational at present, even among which the Birgunj–Raxaul and Bhairahawa–Sunauli customs points are most active. Three ICDs of Biratnagar, Birgunj and Bhairahawa[4] have been completed by the Nepal Multimodal Transit and Trade Facilitation Project so far. This project was initiated in 1998 to construct a rail-based ICD in Birgunj and

---

[4] *Note:* Birgunj, Biratnagar and Bhairahawa are Nepali bordering towns in the Indo-Nepal border. These cities are adjoined with Raxaul, Farbeshgunj and Sunauli–Gorakhpur on the India side.

road-based ICDs in Biratnagar and Bhairahawa, and at the same time, procure *four rapid loading equipment* called 'reach stackers'[5] for the Birgunj ICD, operate Automated System for Customs Data (ASYCUDA) and Advance Cargo Information System (ACIS), facilitate trade and transport and reform and introduce transport and multimodal legislation. Railway lines from Raxaul to ICD Birgunj were constructed under the assistance of grants from the Indian government.

Despite these significant features, the ICDs have been under-utilized. Some traders have complained that these are not user-friendly,[6] while others have suggested certain procedural modifications such as shifting all official formalities from the seaport of Kolkata to the Birgunj ICD itself.[7] If, despite the establishment of ICDs, the traders still have to go to the gateway port to process for cargo clearance, then obviously the expected reduction of transit transport cost by 30–40 per cent is not fulfilled. Thus, ICDs need to be allowed to expand to their full capacities and should serve as the final point of delivery for third-country goods (both imported and exported). If the Bhairahawa–Nepalgunj, Biratnagar and Birgunj points are developed, these can provide enormous advantage to traders from both the countries.

Additionally, New Delhi has agreed to Nepal's request of constructing an east–west railway line parallel to the East-West Highway, which will turn out to be another milestone not only for bilateral trade and tourism but also for transit transport between India and China. The East-West Highway, which runs from Mahendranagar in the west to Kakarbhitta in the east, is Nepal's principal road artery. The proposed railway will alter the whole dynamics of the current state of trade and transit of Nepal and indeed prove to be a milestone in the annals of Indo-Nepal relations. Indian goods bound for China can be transported to Nepal using this railway and then bifurcated along the various roads being constructed by Nepal in the mid-hills, for instance, via Chitwan, Dhading, Kathmandu and then to Khasa or Sindhuli–Dhulikhel–Khasa.

---

[5] *Note:* A reach stacker is a vehicle used for handling intermodal cargo containers in small terminals or medium-sized ports.

[6] *Note:* Interview with Suraj Aggarwal on 12 March 2011, local trader in Birgunj. Also based on interactions with officials of NICCI.

[7] Nisha Taneja, Nishchal N. Pandey, Subhanil Chowdhury, 'Nepal-India Economic Cooperation' (New Delhi: ICEAR, November 2009).

After the completion of the Syafrubesi–Rasuwagadhi highway, an easier access via the Trishuli highway straight to Nuwakot–Rasuwagadhi can be considered. This will be the most direct link from the Indian side to the already operational Gormu–Lhasa railway line in China. There are also proposals of extending the proposed railway line from Birgunj to Kathmandu. While trucks carrying Indian goods from Birgunj to Kathmandu have to travel 220 km, a train from Birgunj to Kathmandu through the mountains would reduce the distance to mere 80 km, cutting travel time and costs.[8] This idea, however, may not materialize in the foreseeable future due to the inertia within the bureaucracies of the two countries. Instead, a Hetauda–Kathmandu fast-track road is on the anvil, and the government of Nepal has earmarked its budget for the financial year 2009–2010 that would reduce transportation cost and time from Hetauda to Kathmandu. Hetauda is a major town in Makwanpur district in Narayani Zone in the southern Nepal. This road is markedly different because it is totally inside Nepal's territory, is partially in use by trucks and is commercially viable.

The trade corridors of critical and strategic importance for Nepal are, however, the north–south connections linking the country's major trade points. The most important north–south links for the flow of trade and goods are Kodari–Barhabise–Kathmandu–Hetauda–Birgunj (part of the Asian Highway [AH] network), and the corridors of Rasuwagadhi–Syafrubesi–Kathmandu–Hetauda–Birgunj. These two routes are effectively linked to its neighbouring countries. Kodari (linked with Tibet) and Birgunj (linked with India) are therefore the most crucial border points for Nepal, and their upgradation is therefore in the country's inherent national interest. In the short term, it makes economic sense to upgrade these points than to strive for further connections at other points along the Indo-Nepal and Nepal–China borders. This also makes for a stronger case as a dry port at Birgunj began operations in 2002.

Nepal's current objective should be to prepare an investment programme that will improve road links from the East-West Highway to the North-South Corridor and thereby strengthen its road connectivity to major economic activity centres and neighbouring countries. A more efficient road network with higher capacity will promote access to rural produce and domestic as well

---

[8] Sudha Ramchandran, 'Nepal to get China Rail Link', www.asiatimes.com, accessed on 24 September 2010.

as regional trade and, therefore, enhance the economic growth. This fast-track road is expected to shorten the travel distance from Kathmandu to the Terai by 150 km, cutting the travel time by about three hours, which is presently more than nine hours. Slope stabilization and road rehabilitation will ensure all-weather traffic from Kathmandu to Kodari, improving the reliability and cost-effectiveness of transport links and bringing considerable savings in both travel time and costs.

In order to evaluate the possibility of Sino-Indian trade via Nepal, one also needs to take into account the tourism inflow which is a major basis for improved connectivity. Both Indian and Chinese tourists to Nepal have been growing in the last couple of years, and if one considers the increase in the number of Indian pilgrims to Mount Kailash through Nepal, the imperative for better infrastructure cannot be debated. Improved access to markets and to health, education and other essential services, as well as development along the highway, will immensely benefit Nepal.

India needs to recognize that a stable and peaceful Terai region is vital for trade and transportation and therefore essential for any future export and import with the Tibet Autonomous Region (TAR) of China via Nepal. As far as air connectivity is concerned, Nepal and India already have numerous daily flights from New Delhi to Kathmandu, and Kathmandu is additionally linked with Kolkata, Mumbai and Varanasi. However, other cities of Nepal are not connected with Indian cities. A direct flight was launched from Biratnagar in eastern Nepal to Kolkata in 2009, but this initiative could not be sustained. Such instances bear witness to the need for cooperation on significant issues such as trade and connectivity between the two countries for the benefit of the region.

Trade and Connectivity with the TAR, China

Much has been discussed about Nepal–China economic relations over the past few decades,[9] but the trade component is beginning to receive priority from governments on both sides only recently.

---

[9] 'Nepal and Its Neighbors: Yam Yesterday Yam Today', *The Economist*, 18 January 2012. See also, 'Nepal-China shall boost business ties: Envoy', Xinhuanet. com, 17 August 2012.

For a long time, Nepal has been requesting for aid and infra-structure facilities to be constructed by the Chinese, who have obliged, without giving adequate focus to building Nepal's own capability. Roads such as the Arniko Highway connecting the border Chinese town of Khasa to Kathmandu, convention centres such as the grandiose Birendra International Convention Centre which is currently being used by the Constituent Assembly, trolley buses in Kathmandu and the Civil Servant's Hospital are illustrations of Chinese help to Nepal.

However, Nepal now intends to export its products to Tibet and make use of its location to emerge as a transit state for China's trade with other South Asian countries. This would instigate Chinese dependency on Nepal rather than the latter constantly asking for aid and assistance. One of the key areas where Nepal has become a major thrust point for Tibet is tourism. Most tourists headed to Tibet go via Nepal as Kathmandu is the only interna-tional sector having direct flights to Lhasa. Even with reference to surface transport, hundreds of tourists and pilgrims bound for Mansarovar and Mount Kailash visit Tibet annually through Nepal. Though political disturbances in Nepal affect tourism in Tibet and vice versa, nevertheless, tourism can form the basis of a sustainable partnership between the South Asian neighbours in the long run.

In sync with their age-old saying, 'If you want to become rich, construct roads', the Chinese have given special emphasis to building roads, bridges and feeder roads connected to main highways all along the Tibetan plateau. And in the recent years, this has been transformed into their willingness to extend these links to the bordering countries as well. The Nepalese have also for many years dreamt of trade and transit across the Himalayas, given the never-ending hassles at the Kolkata port. With the mod-ernization wave of the 1990s, cheap Chinese goods have begun to flood the Nepalese market and through Nepal found their way into the northern cities of India. This is how the Chinese realized that there was huge potential for trade, if the otherwise formi-dable Himalayan passes could be opened at several places along the Tibet–Nepal border. Several blacktopped roads already exist within Nepal connecting Bihar, West Bengal and Uttar Pradesh.

The benefits of trade are already visible as trade with China is turning out to be a critical factor for trade diversification as well as for supplying the Nepalese people with necessary household items at reasonable prices. The Chinese side has been assisting Nepal with the following roads vital for Nepal–TAR trade that can also prove useful for transit trade:

1. Construction of Syafrubesi–Rasuwagadhi road (18 km)
2. Construction of Trishuli–Galchi road inclusive of three bridges (17 km)
3. Construction of Baglung–Jomsom road via Beni (72 km)
4. Construction of an Inland Clearance Depot at Kodari for transit facilitation.[10]

Of these, the most crucial will be the Syafrubesi–Rasuwagadhi road in Rasuwa district which will be the second road-link between Nepal and China, the first being the Arniko Highway discussed earlier in this chapter. Once the road comes into full operation, it will be the shortest route for transportation of goods between China and India via Nepal, making Nepal a feasible entrepôt for trade between the two Asian economic giants. The only route for transit trade at the moment is Tatopani in Sindhupalchowk district. This road was connected with the Japanese-aided Dhulikhel–Sindhuli road via Dhulikhel. It must be recalled that the Chinese constructed the Arniko Highway back in 1962 and cheap Chinese goods have been passing through this road to Sindhuli and then further on to Indian border towns.

Nepalese traders also use the traditional Khasa-Tatopani-Kathmandu-Mugling–Birgunj road for selling Chinese goods to Indian businessmen in major commercial towns in Nepal along the Indo-Nepalese border, mainly Birgunj, Bhairahawa, Biratnagar, Janakpur and Nepalgunj. Goods are first ordered in Guangzhou, trucks are arranged and it generally takes 7–10 days for the consignment to reach the Khasa town in Tibet where it has to pass check posts both at the Chinese side and at Tatopani on the Nepalese side of the border. Border facilities at Tatopani are, however, not up to the standard; there is no warehouse facility, bureaucrats are corrupt and the Kodari Highway along the river is blocked by frequent landslides.

---

[10] For details on the construction of the Port: Online Web URL: http://www.mocs.gov.np/uploads/Treaty%20of%20Trade%20and%20Transit%20_Final_.pdf.

The Birgunj–Kathmandu–Nuwakot–Rasuwagadhi route,[11] comparatively shorter than the route connecting the Tatopani checkpoint from the Janakpur–Sindhuli–Dhulikhel, will be the second blacktopped road link between Nepal and China after the Kodari Highway. This would allow the government to collect revenues and toll taxes, and the locals of Rasuwa district would also be able to easily export their local products to China (small-scale trading is already taking place through a muddy road). The total length of the new road will be around 16 km and 4.5 m wide flagged by 11 bridges, and the total carriageway being 7 m. It initially traverses along the Bhote Koshi River and passes by Linlin and Timure villages that are situated 1,698 m and 1,736 m above the sea level, respectively. The road ends at the 1,819-m-high Rasuwagadhi. Till Dhunche of Rasuwa district, which is 70 km from the Trishuli bazaar, there already exists a pliable road.

Nepal's strategy should be to optimize the benefits accruable from the 1,118-km Gormu–Lhasa railway link both for easy export of Nepalese goods to the mainland and for diversifying imports from China, which comprise batteries and toys to heavy vehicles and other items. If planned properly, this railway line which is now being extended to Shigatse (Xigaze) will have positive effects for the ailing Nepalese economy. China's railway minister Liu Zhijun was quoted in the *Xinhua News Agency* that 'the US$1.98 billion construction would play a vital role in boosting tourism and promoting the rational use of resources' which is expected to be completed by 2014 and is designed to transport 8.3 million tonnes of freight annually.[12] The Shigatse prefecture borders India, Bhutan and Nepal and is 270 km towards Nepal from Lhasa. This extension has brought the Nepal border closer to the railway line. This link could be utilized in two ways: either by extending the line to Khasa or by extending it to Syafrubesi in Rasuwa district. Both ways, the road linkage and infrastructure facilities in the Nepal side of the border are reasonably up to the mark for linkages with the Indian roads. But, when will this materialize? It remains to be seen. The idea of a railway linkage from Tibet has been quite glamorous, yet nobody has been able

[11] For more on the construction of this road on the Chinese side, see 'Highway will bring Nepal and Tibet "in from the cold"', http://news.bbc.co.uk/2/hi/8480637.stm, accessed on 27 September 2010.

[12] 'China building rail link to Lhasa', *The Himalayan Times*, 27 September 2010.

to give a definite answer to the question that which year will the Nepal border be touched by a rail line. It will be a welcome gesture if the Chinese side, as a friendly neighbour of Nepal, continues to update the information on the progress of the rail construction from Lhasa to Shigatse and from Shigatse to the Nepal border. Only then can Nepal, despite its instability and bureaucratic hassles, be able to plan ahead on how to maximize the use of the railway line.

Development of 'a landlocked Nepal' as a transit state between India and China holds tremendous potential for its economic prosperity, and this could be developed as a strategic leverage by Nepal vis-à-vis both its giant neighbours. If harnessed properly, Nepalese towns can turn into equivalents of the state of Monaco that lies between Italy and Southern France. Both India and China stand to gain tremendous benefits from this. Unfortunately, there is not enough interest from the governments of these two countries for inexplicable reasons. It could be because both are quite satisfied with their bilateral trade through the sea lanes, even if it is more expensive and time-consuming, but strategically safer for them.

Although the Nathu La in Sikkim has been reopened, it is proving to be impracticable due to cost, topography and the distance from the main industrial cities of India.[13] For these reasons, Nepal's corridor will be of great economic significance to both India and China as it will give easy access to the regional markets of Tibet and Sichuan for India and the entire north Indian belt for China. A glimpse of Chinese goods swamping the north Indian markets via Nepal is provided by the volume and direction of Sino-Nepalese bilateral trade. In fact, quite a number of Marwari businessmen based both in India and in Nepal have perfected the art of importing Chinese goods for Nepalese consumption alone as well as export to India.

Although China–Nepal bilateral trade has grown by leaps and bounds in the previous decade, Nepalese export to China has been dismal, and currently, the balance of payments is in favour of China. In fact, during the fiscal year 2010–2011, Nepal recorded its highest ever trade deficit with China which rose to

[13] Tara Dahal, 'Nepal as a Transit State: Emerging Possibilities', in Nishchal N. Pandey (ed.) *Nepal as a Transit State: Emerging Possibilities* (Kathmandu: Institute of Foreign Affairs, 2006), 56.

₹44 billion.[14] Only in May 2010, the two countries signed an agreement under which China would provide duty-free access to 361 Nepalese products. However, this access was a part of Chinese duty-free access to 4,721 products from least developed countries (LDCs)[15] and hence did not make much of difference for China's bilateral trade. Nepal has since been pursuing a bilateral agreement with China, asking the latter to provide duty-free access to 497 items. Most of the goods that can be exported to China are agricultural items such as trout fish, milk products, natural honey, incense, essential oils as well as mint, paints, tubes, raw skins of sheep, other leather goods as well as handicrafts, including jewellery, scaffolding equipment and threaded elbow pipes. Among exports, handicrafts topped the chart in total export to China in the financial year 2009–2010 (Nepal Trade Promotion Centre Statistics).

Since it is the Indian businessmen in huge numbers who are engaged in the trans-Himalayan trade, it is for the Government of India (GOI) to realize the pitfalls of not permitting transit for its products to TAR through Nepal. While Chinese goods are entering the Indian market through an open border, the same is not happening for Indian goods. India is losing trade due to its own improper policy and vision. In fact, cement, tobacco, raw fish, iron ore, incense and herbal products could easily find a market in the TAR and via TAR to the Chinese mainland, making use of the Lhasa–Golmud railway. Tibet is perennially short of cement which can be supplied by India. Even Japanese vehicles in Tibet have mostly gone through the Kolkata port to Nepal and then to Tibet.[16]

Among the possible routes, the Birgunj–Naubise–Kathmandu–Tatopani–Nyalam road is already operational, although the road is incapable of holding the increased volume of India–China goods on a sustained basis in the long run. Similarly, the Kodari–Sindhuli–Janakpur road has already been inaugurated and is operational due to Japanese assistance; it connects Nepal's Terai with Khasa (Tibet). The Galchi–Rasuwagadhi sector of the Birgunj–Syafrubesi corridor is being constructed with financial

[14] 'China ready to support Nepal bring down trade deficit', *Republica Daily*, 13 August 2012.

[15] 'Duty-free and quota-free market access for LDCs', David Vanzetti and Ralf Peters in http://ageconsearch.umn.edu/bitstream/47646/2/Vanzetti.Peters.pdf

[16] Statistics from the United Traders Syndicate that sells Toyota vehicles in Nepal.

assistance from the Asian Development Bank (ADB), while the construction of the Dakshinkali–Hetauda fast-track is also set to begin soon. All these roads will bring north India in proximity with Tibet via Nepal, and it is for the Indian private sector to make the best use of this new vista of opportunity.

India stands only to gain from the opening up of new border points for trade between the TAR and Nepal as these border points could be used for trade of Indian goods with China and vice versa. There are, of course, security-related sensitivities, but these issues can be sorted out by a tripartite agreement between the three countries. Currently, the long cumbersome sea route takes several weeks for the goods to arrive in India and vice versa. At least a portion of the trade could be diverted through a land route via Nepal. It will be not only cheaper but also in the long-term strategic interest of India, as very few Indian items are actually available in Tibet and the manufacturers will stand to gain by trade facilitation in South Asia.

Table 7.1 shows that the shortest potential transit routes would be Birgunj–Syafrubesi and Janakpur–Lamabagar. The Bhairahawa–Pokhara–Jomsom–Korala routes and Birgunj–Galchi–Syafrubesi roads are currently under construction and are expected to be completed within a few years. The Mohana–Tinker

Table 7.1
Possible routes of north-south roads through Nepal

Transit road corridors	Total length[17]
Mohana–Dhangadhi–Atari–Baitadi–Darchula–Tinker	415
Nepalgunj–Surkhet–Jumla–Hilsa–Yari–Purang	581
Bhairahawa–Pokhara–Jomsom–Lizhi	467
Birgunj–Galchi–Rasuwa–Syafrubesi	340
Birgunj–Naubise–Kathmandu–Tatopani–Nyalam	393 (already exists)
Janakpur–Dolakha–Lamabagar–China border	295
Rani–Itahari–Hile–Kimathanka–China border	419
Kechana–Taplejung–Olangchungola	460

Source: National Planning Commission, Nepal, 2005.[18]

[17] Some of these roads are already blacktopped to a certain distance.
[18] Three-year plan document, 132.

Pass road is also under construction; only 107 km remains to be further constructed in the Surkhet–Jumla sector. After completion, this road will prove important for religious tourism, connecting Mansarovar in Tibet. The Jomsom–Lo Manthang–Korala road is only 80 km long and is targeted for completion within two years (by 2016). However, even though these constructions are of strategic interest, corruption, red tape and the indifferent attitude of Nepalese officials substantially hindered timely implementation of such projects.

While several tourists are interested in visiting Tibet, a lone carrier operates from Kathmandu, that is, China Eastern, and this has not been able to cope with the growing demand. Airfare is high and only caters to foreign tourists rather than South Asian Association for Regional Cooperation (SAARC) nationals. Moreover, presently, the route stands cancelled due to political unrest in Tibet. China too can mull over the proposition of granting permission to Indian carriers to fly in the sector of Delhi–Kathmandu–Lhasa with a stopover in Kathmandu which would sustain Nepal's aspiration to become a feasible transit air corridor between India and China. The permission that was granted to Nepal Airlines in 1987 has been rendered meaningless as it has just two aircraft in its international fleet. Thousands of travellers flock to Tibet via Nepal annually which abets TAR's progress and prosperity of the Tibetan people. The Chinese government surely must be aware of this phenomenal increase in traffic on the Kathmandu–Lhasa sector. Security issue should no longer hinder these cultural contacts as evident in the Indian example, whereby Tribhuvan International Airport is already allowing Indian security personnel to recheck passengers aboard flights to India which can also be replicated for the flights that disembark in Tibet.

Legal and Security Imperatives

Local people, especially businessmen, in Birgunj, Bhairahawa and Biratnagar along the Indo-Nepal border and at Tatopani and Rasuwagadhi on the Nepal–China border are of the view that transit countries can enjoy rapid reduction in the cost of delivery of imports. However, they caution that these advantages cannot be achieved without addressing problems of customs and port authority or bureaucracies, delays and uncertainties in trade routes and seeking low-cost alternative corridors without consideration of satisfying certain influential constituencies of political leaders. There is also a need to address the issue of loss, damage, pilferage and deterioration en route while making sure that social problems such as HIV AIDS, molestation of women by drivers, alcohol abuse, environmental degradation, rise in pollution and road accidents are taken care of by the Nepalese government once big trucks from both the sides of the border scurry in. In fact, some even suggest that Indian and Chinese trucks should not be allowed in; instead, they must be stopped at the respective border points and the cargo transferred to Nepalese trucks.[19] The road quality also needs to be regularly checked to control damages due to heavy traffic.

Yet, all these lofty ideals and propositions cannot materialize unless the three countries—Nepal, India and China—come together in a workable format for an effective trans-Himalayan trade and transit agreement. Without such understanding, Nepal will have to depend on bilateral agreements and international conventions. The only transit accord on third-country imports and exports, currently, allows transfer of products through the Kolkata port under a bilateral treaty with India that is renewed periodically. The protocol of this treaty clearly stipulates that there are 15 entry and exit points for trade and transit between India and Nepal. Similarly with China, the overland trading is conducted mainly from the Tatopani point, in addition to the four customs points that have been demarcated for commercial purposes, though the Rasuwagadhi point is also fast catching up. It is, therefore, imperative that a trilateral treaty is framed for this purpose with special focus on facilitating trade rather than stressing on documentation requirements.

Conclusion

Facilitating cross-border connectivity is one of the main thrust areas of Indo-Nepal and Sino-Nepal economic relations and unquestionably essential if bilateral relations are to be cemented

---

[19] Author's interview, Birgunj, Nepal, March 2011.

at the level of the common man on both sides of the border. In 2010, India accepted Nepal's request to upgrade the four major custom checkpoints at Birgunj–Raxaul, Biratnagar–Jogbani, Nepalgunj–Rupedia and Bhairahawa–Sunauli as well as construct approaching highways towards the border on the Indian side and expand roads on the Nepalese side and broad-gauge rail links to Nepal. According to Kheya Bhattacharya, the then joint secretary (SAARC) at the Ministry of External Affairs in India, rail corridors at Birgunj–Katiyar–Singhabad–Rohanpur–Chittagong to Jogbani–Biratnagar–Agartala were identified which would link Nepal, India and Bangladesh, and through these, further connectivity with Chinese infrastructure was envisioned.[20] Infrastructure development in Nepal will also have a bearing on Bangladesh by helping that country to link its market with that of China.

Not many Indian policymakers realize that it is India that gains if Nepal emerges as a viable transit state between India and China. In the same light, the Chinese side must also give adequate support to building infrastructure at border points with Nepal as this will have a positive long-term impact on its exports not only to Nepal but also to the entire South Asian region. Therefore, it must redouble efforts to link up the Lhasa railway with the Nepal border. Nepalese traders have been adept at making maximum use of their country's strategic geographical location for their economic benefit since the early 17th and 18th centuries. History has turned full circle and the time has come now to convince both its neighbours that Nepal can prove a strategic strength for the South Asian region as a whole.

---

[20] Address by Dr Khea Bhattacharya in *SAARC: Towards Greater Connectivity*, Dipankar Banerjee and N. Manoharan (eds.) (New Delhi: Konrad-Adenauer-Stiftung Publications, 2008), 39.

8

Bridging the Karakoram: From Ladakh, Tibet and Kashgar to the Further West

D. Suba Chandran

Introduction

Until 1947, parts of Jammu and Kashmir (J&K), Tibet and Kashgar interacted closely with each other and formed a whole region within them. In particular, the Ladakh–Skardu–Gilgit sectors had been culturally and economically intertwined with Tibet and Kashgar. The graves of Yarkandi merchants in the Nubra Valley of Ladakh across the Khardung La and the myth of a Mongolian demon in the Diskit monastery highlight these historical trans-Karakoram linkages. Daulat Beg Oldi (DBO), the last military post in India above the Nubra Valley, which was in news for opening of an airfield by India,[1] has a historical connection between Ladakh and Yarkand and is named after a Yarkandi businessman, who, according to local legends, died here after descending from the mighty Karakoram Pass.[2]

Though politically under different regimes, these three regions interacted closely in economic and cultural terms, as a part of the much famous Silk Route. While the economic and trade aspects

---

[1] 'Airfield to be reopened in east Ladakh itself will reveal', *The Hindu*, 7 April 2009.

[2] In fact, in local language, Daulat Beg Oldi means 'Daulat Beg died here'!

of the Silk Route have been amply described and explained elsewhere, the cultural linkages have not been adequately covered. Thus, this chapter attempts to explore the physical and cultural connectivity in these regions in a more in-depth manner.

Reopening Old Routes: From the People's Perspectives

The primary focus for the above-mentioned three regions cannot be in terms of improving connectivity. For there are no 'existing' routes which are 'in use' that could be 'improved' upon. Instead, there were a few routes which 'were in use' at some point of time in history but were closed in the recent past, which can be now 'reopened or revived'.

Voices for reopening the routes emanate from two different sub-regions within Ladakh, belonging to two distinct communities. Politically and ethnically, Ladakh is divided into Leh and Kargil districts, inhabited by the Buddhist and Shia communities.[3] Though there have been occasional differences between the two communities, yet they have shared the same space and lived harmoniously in the Ladakh region for ages.[4] Their aspirations vis-à-vis connectivity with the neighbouring regions are notably different. The reasons for this divide are purely historical, social and economic rather than communal.

Historically, the Kargil district has been in close contact with its neighbouring Skardu and Gilgit regions in the Northern Areas; there were, and continue to exist, numerous divided families across the Line of Control (LoC) between India and Pakistan occupied Kashmir (PoK). Hence, their primary desire is that the Kargil–Skardu road be opened; on the other hand, the Leh district has

---

[3] Though this divide is not neat, Leh district has a Buddhist majority with a small Shia population in Leh city and Kargil has a Shia majority with a small Buddhist population, primarily living in the Zanskar Range.

[4] For the communal divide between the communities, see Martijn Van Beek, 'Dangerous Liaisons: Hindu Nationalism and Buddhist Radicalism in Ladakh', in Limaye, S., Malik, M., Wirsing, R.A. (eds), *Religious Radicalism and Security in South Asia* (Honolulu, HI: Asia-Pacific Center for Security Studies, 2004), 193–218; and Martijn van Beek, 'Beyond Identity Fetishism: "Communal" Conflict in Ladakh and the Limits of Autonomy', *Cultural Anthropology* 15(4): 525–569.

become a tourist destination over the last two decades, and tourism has become the primary economic activity. Hence, a majority in this district prefers that the Leh–Mansarovar road be opened.

The demarcation of the LoC between India and Pakistan in J&K led to the division of families not only between the Paharis in Rajouri and Poonch and the Kashmiris in the Valley but also among the Baltis in Kargil and Skardu regions. There are hundreds of divided families in Kargil, Batalik and Turtuk regions who aspire to visit the other side and see their relatives. While the voices of the divided families in the Kashmir Valley and Jammu region are heard often through the print and electronic media, unfortunately the latter regions do not get enough attention in the media. This can be partially attributed to the treacherous condition of roads in the region, which makes it difficult for the media to get access to the people in both Srinagar and Leh.

Numerous estimates have been made about how much it will cost to travel from Muzaffarabad and Mirpur to Baramulla or Jammu. The current route from Skardu is through Gilgit, Islamabad and then to New Delhi, Jammu, Srinagar and finally Kargil. One could easily go around the world and return to the starting point by the time someone starts from Skardu and reaches Kargil, which are separated by only about 130 km; if the road is opened from Kargil to Skardu, it would take just five to six hours.

People of this region (from Leh to Gilgit) believe that they are distinct, historically and politically. Ismail Khan, an eminent writer from the Northern Areas, holds that the conflict and violence witnessed in Kashmir has nothing to do with the people of this region. He wrote:

> The fact is that neither the people of Ladakh nor from Gilgit-Baltistan are 'Kashmiri'. The locals do not eat, dress or speak like the Kashmiri, and have much more in common with each other in every way in terms of culture and sensibility than with Srinagar valley or Azad Kashmir. The people of Ladakh and Gilgit-Balitistan have been dragged unwillingly into the Kashmir conflict, the major continuous flashpoint of South Asia, simply because a confluence of geography and history brought them under the state of Jammu and Kashmir.[5]

---

[5] Ismail Khan, 'Righting the Wrongs in Ladakh-Baltistan', http://www.claudearpi.net/maintenance/uploaded_pics/RightingtheWrongs.pdf.

Therefore, a general query of the people in this region is: why should the people and divided families in the Northern Areas and Kargil suffer for a conflict that has nothing to do with them?[6] One of the main reasons why they posit this question clearly is due to the fact that they feel alienated by and unrepresented in the discussions that are being held between India and Pakistan on J&K. The discussions in New Delhi and in Islamabad rarely take into account the people of Leh–Kargil–Skardu–Gilgit region.

Also consider the geographical extent of this region — Ladakh and Northern Areas comprise two-thirds of the entire J&K territory. This is why opening Kargil–Skardu road becomes important for India and for the Indo-Pak cross-LoC confidence-building measures (CBMs) over J&K. It would not only address the issues of the divided families of this region but also help set right the lopsided nature of cross-LoC interactions, which are now heavily tilted towards the people in Jammu, Kashmir, Mirpur and Muzaffarabad regions.

As far as the role of the opening of the Kargil–Skardu road for improving the linkages between India and China is concerned, it assumes immense significance. Clearly, Kargil–Skardu is within J&K and the agreement has to be between India and Pakistan. First, historically from times immemorial, these regions from Leh to Central Asia and Kashgar have been interconnected economically, politically and culturally through Kargil, Skardu and Gilgit. Until 1947, trade and the movement of people took place continuously from Tibet to Central Asia through Leh, Kargil, Skardu and Gilgit. Traders, caravans, people and religious patterns moved along the Silk Route. Even for this section of the Silk Route to be opened, the Kargil–Skardu sector needs to be finalized first.

Second, the Northern Areas are today well connected (relatively) with Xinjiang, the neighbouring Chinese province. According to Ismail Khan,

> Today, under an agreement, bonafide residents of the Northern Areas have visa-free unlimited access to the Sinkiang (Xinjiang) Province of China. The Karakoram Highway (KKH) has brought with it trade, economic, social transformation and above all — political awareness. Pakistan and China have agreed to further expand the road network, construct railways and set up an oil pipelines and fiber optic links from the Chinese border to the

---

[6] General observations during the field trips.

Gwadar port in the Arabian Sea. The Northern Areas are highly strategic, since only this region in South Asia borders five countries that of China, India, Pakistan, Afghanistan and Tajikistan, and remain a highly favourable future spot in terms of providing trade, oil corridors, water routes and dams. A survey to link up the other parts of the world with Central Asian oil reserves through the Northern Areas is already underway.[7]

Reopening the Kargil–Skardu road will help the people of the Kargil region, which is also their primary expectation. On the other hand, people in the Leh district primarily want to open the Kailash Mansarovar route.[8] Unlike the other routes in J&K, which are across the LoC between India and Pakistan, the Leh–Mansarovar route lies across the Line of Actual Control (LAC) between India and China. However, opening this route is important for historical and popular reasons. As mentioned earlier, the Silk Route was the only outlet for the people of Ladakh, until the Zoji La and Leh–Manali roads were opened for regular traffic in the recent years.

Economically, the local population will greatly benefit from this route, mainly through tourism. Kailash Mansarovar, one of the most revered Hindu pilgrim destinations, is only about 300 km from Demchok on the LAC. The road up to Demchok is well laid, and much of the road from there to Mansarovar, which is under the Chinese control, is also commutable.[9] Thus, opening this route will greatly benefit the local population in the Leh region, which is primarily dependent on tourism for its survival.[10] This needs emphasis also in the light of the fact that the Zoji La is closed for six months in a year and the road from Leh to Srinagar via Kargil is one of the most dangerous in the entire region.

Prospects seem viable given that along with the peace process with Pakistan, India is also engaged in talks to resolve the boundary dispute with China. Until Vajpayee's visit to China in 2003, China had not even accepted Sikkim as a part of India. China's acceptance of Sikkim as an inalienable part of India remains a

---

[7] Ismail Khan, 'Righting the Wrongs in Ladakh-Baltistan', http://www.claudearpi.net/maintenance/uploaded_pics/RightingtheWrongs.pdf.

[8] Invariably, the people of Leh district underline that they want the opening of Kailash-Mansarovar route, but not against the opening of Kargil–Skardu road, and the people of Kargil region say the vice versa.

[9] Observations based on field trips.

[10] Interviews with tourist operators.

debated issue even now. However, China's acknowledgement of the same of late and with the Nathu La in Sikkim being opened for border trade between India and China in July 2006, a similar arrangement could be reached with respect to Demchok also, this time for pilgrim traffic.

Prospects and Feasibilities

Clearly, there are three primary axes that could help linking J&K and China:

1. First, a link from Leh to Kailash Mansarovar in Tibet,
2. Second, a link from the Nubra Valley in Leh district to Yarkand in Xinjiang across the Karakoram Pass and
3. Third, a link between Kargil and Kashgar via Gilgit.

Of the three, the first route, Kailash Mansarovar, should be the most viable in terms of physical networking, though politically it could prove to be a landmine given the present situation. However, a route, if constructed, will be one of the greatest CBMs in this region, given the local and the Sino-Indian components attached to it. Recognizing the tourist potential attached to this route, all components from the Leh district have been urging the governments of India and China to open this route. Opening the Kailash Mansarovar route will bring a huge tourist inflow, which is otherwise routed through a long, circuitous and treacherous route from Himachal Pradesh and Nepal.

Kailash Mansarovar is an important pilgrim destination for the Hindu community; if the route via Ladakh is opened, it would be easy for the pilgrims to fly into Leh, and take a vehicle via Demchok and reach Kailash Mansarovar, with relative ease reducing a more than two-week destination via Himachal Pradesh into two days via Leh by road. From the religious perspective, opening this route is equally important for the Buddhists of Ladakh as well. More importantly, the Leh–Demchok–Mansarovar route does not involve any trekking. Linking Leh with Kailash Mansarovar physically should not be a problem according to the rough estimates proposed by local tourist operators.[11] They believe so, as unlike the other routes from Leh to the outside world, via either Kargil or Manali or Khardung La, the road to Mansarovar is almost on the banks of the Indus and is already metalled up to Nyoma. Thus, though it may be a little difficult, with some attention it will prove much more beneficial to all concerned.

The second route, via the Nubra Valley and DBO, is perhaps the most difficult, in political, security and physical terms. This region is militarily sensitive for the Indian establishment; Indo-Pak conflict over Siachen further complicates the security environment in this region. DBO is particularly militarily sensitive to India, and Indian security forces have been attempting to prepare an airstrip in this region to rein in difficult situations.[12]

Besides the military sensitivities, this route across the Karakoram Pass has been physically the most dangerous in the past.[13] Elders in the Leh and Nubra Valley, who have either travelled or listened to stories narrated by their relatives, consider that reopening this route via Karakoram Pass may be physically the most challenging.[14] Even if the Karakoram Pass is opened, keeping it open throughout the year will cost more. Currently, the Indian security forces and the Border Roads Organisation (BRO) have spent a huge amount of money and have made enormous sacrifices to keep the Khardung La open.

Moreover, there is not much of a demand from the Nubra Valley or the rest of Leh district to open this route. One of the reasons, perhaps, could be the movement of population from the Nubra Valley into Leh, given the harsh conditions and lack of connectivity. Second, except for adventure tourists, not many tourists are keen to cross the Khardung La. Most of the tourists restrict their voyages to a 25-km trip up to the Khardung La — take a photo and get back to Leh the same evening. Though there are places of tourist importance in the Nubra Valley, for example, in

---

[11] Interviews with tourist operators in Leh.

[12] Prashant Dikshit, 'Daulat Beg Oldi: Taking Wing Again', 10 June 2008, http://www.ipcs.org/article_details.php?articleNo=2595. Also see, 'Now, another Air Force base on the China border', *Business Standard*, 2 October 2010.

[13] Janet Rizvi, *Trans-Himalayan Caravans: Merchant Princes and Peasant Traders in Ladakh* (New Delhi: Oxford, 1999).

[14] Interviews with elders in Leh and Nubra Valley. Many elders in Nubra Valley even comment, Karakoram Pass is perhaps the most treacherous for both the travellers and the mules that were carrying the goods.

the hot springs of Panamik and the monastery in Diskit, not many tourists travel across the Khardung La.

The third route from Kargil to Kashgar via Skardu and Gilgit, though physically not a problem, is politically a highly sensitive issue. Historically, it has been a part of the much famed Silk Route; in fact, in comparison to Leh, Kargil used to be the most important town in this sector. While Leh was more of a transit town, Kargil served as a major trading depot. Goods from Kashgar, Central Asia, Kashmir and Punjab all congregated at Kargil. The Munshi Museum in Kargil today will highlight the goods traded in this route via Kargil.[15]

Politically, the Northern Areas serve almost as a colony of Pakistan, with no specific political status or representation in Pakistan. While the other Kashmir entity, referred to as Azad Jammu and Kashmir (AJK), has a separate political structure, however flawed it may be; unfortunately, the Northern Areas have no such political representation and are considered by and large a black hole in Pakistan's political structure.[16] Though Pakistan termed the Northern Areas as Gilgit-Baltistan in 2009,[17] in terms of political structure, this region remained totally under the control of Islamabad. Hence, Pakistan remains extremely apprehensive about opening this region to the rest of J&K, which otherwise became the primary reason behind Islamabad agreeing to open the LoC across Poonch and Muzaffarabad.

Additionally, there is an active Chinese presence in the Northern Areas. According to Selig Harrison,

> the entire Pakistan-occupied western portion of Kashmir stretching from Gilgit in the north to Azad (Free) Kashmir in the south is closed to the world ... a simmering rebellion against Pakistani rule and the influx of an estimated 7,000 to 11,000 soldiers of the People's Liberation Army. China wants a grip on the region to assure unfettered road and rail access to the Gulf through Pakistan.

---

[15] The Munshi Aziz Bhatt Museum in Kargil contains numerous articles from the hookah pipes from Yarkand, rugs from Kashgar, dyed and raw silk from Khotan, shoes and dyes from Amritsar, etc.

[16] See the report by Baroness Emma Nicholson titled 'Kashmir: Present situation and future prospects', passed by the European Union in 2007, and International Crisis Group, 'Pakistan: Discord in Northern Areas', April 2007.

[17] 'Autonomy package for NAs approved', *Dawn*, 30 August 2009.

It takes 16 to 25 days for Chinese oil tankers to reach the Gulf. When the high-speed rail and road links through Gilgit and Baltistan are completed, China will be able to transport cargo from Eastern China to the new Chinese-built Pakistani naval bases at Gwadar, Pasni and Ormara, just east of the Gulf, within 48 hours.[18]

Besides, Pakistan and China have an agreement on the Aksai Chin, a territory on which India holds a legal claim. For China, the Aksai Chin is of extreme importance, as its national highway (NH G219), which links Xinjiang and Tibet, runs cutting across the Aksai portion in China. Technically, this road can be taken to travel up to Kathmandu in Nepal, as the Nepal–China Friendship Highway is linked to G219. Hence, for strategic reasons, both Pakistan and China will be extra cautious in linking the Northern Areas with Ladakh, and extending further into Xinjiang.

Recommendations for Future Cooperation in the Region

This chapter proposes two strategies that could be pursued by India, China and Pakistan in reaching some kind of consensus on regional collaboration: opening the two routes between Kailash Mansarovar and Kargil–Kashgar, and developing the J&K–Kashgar–Tibet route as an integrated region.

Opening the Kailash Mansarovar and the Kargil-Kashgar Routes

From a regional perspective on the J&K region, opening the Leh–Mansarovar and the Kargil–Skardu–Kashgar routes is very important. Reopening these two routes will revive the much famed Silk Route, thereby linking Tibet with Kashgar via Demchok, Gilgit and Sust. Skardu is already well linked with Gilgit, which is situated strategically along the Karakoram

---

[18] Selig Harrisson, 'China's Discreet Hold on Pakistan's Northern Borderlands', *New York Times*, 27 August 2010.

Highway (KKH). From Gilgit, one will be able to reach Xinjiang and Central Asia turning northwards or the Karachi and the Gwadar ports by turning south.

A question of much more significance here would be whether India and China could jointly consider developing the entire region—comprising Xinjiang, Tibet, Ladakh and the Northern Areas. The political stakes are high for both India and China. For China, peace and stability in Xinjiang and Tibet is of extreme importance. In Xinjiang,[19] the Central Asian linkages and the Islam factor play a crucial role in the perception of the Uighurs vis-à-vis Beijing. In fact, Xinjiang is seen as China's Wild West. The 2009 uprising of the Uighurs in Xinjiang reflects the unrest which local perceptions on official discrimination and deliberate settlement of the Han Chinese can stir in the region. Though the 2009 uprising was quelled by ruthless use of force, there is a huge divide, which persists even today between the province and Beijing, and within the communities inside Xinjiang—between the Uighurs and the Han Chinese. This leads to reluctance on part of the Chinese authorities to consider any joint programmes on the region with its neighbours.

Alternately, though Aksai Chin has a minimal population, mostly comprised by nomads, it is strategically important for China, as it has built an NH linking two of China's most restive provinces in the West, that is, Tibet with Xinjiang (China's NH G219). As far as Tibet is concerned, though China seems to be waiting for Dalai Lama's exit from the political scenario, one cannot be sure which way the next generation of Tibetans would grow up and lean to. This should be a big worry for India as well; Ladakh and Himachal Pradesh in India host substantial Tibetan refugees. An unstable Tibet will not be in India's interests, especially in the post-Dalai Lama scenario.

At other times, various negative consequences of improved connectivity have been seen in these regions. There have been reports linking radical Islam in Xinjiang to Pakistan; thus, the KKH

---

[19] Predominantly Muslim, the Xinjiang province of China has a mixed population that includes the Uighurs, Uzbeks, Kyrgyz and Kazakhs. The Uighurs have been unhappy with the Chinese government for the last few decades; the Uighur uprising in 2008–2009 has only increased Beijing's sensitivity towards this frontier region, which shares borders with J&K and Tibet.

and Pakistan connection has not been entirely productive for China and its Muslim-dominated Xinjiang province.[20] In one of his commentaries, Ziad Haider had commented on the negative impact of KKH on Sino-Pakistan relations, especially on Xinjiang:

Since its opening in 1982, the Highway has facilitated trade and people-to-people contact between the two countries. It has increased China and Pakistan's control over their frontiers and capability to deal with security threats from India and elsewhere. Upon its completion, China's deputy Premier Li Xiannian publicly stated that the Highway 'allows us [China] to give military aid to Pakistan'. What Li had not foreseen is that China's opponents could also go in the other direction — bearing arms and threatening China's security. That new threat has emerged in part from Pakistan's religious links with the Uighurs, who have long agitated against Chinese rule.[21]

A more nuanced understanding of the existential quandaries are reflected by Zaid Haider remarks:

Many Uighurs who crossed into Pakistan in the eighties enrolled in madrassas that promoted radical views. They studied under the patronage of groups such as the Jamiat-i-Ulema Islam and were recruited to fight in the Soviet-Afghan war. At the end of the war, the Highway funnelled them back into Xinjiang where they joined violent Uighur nationalist movements. With the rise of the Taliban in Afghanistan, China's fears were further compounded. The Taliban and the Islamic Movement of Uzbekistan (IMU), a jihadi group with ties to Al Qaeda, began to recruit Uighurs from the vast network of Pakistani Deobandi madrassas. Chinese authorities have claimed that more than one thousand Uighurs fought in Afghanistan alongside the Taliban and Al Qaeda during Operation Enduring Freedom.[22]

On the contrary, unlike in Pakistan, Islam in J&K still remains Sufi in nature; perhaps the Sufi Islam in J&K is the most liberal

---

[20] Ziad Haider, 'Sino-Pakistan Relations and Xinjiang's Uighurs: Politics, Trade, and Islam along the Karakoram Highway', *Asian Survey* 45(4) (July–August 2005): 522–545.

[21] Ziad Haider, 'Clearing clouds over Karakoram', *Daily Times*, 4 April 2004.

[22] Ibid.

of all versions in the entire South Asia. Kashmir's Sufi Islam, in fact, can be of soothing influence on Xinjiang, if China agrees to extend the travel between Kashgar and Gilgit, up to Kargil and Srinagar. Traditionally, the princes and nobles of Gilgit and Baltistan came to Srinagar for their education via Kargil and Gurez Valley. Such linkages, if renewed, could provide the much needed another opening for India to its Kashmir Valley and connecting it to the outside world. One of the primary reasons for the present Kashmiri unrest is their physical suffocation. Frustrated by unsuccessful attempts in establishing viable business linkages, the locals are forced to agitate against the government; the business community in particular, which gave the 'Muzaffarabad Chalo' call during 2008–2009, received widespread support for this reason alone. Linking the valley and Ladakh with Kashgar will also give the local people access to Central Asia. Therefore, linking Xinjiang with J&K will be a huge win–win situation for the entire region.

A bus service between Gilgit in Pakistan and Kashgar in Xinjiang has already been mooted. Also during General Musharraf's period, it was announced that Pakistan and China were planning to build a railway and pipeline along the highway. He declared that the project when completed would be one of the new wonders of the world. With China already constructing a railway line to Lhasa connecting Tibet with rest of China all the way up to Beijing, such a railway line along the KKH is no longer unthinkable. Such a line could also join up with the already existing rail networks between Beijing and Central Asia, via Urumqi, the capital of Xinjiang.

A SWOT Analysis

What are the strengths, weaknesses, opportunities and threats (SWOT) of opening these routes? These would become clearer from Table 8.1.

J&K-Kashgar-Tibet as an Integrated Region

The rationale for proposing the establishment of a region comprising the three above-mentioned geographical entities stems

Table 8.1
SWOT for Opening the Kailash-Mansarovar and the Kargil-Kashgar Routes

Strengths	Weaknesses	Opportunities	Threats
• Popular support in Kargil and Leh • Historical and cultural precedence (the Silk Route)	• Reluctance of Pakistan to open even Kargil–Skardu road • Reluctance of the intelligence agencies	• Existence of KKH and the Gilgit–Kashgar bus service • Agreement between India and China on Kailash Mansarovar Yatra through other routes • Chinese gas and rail networks • India's efforts to link J&K with the rest of India	• Movement of radicals • Smuggling of goods • Misuse by intelligence agencies

from the following: all these three sub-regions, historically, economically and culturally, shared a close relationship until 1947–1962; all three sub-regions are the peripheries of India, Pakistan and China facing certain peculiar problems; all three regions share and are divided by the Himalayan belt, where they experience certain similar issues relating to environment, energy and connectivity; and more importantly, all three regions have their own political problems, with a small but considerable radical section.

The Silk Route used to link all these three regions at a given time in history. Today, China is already engaged in improving the connectivity in Kashgar and Tibet with the rest of China and between these two regions as well. India is also trying to improve its connectivity projects in J&K, though at a painfully slow pace the rail projects in Kashmir are progressing. A rail service within Kashmir Valley has been made operational, and there are efforts to link Kashmir Valley with the rest of India, by breaching the Pir Panjal across Banihal.

Pakistan and China are working together to build the KKH linking Kashgar with Gwadar. China has also invested heavily in improving the connectivity in Gilgit-Baltistan, besides cooperating on multiple energy-related projects. Moreover, Kailash Mansarovar, in particular, is the source of three major river systems of South Asia—the Indus, the Ganges and the Brahma-putra. With water becoming a crucial issue in this region, it is imperative that the three countries work together. Finally, all three regions have their own problems of radicalism.

China has also been investing heavily in energy in Central Asia and has been laying a network of gas pipelines, besides upgrading its rail network. There have been reports on China building a series of networks linking Beijing with London, linking King's Cross with Beijing.[23] As stated earlier, China is also planning to convert the KKH into a rail line and a gas pipeline. These proposed projects reflect that the Chinese understand the significance and the benefits that can be gained from developing connectivity in the region. Yet political jockeying and mistrust continues to mar the efforts of these countries from successfully formulating a regional mechanism to avail these opportunities.

A SWOT Analysis

Efforts of sub-regional cooperation or growth triangles are not totally new to India and China. What are the strengths, weaknesses, opportunities and threats of envisaging the three peripheries as an integrated whole? These are illustrated in Table 8.2.

Table 8.2
SWOT for J&K-Kashgar-Tibet Routes

Strengths	Weaknesses	Opportunities	Threats
• Historical and cultural	• Lack of support from Pakistan	• Existence of bus, rail and gas pipelines in the sub-regions	• Movement of radicals
• Popular support	• Lack of internal infrastructure		• Smuggling of goods
	• Support from the intelligence organizations	• Support for sub-regional initiatives by India and China in Mekong and Brahmaputra basins	• Misuse by intelligence agencies

[23] 'King's Cross to Beijing in two days on new high-speed rail network', *Daily Telegraph*, London, 8 March 2010.

Conclusion

Though to envision gas pipelines and rail networks through the KKH into Srinagar or Ladakh on the similar lines of China would be too early, one has to plan ahead for future, such as linking Sikkim and Kathmandu with Kolkata. Especially when China is planning to build gas pipelines and rail network along the KKH, hooking into it from Baramulla will not be a big problem for India. Even current routes exist from Srinagar to Gilgit via Gurez, Burzil Pass and the Astore River which can help improve the vision of better connectivity among nations. In fact, opening the route from the Gurez Valley, which has been historically a part of the Silk Route, was envisioned as early as 2007 in the rec-ommendations of the working groups on J&K set up by Prime Minister Manmohan Singh. With the Afghan transit becoming a pipe dream, India has to consider alternative rail and gas net-works to reach Central Asia. India also has to consider getting access to the Asian Highway (AH) and Asian Railway, linking Central Asia and Europe with Southeast Asia. Given the politi-cal instability in the Afghanistan–Pakistan region, it is important for India to find alternative routes to realize its Look East Policy (LEP).

It is in the political and economic interest of India, Pakistan and China to ensure that these three sub-regions, which form their peripheries, are developed and various sensitive issues addressed, paving the way for peace and stability. An integrated region developed together will be in the interest of all three countries. Making use of rail and gas pipelines could be an effec-tive strategy to achieve this objective.

Linking India and China across the Karakoram by linking it with Tibet and Xinjiang, opening the Kailash Mansarovar route and extending the Kashgar–Gilgit bus link into Skardu and Srinagar will be one step in this direction. In short, reviving the Silk Route and reimagining rail and pipelines will benefit one and all. This has the potential to transform this entire region—a circle linking Leh, Kargil, Gilgit, Kashgar and Lhasa.

Also, to achieve these objectives, New Delhi has to ensure that its own territories and peripheries in J&K are linked with the rest of India. Its performance in linking the Kashmir Valley with the rest of India by rail has been far from satisfactory. Similarly, its efforts to link Ladakh with the rest of J&K across the Zoji La and with the rest of India via Manali and the Rohtang have also not yielded results. It is unfortunate that Ladakh is not connected internally as from Turtuk to Kargil, which is in the same district in Ladakh, and it takes two days. India has to build adequate infrastructure inside its own territory, before linking up its peripheries with the Chinese.

9

Arunachal Pradesh: A Barb or Bridge between India and China?

Sanasam Amal Singh

Introduction

Once referred as the Northeast Frontier Agency (NEFA), Arunachal Pradesh is the largest state in terms of area in northeast India. It is a mountainous frontier state sharing its international borders with Myanmar (520 km) on the east, Bhutan (217 km) on the west and China (1,126 km) towards the north, and is inhabited by 26 major tribes of which over 110 sub-tribes live in 3,857 different villages spread across 83,743 sq km. Arunachal Pradesh has a complex hill system traversed by numerous river valleys and is part of the great Himalayan ecosystem as well as recognized as one of the 18 biodiversity 'hot spots' in the world.[1]

Broadly, on the basis of their socio-religious affinities, the people may be divided into three cultural groups.[2] The Monpas and Sherdukpens of Tawang and West Kameng districts follow

---

[1] The state comprises 16 districts: Tawang, West Kameng, East Kameng, Papum Pare, Lower Subansiri, Upper Subansiri, Kurung Kumey, East Siang, Dibang Valley, Lower Dibang Valley, Lohit, Changlang, Tirap, Anjaw, Upper Siang and West Siang.

[2] The population of Arunachal Pradesh was 1,091,117 according to the 2001 census. The population density at 13 per sq km is the least in the country, and for some of the districts such as Dibang Valley, it is as low as one person per sq km.

the Lamaistic tradition of Mahayana Buddhism. Noted for their religious fervour, the villages of these communities have richly decorated Buddhist temples, locally called 'Gompas'. Though largely agriculturists, practising terrace cultivation, many of these people are also pastoral and breed herds of yak and mountain sheep. Culturally similar to them are Membas and Khambas who live in the high mountains along the northern borders.

The second group of the people comprises the Adis, Akas, Apatanis, Bangnis, Nishis, Mishmis, Mijis, Thongsas and so forth, who worship the sun and moon god, namely, Donyi-Polo and Abo-Tani, considered the original ancestors for most of these tribes. Their religious rituals largely coincide with phases of agricultural cycles. They invoke 'nature' deities and make animal sacrifices. They traditionally practise 'jhumming' or shifting cultivation. Adis and Apatanis extensively practise wet rice cultivation and have a considerable agricultural economy. Apatanis are also famous for their paddy-cum-pisciculture.

The third group comprises Noctes and Wanchos, adjoining Nagaland in the Tirap district. These are resilient people known for their strictly structured village society in which hereditary village chief still plays a vital role. The Noctes also practise elementary form of Vaishnavism. Most of these communities are ethnically similar, having derived from an original common stock, but their geographical isolation from each other has brought among them certain distinctive characteristics in language, dress and customs.

In terms of connectivity, the Tawang district offers a strategic pathway for the region to develop infrastructure and networks. Situated at the height of 3,500 m from the sea level on the mountainous range of the northern Himalayas in the westernmost part of Arunachal Pradesh, Tawang is inhabited by the Monpas.[3] The shortest connectivity point to China from Tawang is Bumla, 37 km from Tawang town, and the second is Kenzamane in Zemithang circle of Tawang, 50 km from Tawang headquarters.

As against decadal growth rate of 21.34 per cent at the national level, the population of the state has grown by 26.21 per cent over the period 1991–2001. The sex ratio of Arunachal Pradesh at 901 females to 1,000 males is lower than the national average of 933.

[3] With 2,085 sq km, population of Tawang is 39,242 (2001 census) and comprises 195 villages.

Alongside, Bomdila, the district headquarters of West Kameng, also shares an international boundary with Tibet in the north, Bhutan in the west, Tawang in the northwest, East Kameng district in the east and thus can provide another major gateway for connectivity. The southern border is shared with Sonitpur district and Darrang district of Assam. The land is inhabited by the Monpas, Sherdukpens, Akas, Mijis and Khawas tribes. At the height of 8,500 ft, Bomdila is considered as a transit point on Tezpur–Bomdila–Tawang highway (it is 165 km from Tezpur).[4]

Border Trade Points

Border trade saw a major setback after the 1962 conflict and was discontinued along the Sino-Indian border. At present, there is no land customs station (LCS), and hardly any traditional trade between the countries is seen. While Zemithang and Bumla in the Tawang region have good prospect for formal trading, none of them have been explored (Zemithang point is geographically more convenient to Indian side, while Bumla is easier from Chinese side for trade route). A comprehensible bilateral agreement between the Government of India (GOI) and China can open up these trade points and mutually benefit the people of both the countries.

Keeping this in mind, the Government of Arunachal Pradesh has identified the below-mentioned border trade points. The State Public Works Department (PWD) has already started constructing road up to Zemithang, and also development of infrastructure is under process in the Indo-Myanmar and the

---

[4] Tawang has the literacy rate of 47.32 per cent and West Kameng, 60.76 per cent (Arunachal Pradesh Human Development Report, 2005, available at http://planningcommission.nic.in/plans/stateplan/sdr_pdf/shdr_ap05.pdf). For health service, see appendix in the report. For three districts, i.e. West Kameng, East Kameng and Tawang, there is only one graduate college in Bomdila. The people of both Tawang and Bomdila look well integrated into the Indian mainstream than most other eastern Himalayan towns such as Darjeeling, Gangtok and Shillong. Hindi, which faces resistance in most of the eastern hills, has become the lingua franca of this frontier region. They have adopted Hindi because it is their national language and because tribal groups here do not have a common language.

Indo-Bhutan sectors. Border trade in the following sectors is being proposed:

1. *Sino-Indian Sector*
   Kenzamane (Zemithang) in Tawang district
   Bumla in Tawang district
   Gelling (Kepangla Pass) in Upper Siang district
   Kibithoo in Anjaw district
   Mechuka (Lolla Pass) in West Siang district
   Monigong (Dumla Pass) in West Siang district
   Taksing in Upper Subansiri district
2. *Indo-Myanmar Sector*
   Pangsau Pass (Nampong) in Changlang district
3. *Indo-Bhutan Sector*
   Bleting (Namtsering) in Tawang district
   Dongshengmang and Bongkhar in Tawang district

Infrastructure Development in the Border Regions

Long-term isolation and separation from the mainstream of the country have posed formidable constraints to the socio-economic development of Arunachal Pradesh. The state inherited almost no infrastructure development at the time of Independence. However, with the introduction of the planning process via five-year plans, development of infrastructure such as roads and bridges, buildings, educational institutions, hospitals, health care units and so on was given top priority. Despite these efforts, the regions, especially the border areas, are still in a dismal state.

It is stated that Arunachal Pradesh still has 22 strategically located administrative centres that are yet to be connected by roads. Due to this lack of infrastructure, the villages at the India–China border area are sparsely populated. With growing aspirations of the younger generations, there is a significant movement and migration of people from the remote border areas to the foothills, rendering the borders depopulated. Thus, from a strategic point of view, the depopulated situation in the border areas can make them highly vulnerable to the outside forces.

In the year 1997–1998, the Border Area Development Programme (BADP) was initiated in Arunachal Pradesh, primarily for the Indo-Myanmar border, with a provision of ₹4 crores. From 1998 to 1999, the programme was also extended to the international borders of India–China and India–Bhutan, with a view to meeting the special needs of the people living in the border areas of Arunachal Pradesh and removing the critical gaps in physical and social infrastructure requirements as well as strengthening the economic conditions and raising the standard of living among the inhabitants of the remote border areas of the state as per the guidelines of the BADP. Over the years, allocation under the BADP has been enhanced; however, the present quantum of allocation is inadequate to bring about any substantial change in the status of infrastructure development and the livelihood pattern in the remote and inaccessible border areas of the state. Besides, being a tribal state, the GOI needs to reconsider suitable enhancement of allocation under the BADP from the strategic point of view and also to achieve balanced development irrespective of the location of the areas.

As per current criteria, the release of the BADP fund is subject to submission of Quarterly Progress Report (QPR) as well as Utilization Certificate (UC). Timely submission of QPRs and UCs sometimes gets delayed due to communication bottlenecks — inhospitable mountain terrain, inclement climate and so on. This in turn creates problem in the release of funds for further construction. Another problem is that the construction materials in the border areas are to be transported on head-load only; therefore, implementation of works gets delayed (as per milestone laid down for the purpose). This has been one of the factors in hindering the provision of basic facilities for the people residing in the border areas.

The officials at the District Collector's (DC) office in Tawang suggested that there should be a separate department or cell to look after or deal with the BADP because the State Planning Department alone cannot handle it effectively. This separate cell under the Home Department should look after the matters of border management, including BADP in the line of Department of Border Management, Ministry of Home Affairs and GOI. It is, therefore, felt that unless a separate department/cell is created with adequate manpower/expertise, formulation of any prospective plan for effective implementation of BADP and proper monitoring and coordination of the programme will not be possible. Such problems have led to an exodus of the population in the border villages, primarily for two main reasons: (i) the people are feeling neglected due to lack of development and income-generating activities and are forced to migrate to the adjoining states such as Assam and (ii) political tensions between the two countries have led to strategic roadblock. Many times, tension arises in the border region that is not published in the media. For instance, during the recent visit of the Dalai Lama in Tawang, the Chinese People's Liberation Army (PLA) became very active and aggressive along the McMahon Line. In such a situation, the villagers felt apprehensive of Chinese intrusion.[5]

Physical Infrastructure: Road and Rail Networks

Highways and rail networks are fundamental segments of infrastructure for connectivity and the backbones of economic growth. But unfortunately in Arunachal Pradesh, connectivity is a major challenge. Since the state has hilly terrain, development of inland waterways and rail connectivity is challenged by topographical hurdles which require substantial investment from the nation. It is, however, important to note that it is road connectivity which would play a dominant role in fulfilling the transportation needs of the public in this region. The main grid of transportation of goods and passengers in the northeastern states of India is the road network of 82,000 km. Of this, Arunachal Pradesh alone occupies 15,000 km. On the other hand, the railway network is limited to 2,500 km and lies almost entirely within the state of Assam (2,466 km), with short stretches in Tripura (45 km) and Arunachal Pradesh (1 km). However, the centre has recently given instructions to the Northeast Frontier Railways (NFR) to commence work to connect all the seven state capitals of the northeast with the railway network (at present, only two state capitals — Guwahati and Agartala — are connected to the railway network, and the government wants the remaining five — Kohima, Shillong, Imphal, Aizawl and Itanagar — to come on the railway map at the earliest). Once the seven state capitals are connected through railway networks, the government would like the NFR to connect the border areas in the seven states as well.

[5] Based on personal interviews with local residents.

In his 2008 visit to Arunachal Pradesh, the then Prime Minister Manmohan Singh also announced a special package for the state which covers the following:

1. 1,840-km-long double-lane Trans-Arunachal Highway at an estimated cost of ₹5,500 crores
2. Four-lane Highway connecting Itanagar
3. Road connectivity to 513 villages under Prime Minister Gram Sadak Yojana (PMGSY)
4. One time grant of ₹265 crores for completing incomplete schemes
5. ₹550 crores for electrification of villages
6. Central assistance of ₹400 crores for reconstruction of flood damaged areas
7. ₹50 crores for strengthening of Ram Krishna Mission Hospital
8. ₹77 crores for drinking water supply project for Itanagar
9. Rail link between Itanagar and Harmuti.

The data given in Tables 9.1 and 9.2 illustrate the current state of infrastructure in the region.

According to the District Planning Officer of Tawang, under the PMGSY, 438 habitations are already connected to the main arteries. Another 513 small villages in remote border blocks are at present being taken up for road connectivity. The Trans-Arunachal Highway of double-lane connectivity to all the district

Table 9.1
Length of NHs in Arunachal Pradesh

S. no.	NH no.	Length (in km) within the state	Agency (km) State PWD	NHAI	BRO
1	37	22.00	22.00	0.00	0.00
2	52	335.00	0.00	0.00	335.00
3	52A	45.00	0.00	0.00	45.00
4	52B	389.00	389.00	0.00	0.00
5	153	33.00	33.00	0.00	0.00
6	229	1,054.00	672.00	0.00	382.00
	Total	1,878.00	1,116.00	0.00	762.00

Source: Ministry of Road Transport and Highways, GOI.

Table 9.2
Status about connectivity of district headquarters with double-lane NH in Arunachal Pradesh

District	District headquarters	Whether already connected to NH
East Siang	Pasighat	Yes
Lohit	Tezu	Yes
Lower Dibang Valley	Roing	Yes
West Siang	Along	Proposed to be connected under Arunachal Pradesh Package of Roads and Highways of SARDP-NE
Anjaw	Hawai	
Changlang	Changlang	
Dibang Valley	Anini	
East Kameng	Seppa	
Kurung Kumey	Koloriong	
Lower Subansiri	Ziro	
Papum Pare	Yupia	
Tawang	Tawang	
Tirap	Khonsa	
Upper Siang	Yingkiong	
Upper Subansiri	Daporijo	
West Kameng	Bomdila	

Source: Ministry of Road Transport & Highways, GOI.

headquarters has also started in full swing. The officer also brought to light the problems resulting in the slow pace of development of road connectivity as being low-quality material and unskilled labour. Due to the poor quality of materials, the newly constructed blacktop roads do not last more than a season. A heavy downpour can easily wash away the blacktop. All weatherproof roads need to be constructed. Also, all the villages at the border areas are sparely populated as migration to the district headquarters is increasing. As a result of thin population, the concerned authorities lack interest in building road linkages.

On the other hand, the construction of a two-lane road on Tezpur–Baluphong–Bomdila–Tawang highway by the Border Roads Organisation (BRO) is now in full swing. This route is very important for the states' social and economic activities as imported goods from Nepal, Bhutan and Burma come through this route.

It is also a lifeline for certain villages in the border areas more so as the Arunachal Transport Corporation is not effective due to poor road infrastructure. Heavy vehicle movement is very tough. Up to Tezpur (Assam), the road is very good and smooth though small in width, but from Baluphong in Arunachal near Assam border, it gets worse. The only areas where road conditions are good happen to be the one maintained by army camps. The stretch up to Tawang has around 13 difficult spots, that is, landslide-prone areas, where transporters face tough times to negotiate travel. The BRO personnel are positioned at every 5–10-km distance to help construct and repair the road and to clear roadblocks caused by landslides.

The Arunachal Pradesh Human Development Report 2005 also points to the need for improvement of road linkages within the state for sound implementation of development. The report includes a composite index of infrastructure for 2000–2001, based on a number of indicators. These include length of roads per 100 sq km, surfaced road as a percentage of total road length, percentage of gross irrigated area to total cropped area, percentage of electrified villages, number of banks per 10,000 population, number of schools per 100 sq km, number of health centres per 100 sq km and availability of several other services. Highlighting the wide gaps in road connectivity between rural and urban areas, the report states that despite continuous efforts to extend the road network in the state, the road density is still very low. This has resulted in high transportation costs and high prices of commodities in Arunachal than elsewhere in the country.

Suitable interventions and faster decision-making are required from the higher political set-ups. For a state like Arunachal which is a strategic point, a clear-cut and strong policy should be implemented in time. Most sections of the society express their disappointment on the slow level of development of roads in the region, including the defence personnel, who believe speedy development will lead to more secure borders. An in-depth discussion with some of them reveals that the presence of Chinese military on the other side of the Line of Actual Control (LAC) has led to a hypothesis that the government felt that it would be strategically important to keep the roadways infrastructure in Arunachal weak.

The rationale behind such a policy was that the inhospitable nature of the terrain would deter the Chinese from furthering their strategy of easy territorial access into a state in which China claims almost around 90,000 sq km (34,750 square miles) of territory. But at present, India has dropped this logic and initiated a policy shift in May 2006 when the Cabinet Committee on Economic Affairs (CCEA) cleared the construction of strategic roads in Arunachal. This sudden change in Indian policy towards the border areas also reversed the post-1962 mindset. This vital Indian policy shift in Arunachal can be seen as a reaction to the Chinese build-up of roads to Aksai Chin in the western sector and to Tibet in the eastern sector.

Under the Special Accelerated Road Development Programme in the North-Eastern (SARDP-NE) region planned by the Ministry of Road Transport and Highways, the Trans-Arunachal Highway length would be 1,839 km, of which 832 km would fall on radial roads, but there is still a gap of around 1,007 km. The central government is planning to take up the missing gaps in 'Phase B', but the state government of Arunachal is urging to finish it in Phase A, because it will give faster connectivity between the district headquarters. Recently, Arunachal received a special package of building 812 km of roads bordering China. The BRO has been given the responsibility for this. This double-lane road construction is in full swing on the Tezpur–Bomdila–Tawang route. However, according to the BRO, apart from the difficult terrain and climatic conditions, there are two major obstacles in constructing these roads. First, the tribal structure of Arunachal Pradesh makes it difficult for the state government to acquire land for these roads. Second, the provisioning of an Inner Line Permit (ILP) for each labourer before entering Arunachal Pradesh makes it highly cumbersome.

Air Connectivity, Telecommunications and Power Transmission

With the strategic location of the region characterized by limited transportation and other infrastructure facilities, it would be essential to construct a civilian airport and power plant and substantially improve the telecommunication facilities to bring it into the national mainstream.

At present, Arunachal does not have a single airport. The state government has requested the centre to be 'liberal' and not consider only profitability as a criterion for the construction of the proposed greenfield airport project in Itanagar. It has asked the centre to accord priority to the airport project, which when completed will be the state's maiden civilian airport. Terming the airport project as being of an 'immense emotional and sentimental value for Arunachalees', the late chief minister Dorjee Khandu expressed that such projects should not be guided by cost–benefit analysis and should be supported more liberally by the central government. Yet, the project has already been delayed by more than two years for which 'in-principle' approval was given by the Union Civil Aviation Ministry in September 2009.

In Tawang, there are two helipads: one at the Tawang town and the other at a lower altitude area called Khirmu. Helicopters with a heavy load take off only from Khirmu where the engines can function more effectively due to higher air density. The state-run Airports Authority of India (AAI) had earlier conducted a detailed feasibility study for the construction of an airport at Tawang. It was found that the construction of an airport there was feasible. It would have been a viable proposition as it is a popular tourist destination. However, the AAI abandoned its plans to build a civilian greenfield airport at Tawang in Arunachal Pradesh after the union government felt it would be too close to the Sino-Indian border. Further, the union government stated that as per the rules, no civilian airport should be built in the area which is within 70 km of the Sino-Indian border.

Regarding telecommunication networks, only Bharat Sanchar Nigam Limited (BSNL) post-paid and prepaid connections operate in the border areas. While the Tawang district headquarters receive good signals, the connectivity is weak beyond the town. BSNL is experiencing heavy financial losses in Arunachal Pradesh. This could also be the reason for private companies to be reluctant from entering the border district. Difficult climatic conditions raise the maintenance cost of instruments and require substantive manpower. Due to this, BSNL has handed over the maintenance duties to the army set up in the area.

The Indian defence forces often complain about the weak telecommunication networks at the border posts. Sometimes, they are forced to use Chinese connections for sending messages to their families. The chief librarian of the Tawang district library informed that even newspapers do not reach Tawang in time due to transportation problems. According to the officials of the electricity department, under the border village illumination programme, also known as rural electric mission, 523 villages in Arunachal have been electrified in 10 border districts. Only two/three villages which are extremely remote in the Dibang Valley district are using solar energy. However, electric supplies in these areas are irregular, even though the state has enough potential for power resources. The chief executive officer (CEO) of National Hydro-electric Power Corporation (NHPC), Tawang region, also informed that 'small hydro projects' for each village could be feasible in Arunachal state but have not been developed. However, in comparison to Tawang, Bomdila has better electricity, telecommunication and Internet facilities.[6]

Regarding cross-border cooperation in power and energy sectors, both India and China can rely mainly on Brahmaputra, also known as Yarlung Tsangpo in Tibet. However, reports on the damming of Brahmaputra by China have raised a big issue in Arunachal and Assam. Environmental activists in both the states allege that the Chinese plan to build 28 large hydel power stations in the Yarlung Tsangpo region to generate 37,000 MW of electricity by constructing dams as well as reservoirs. The GOI has shown its apprehension about such Chinese initiatives and asked China to share information and hydrological data with India regularly. Suggestions have also been made that New Delhi should initiate dialogue for signing a Brahmaputra water-sharing treaty with China such as the Indus Waters Treaty with Pakistan or the Indo-Ganga Water Treaty with Bangladesh.

According to some prominent journalists and experts on dam and displacement, the Chinese government is not likely to agree on regional cooperation in this regard because they are believed to wanting to divert the water to irrigate the north-western part of the Gobi desert in Xinjiang and Gansu provinces. The western part constitutes almost 45 per cent of China's total land mass and has only 7 per cent of its own water resources. Moreover, with the China's population touching 1.6 billion, the Government of

---

[6] The chief minister of Arunachal laid the foundation of three small hydro projects for Tawang district, namely, Nyuri Mago (2 × 2,000 kW), Thingbu (2 × 1,500 kW) and Tawang Gompachu (2 × 1,500 kW). These small hydro projects will also enable to give enough power to the adjoining districts like East and West Kameng.

the People's Republic of China (PRC) thinks it is imperative to supply more water and increase food production. Another point that concerns these experts is that the Yarlung Tsangpo gorge is the biggest gorge in the world; it traverses a long distance before ending at Pasighat, in the state of Arunachal in India. Thus, at any time the Chinese may release water and cause flood to the Upper Siang division in Arunachal. According to NHPC officials, Brahmaputra, which is 2,906 km long, has a stretch of 1,625 km in China, while the next 918 km in India and the remaining 363 km in Bangladesh, which means it is essentially controlled by China.

Lastly, China is also believed to be developing a mega tourist infrastructure north of the McMahon Line. Beijing plans to bring three lakh tourists every year to visit the gorges of the Brahmaputra, and the Chinese authorities do not bother their tourists with an ILP System like that in India. Both Brahmaputra and Sutlej rivers flow from Tibet; therefore, it is necessary for India to have a continuing stable relationship with China. Unfortunately, Indian knowledge on hydel projects is much less compared to China; thus, talks between the technical delegates of the two countries would help in better cooperation.

Implications of Increased Infrastructure Connectivity

Development of infrastructure for connectivity, especially through roads, possesses more merit than disadvantages and hence is warmly welcomed by local people in the region. Nor is there an opposition from any section of the state. Unlike other states in the northeast, Arunachal is not a conflict state, and it is free from demand, extortion and any form of violence. Insurgency in Arunachal Pradesh is not a home-grown trouble, but a spillover from neighbouring states and countries. The only hurdle then is its difficult geographical terrain and unpredictable climatic conditions. To tackle this, the local people demand better management of resources and infrastructure for efficient trade and transport. Good infrastructure will not only better connect the people in border areas but also ensure greater security, benefiting not only Arunachal alone but also the entire northeast region in the long term.

However, some bureaucrats suggest that three points of disadvantage may arise: First, there is a possibility of increased demands for Autonomous District Council (ADC) based upon the existing two committees, namely, Mon ADCs (comprising Tawang and West Kameng districts) and Patkai ADC (comprising Tirap and Changlang districts). The idea behind is that easy connectivity between district headquarters will increase interaction among the same tribes settled sporadically across the state and help them in mobilizing for autonomous demands. Second, since Arunachal is surrounded by militancy-infected states, insurgents from Nagaland and Assam may sneak into Arunachal and use it as a hideout. Lastly, the neighbouring countries may send spies through the border roads disguised as porters coming for barter trade. Due to similar physical appearance with the Monpas, they can naturalize and masquerade as locals in no time.

According to the police department of Bomdila, militants from neighbouring states and intruders from neighbouring countries often come into Arunachal pretending to be labourers. Thus, they keep strong vigil on every single labourer and make the contractor responsible when they commit any crime. To check such illegal intrusion, state bureaucrats continue to enforce ILPs strictly in Arunachal. However, government officials and students from other states are allowed to show only their relevant documents. The above-mentioned problem is not new and has been successfully foiled by the Indian armies and state police in the past. The task for the government now is to go beyond traditional concerns and develop mechanisms to help connectivity and trade issues.

Concerns among Local Communities

The local organizations, journalists, activists and individuals from different communities in Tawang and Bomdila often hold a common opinion: *It is only as recently as five years ago that India woke up and started beefing up both military hardware and border infrastructure.*

This reflects that the Indian government has neglected the border areas for many decades. After 1962, the national attention was focused on development of border areas from the point of defence architecture. But infrastructure developments in civilian areas were given much less importance. The old concept of Himalayan range as a natural barrier against any invader from the north dominated Indian government's policy for a long time. This mindset has changed recently after watching China construct strategic roads and railway links in the Tibet Autonomous Region (TAR) and make wasteland areas inhabitable for the villagers. As a reaction of these dynamic developments, the Indian government has started constructing strategic roads under the SARDP-NE from 2006.

Another main concern is that the centre allocates based on the number of people and not area, which disadvantages Arunachal in many respects. Ninety per cent of the local population in Tawang and Bomdila is in favour of re-establishing border trade between India and China, but only after boundary dispute is fully resolved. Bilateral trade relationship will augur economic growth for both the sides—TAR and Arunachal; consequently, Arunachal could become a gateway to East Asia.

Infrastructure Connectivity between India and China through Manipur

Manipur is a landlocked, isolated and mountain-girt state, situated in the easternmost part of northeast India bordering Myanmar.[7] India and Myanmar share a boundary of 1,643 km in Manipur, while the total length of the boundary line that Manipur shares with Myanmar alone is 398 km. Out of these 398 km, only 52 km are manned by security personnel. For the purpose of this study, a field visit to Moreh was undertaken and the following observations were made based on personal interviews. Moreh is a small border town situated on the south-east border of Manipur at a distance of approximately 109 km away from Imphal, the capital city of Manipur. It falls within the Tengnoupal subdivision (SD) of the

---

[7] The state of Manipur comprises nine districts: Bishnupur, Chandel, Churachandpur, Imphal West, Imphal East, Senapati, Tamenglong, Thoubal and Ukhrul, with a total population of 2,388,634 and 22,327 sq km area.

Chandel district. Its neighbouring town of Myanmar is Tamu, which falls within the Saigang SD of the country.

Today, with its multiracial population, Moreh has assumed a cosmopolitan character. On the basis of the electoral roll issued for the recent ninth assembly election in Manipur, Moreh has a total voter count of 14,584 people. The communities inhabiting Manipur include Kuki, Meitei, Meitei-Pangal (Manipuri Muslim), Tamil, Punjabi, Nepali, Marwari and so forth. The whole of Moreh has been classified into nine wards. Due to conflicting interests between the non-tribal populations and the Kukis, and the opposition by the latter, elections for small town committee have not been held for quite some time. Even though elections for small town committee have not been held, development funds and projects have been pouring in to Moreh.

Border Trade Routes

Since time immemorial, local traders from India and Myanmar have illegally crossed over to conduct border trade which continued till as late as 1994. They accessed several routes which present opportunities for improved connectivity today. First and foremost, a route reaches India from Myanmar through Mandalay, which split northwards at Tamu–Manipur border and connects with the NH 39, also known as the Indo-Myanmar Road, acting as a springboard to Imphal, then to Nagaland, from where it goes to Assam and is finally connected to Kolkata and other parts of India. The other direct routes reach Myanmar from places called Noklak and Tobu situated in eastern Nagaland bordering Myanmar. This route is the most preferred option by illegal traffickers. Apart from these two well-known routes, there are also two other trade routes which have been in use since ancient times. For instance, a route reaches Somrah tract of Myanmar from the Chingai SD of Ukhrul district and another one reaches Somrah tract of Myanmar from the Kamjong SD of Ukhrul district.

For the first time, the GOI and the Myanmarese government signed a border trade agreement for exchanging locally produced commodities among people living along the border in 1994. Later, on 12 April 1995, the Indo-Myanmar cross-border trade was formally opened by P. Chidambaram, the then Indian Union Minister of Commerce, and Myanmar counterpart Lt General Tun Kyi, Minister of Trade. Since then, formal trade between the two countries has started with expectations of extending it beyond Myanmar to other Southeast Asian countries. However, after 1998, with the coming up of Namphalong trade centre on the Myanmar side of the Indo-Myanmar territory, the once flourishing trade centres in Moreh have steeply declined.

Infrastructure for Connectivity

The state of Manipur has three national highways (NHs)—NH 39, NH 53 and NH 150; the former connecting Assam and Nagaland, the latter two running through its own SDs, Jiribam and Mizoram. The Ministry of Road Transport and Highways is planning to upgrade these highways into double-lane roads on agency basis. Out of the three, NH 39 is the shortest to reach the Moreh LCS and is the most important lifeline through which economic activities are carried out. The disadvantage is that the Moreh LCS is not linked by rail. The nearest railhead is at Dimapur (Nagaland), which is about 329 km from Moreh (Table 9.3).

At present, the NHs are in pathetic condition and have been deteriorating over the years. The NH 39 which is most convenient for import–export transportation is plagued by potholes in winter and landslides in summer. The road is far better from Guwahati to Dimapur to Kohima than from Mao–Imphal–Moreh. The bridges along the Imphal–Moreh road constructed

Table 9.3
Length of NHs in Manipur

S. no.	NH no.	Length (in km) within the state	Agency (km)		
			State PWD	*NHAI*	*BRO*
1	39	217.00	185.00	0.00	32.00
2	53	221.00	0.00	0.00	221.00
3	150	523.00	86.00	0.00	437.00
	Total	961.00	271.00	0.00	690.00

during World War II are still being used without any upgradation or renewed construction.

However, in the last five to six years, the state government with
funds from the centre has begun undertaking works for the expansion and improvement of all the three highways—NH 39, NH 53
and NH 150—passing through the state.[8] The Directorate of Transport, Manipur, staved off the responsibility by blaming insufficient
bids for the development of the Imphal–Moreh road. Despite efforts
being made by the Ministry of Surface Transport and Highways,
none of the local contractors have qualified in the pre-qualification
in the bidding, and outside firms which qualified in the bidding are
hesitant to come because of bad law-and-order situation. On the
other hand, the local communities want the Imphal–Moreh stretch
(NH 39) to be totally handed over to the BRO/Border Roads Task
Force (BRTF), an accord towards which was established previously
but has not been brought into practice.

On the Tamu side in Myanmar, a bridge has been constructed
over the Mynal River on the Manipur sector of the Indo-Myanmar
international boundary with Chinese assistance which has benefited the Myanmarese traders. Social organizations based in
Moreh have often accused the GOI of having limited objective
on development projects, that is, to enhance political ties with
Myanmar and not taking keen interest in the development of
infrastructure in the border regions. Geographically, Manipur has
good prospects for road connectivity with Association of Southeast
Asian Nations (ASEAN) and East Asian countries. The TAR across
Manipur from Silchar (Assam) via Moreh further to Mandalay,
the old capital of Myanmar, and beyond to the other South East
Asian countries, can increase connectivity and trade with East
and Southeast Asian countries.

The Indian government's proposal of setting up a rail corridor
between India and Myanmar can also give the people from the
northeast access to Southeast Asia and to China and Russia. In
this regard, a 350-km-long distance needs to be bridged through
rail to connect India with Myanmar. Out of this, roughly 150 km
are on the Indian side. So, just as Myanmar is getting a rail link

---

[8] The eviction of encroachers along the Indo-Myanmar section of the NH 39
under the project of constructing four-lane highways was in progress for some
time, but at present, it has stopped. Right now, only temporary repairing is
going on.

with China in two years, a link with Myanmar could help India to gain access to China as well. On a brighter note, India has already done some feasibility studies on the India–Myanmar rail link. This study recommended the construction of a rail link between Tamu, Kalay and Segyi on the Myanmar side and the construction of a link between Jiribam, Imphal and Moreh on the Indian side.

The centre had also agreed to start a regular bus service between Imphal and Mandalay in Myanmar via Moreh, following a resolution adopted by the Manipur Assembly on 1 August 2003, with a view to boosting trade between the two countries. But New Delhi is yet to get a positive response from the Myanmarese government on the commencement of this bus service.

Regarding air connectivity, Moreh also does not have an airfield, so tourists or businessmen have to depend on the Imphal airport, which is the second largest in the northeastern region. From Imphal, the possible overland route can be Imphal–Mandalay–Ruili–Kunming. The Yunnan foreign affairs office is currently lobbying for India and Myanmar to conduct a joint survey of this overland route, which, it believes, can be opened to trade within months, provided political will exists.

Other infrastructures such as telecommunication, banking, Internet and electricity are also limited in availability in Moreh. Besides BSNL, telephone service operators from other private companies such as Aircel and Airtel are also operating their telephone networks. All the networks reach beyond Namphalong market in Myanmar side. Banking service is gradually improving as SBI and UBI branches are functioning well; however, Internet banking and ATMs are currently in the process of being installed. There is a hope that after the completion of integrated check post (ICP), banking, Internet service and postal delivery will improve.

Hindrances to Infrastructure Development

The improvement of physical infrastructure such as road connectivity should be the topmost priority of the Indian government in this border state because of its economic importance. But the local communities are disappointed that it is not so, and the government is more concerned about disturbances from militancy. First, the main obstacle for development of infrastructure for connectivity is the problem of insurgency. More than 20 insurgent groups are operating on the NH 39 stretch in Manipur, extorting and demanding money from contractors, traders and transport owners. From Nagaland to the Senapati district, the stretch is controlled by Naga insurgent groups, the Imphal Valley stretch is controlled by Meitei insurgent groups and from Palel to Moreh by Kuki insurgent groups as well as the Meitei groups. The Kuki National Army (KNA) and United National Liberation Front (UNLF) are involved in a tussle for domination in the Moreh town. Thus, ethnic tensions can easily derail the government's efforts towards development.

Second, even though there are 53 check posts of various departments/organizations of the governments of Manipur and Nagaland from Dimapur to Moreh on NH 39, extortions remain in full swing. The peace agreement of Naga militants and Soo (Suspension of operation) of Kuki militants with the government has had no impact. Collection of illegal tax forcibly from contract works continues unabashedly in the region. Third, the failure of Myanmar to flush out northeast militants from its soil despite 38 rounds of Indo-Myanmar biannual liaison meetings adds to the problem. Lastly, the politics of ethnicity and misgovernance by state machineries remains a crucial deterrent.

Conclusion

Nature has provided the northeast region of India with abundant resource. A clear developmental strategy can bring adequate infrastructure for connectivity and in turn boost regional economy through these states. Concrete proposals like that of the 'Kunming Initiative' started in 1999 during a conference on regional cooperation and development should be brought into practice. The proposal centres on integrating the BCIM economies, especially along border areas, primarily through cross-border infrastructure development, including rail, air and river links but in particular roads. Thus far, China has been the most enthusiastic proponent of the initiative; India its least. This shows that India lacks a strategic mission towards its neighbours. India could benefit much from learning from other countries, especially the Yunnan model, which is much similar to the northeast region of India, and consistent development in that region has led it to become China's gateway to South Asia and Southeast Asia.

On the same lines, with adequate infrastructure, Arunachal Pradesh and Manipur can also become India's gateway to East Asia. The people of Tawang and Bomdila have many cultural affinities with the TAR (China) and still have relatives across the border. A close interaction between them could bring social and political harmony between the two countries. Manipur too has been considered as a gateway to Southeast Asia since early period. With proper implementation of the Look East Policy (LEP) on security and economic cooperation and improved infrastructure, this region can be transformed into a tourist hub and integrated it into the China–ASEAN tourist circuit, along with obtaining other trade-related gains.

10

Border Trade and Connectivity in South Asia: A Sub-regional Approach—Some Conclusions

Bhavna Singh

Trade and transport corridors passing through myriad assorted geographies have the potential to connect people from different regions, ethnicities and linguistic backgrounds in both physical and material realms and become the harbingers of change through dissemination of fresh ideas. Trade and connectivity have the capacity to work not only within but also despite the constraints presented by any given topography. In fact, they operate as the 'instruments' of creating 'borderless worlds' since they are believed to promote economic integration even among states enduring conflict and help to overcome political antagonism through transborder economic cooperation.[1] They also debunk the artificial nature of boundaries created by political entities, which takes into consideration neither the traditional modes of community engagements along the bordering regions nor the exchange of traditional mores and practices.

Nevertheless, while broadcasting an array of products, services and information, it becomes essential to develop a culture of agreements, formal or informal, customs and institutions that can administer trading relationships and structures for minimizing conflict

---

[1] Mayumi Murayama, 'Borders, Migration and Sub-regional Cooperation in Eastern South Asia', *Economic and Political Weekly* 41(14) (8–14 April 2006): 1351–1359.

of national interests. It is the lack of these established norms that leads to sporadic instances of mistrust and mutual suspicion in case of any mishap. Thus, it is very essential that the South Asian countries work towards establishing such parameters.

Both India and China, with a combined gross domestic product (GDP) of more than US$14 trillion and a combined population of more than 2.5 billion people, have emerged as key drivers for global and regional economic structures. Growth characterized by immaculate speed and efficient delivery as far as China is concerned and a sustained momentum along with thorough policy guidelines in case of India has led many to believe in the era of Asian economic dominance or Asianomics. Though occasional hiccups have surfaced about their success stories on sustained economic growth, as seen in the aftermath of the 2008–2009 recession which necessitated government intervention through fiscal stimulus, it is undeniable that these two countries hold the potential to shape the economic infrastructure of the globe and the South Asian sub-region in the near and long term.

This change in attitude and approach is already evident in the way China is asserting the strength of its currency and also experimenting with new models of economic development for its peripheral regions. For instance, China's strategy through the Western development campaign in Xinjiang, Tibet and other south-western provinces and the regional economic models of Yunnan and other south-eastern coastal provinces allow them certain amount of autonomy while conducting trade across borders. Similarly, Indian economic giants are making their mark all over the globe through a slow and steady process of acquisitions and partnerships, gradually conquering uncharted markets, as well as its Look East Policy (LEP) is a mark of the growing alacrity within Indian establishment to engage in cross-border trade through its northeastern states. Their expanding economic ties could prove even more significant in the regional and sub-regional contexts with regard to neighbours such as Nepal, Bangladesh, Pakistan, Bhutan and Myanmar.

Yet, it is rather disheartening to see how little the two neighbours have achieved in terms of bilateral and regional confidence-building mechanisms (CBMs) for furthering trade and connectivity. The growth stories of the two economic giants in Asia have failed to transform the shape of the South Asian sub-region. Smaller (geographically) neighbours are treated as transit nations and often experience dominance and sometimes nonchalance from their two giant neighbours as per the prevalent geopolitical scenarios. This chapter aims at exploring the incentives and viabilities of multilevel cooperative mechanisms between the two Asian giants and their geographically smaller neighbours in the realm of border trade and infrastructure connectivity. It attempts to decipher a regional solution for these issues in the trans-Himalayan region and suggests a more obligatory regional approach towards resolving outstanding concerns. For this purpose, it is divided into two sections discussing trade first and connectivity later.

Border Trade in South Asia: Prospects and Obstacles

There are two crucial distinctions that need to be made while discussing the ramifications of border trade for a country. First, border trade in general is sought to imply the flow of goods and services across international borders between jurisdictions. Second, it also encompasses the illegal economy of trade in the areas where crossing border is relatively easy and products are relatively cheaper. In this reference, the districts and passes across the trans-Himalayan range in India, China, Nepal and other neighbouring areas such as Bangladesh and Myanmar provide immense opportunities as well as challenges for the augmentation of border trade.

These areas have enjoyed trade relations since historical times, which have been unfortunately disturbed of late, due to geopolitical considerations and narrow-minded decision-making, but stand at the threshold of revival with optimistic signs from the new leaderships. Certain endeavours are particularly noteworthy as they reflect the growing alacrity among these neighbouring countries to rekindle their traditional trade links.

Border Trade between India and China

There are three main sectors through which border trade has been carried out between India and China: first, the Jammu and Kashmir (J&K) sector, which accounts for the larger part of the traditional 'Silk Route' trade connecting India to China and further to Central Asia; second, the Himachal sector, which forms an alternative trade link with China through Tibet; and third, the Sikkim sector, mainly through the Nathu La pass, which currently exhibits the most dynamic region for both legal and traditional border trade with China.

Historically, trade across all the three sectors flourished enormously, so much so that the British even envisaged constructing railway lines from Indian districts to centres in China (Siliguri to Chumbi Valley) to facilitate greater border trade between India and Tibet.[2] However, border trade was discontinued following the 1962 war between India and China.[3] Revival of this trade was sought only by the early 1990s when both the countries reached a consensus on exit and entry procedures for border trade. In 1992–1993, two mountain passes at Shipki La in Himachal Pradesh and Lipulekh in Uttaranchal were opened which paved the way for an overall expansion of border trade.[4] Further on, a memorandum of understanding was signed between the two countries to resume border trade between Sikkim and Tibet and establish Changu in Sikkim and Renqinggang in Tibet Autonomous Region (TAR) as trade markets for India and China, respectively.

Nathu La was finally reopened in 2006, coinciding with the declaration of India–China 'year of friendship'. Till then, most of the trade between Sikkim and Tibet took place through sea routes via the port of Tianjin.[5] Strategists and economists believed that it signalled the improvement in bilateral ties of the two neighbours at that particular time, and that over the years, in comparison to the trade through Lipulekh and Shipki La, border trade through Nathu La has proved to be more beneficial and continues to posit great potential in the future as well. This can be attributed to several geographical disadvantages in the former regions which are not so evident in the latter region.

---

[2] Pushpita Das, 'Nathu La: Pass to Prosperity but Also a Challenge', 4 July 2006, IDSA Comment, Online web URL: http://www.idsa.in/idsastrategiccomments/NathuLaPassToProsperityButAlsoAChallenge_PDas_040706, accessed on 10 March 2012.

[3] Ibid.

[4] Ibid.

[5] 'China, India to reopen border trade', *Xinhua*, 19 June 2006, Online URL: http://www.china.org.cn/english/features/poverty/171927.htm, accessed on 26 March 2012.

A study group constituted by the state government of Sikkim headed by Mahendra P. Lama in its report titled 'Nathu La Trade: Prospects, Potentials and Opportunities', highlighted the huge potential of trade through Nathu La. The report projected that the cumulative trade flow through Nathu La would reach US$580 million (₹2,266 crore) by 2010 and US$2 billion (₹12,203 crore) by 2015.[6] Yet on the ground level, the trade figures did not reach the projected amount which exposes the inertia and the lackadaisical attitude of the governments on both sides and their unwillingness to open trade citing security reasons. China's inhibitions regarding Tibet's engagement with India are widely known, while India's reticence seems to surface from the fear of its inability to protect the interest of local traders and inhabitants.

Despite substantial recommendations being made by the Nathu La study group, the conditions at the ground remain dismal. Enhancement of infrastructure facilities, which is a prerequisite for improvement of trade relations, remains constrained by bureaucratic hiccups. Neither have these bureaucratic procedures been updated or relaxed for desired outcomes in trade nor has the trade basket been improvised. While cross-border trade in Tibet had risen by 88 per cent in 2010, much of this was on account of its exchanges with Nepal. Its trade with Sikkim constituted only 5 per cent, which shows the huge potential that can be exploited but is currently not being harnessed.[7]

Besides, there are often reports of non-trade groups intervening in the business operations. For instance, in May 2007, traders complained of harassment by army officials and undue interference in trade activities, which do not fall in the army's purview of functions. The state government raised the issue with the Ministry of External Affairs after a month's delay, and called for boycott by trade associations, while no such interference is heard of on the Chinese side.[8] Another factor affecting trade in the region is

[6] Nathu La Trade Study Group, Sikkim-Tibet Trade via Nathu La: A Policy Study on Prospect, Opportunities and Requisite Preparedness, 2005.

[7] Tibet to invest in border trade with India, *The Hindu*, 31 October 2010, Online URL: http://www.thehindu.com/business/Economy/tibet-to-invest-in-border-trade-with-india/article861691.ece, accessed on 31 June 2012.

[8] Ankur Mahanta, 'Regional Cooperation and Cross-Border Trade: A Study on the Reopening of Nathu la for Cross-Border Trade between India and China', Unpublished dissertation submitted to the Tata Institute of Social Sciences, 2008, 102.

the internal ethnic discrimination between the original inhabitants such as the Lepchas, Bhutias and the settlers from outside, largely comprising Marwari, Bihari and Bengalis who have been integrated over long periods of time. The business transactions are largely controlled by the latter, while the former feels marginalized in their own territory.

In addition, the basic handicaps relating to inadequate infrastructure facilities such as power, roads and communication, lack of knowledge of the entrepreneur regarding manufacturing activities, lack of raw material, inadequate land availability and absence of proper manpower largely contribute to the negative influence on cross-border trade in this region.[9] Even the revision of list of tradable items in 2012, though relevant in today's market, has been arbitrary without giving tax exemption on the recently included items of trade.[10] The government has by and large failed to provide a logistically sound trade atmosphere buttressed by good marketing network and enabling laws for private investment and in removing technological and financial blockades to improve cross-border and sub-regional interaction. Efforts of the Border Roads Organisation (BRO) which operates the project 'Swastik' have been found to be extremely slow despite the urgency of their requirement (based on field trip observations around Nathu La, 2012).

Thus, due to these obstacles, trade has failed to pick up across the Sikkim–Tibet border and remains much below the predicted standards. The abovementioned bottlenecks also hinder cross-border trade along the previously mentioned border regions of

[9] These basic requirements which remain unfulfilled include: infrastructure build-up through development packages—build-up and upgrading of storage facilities, parking bays, security and medical facility at Sherathang and Nathu La; improvement of existing highways and exploration of alternative routes to Nathu La; restructuring of transport services—freight business, passenger, container and warehousing; installation and upgradation of banking services, taxation, custom facilities; sustainable and ecological management of the region; and construction of airport facilities, museum and, more importantly, centre—state coordination and protection of local Sikkim's interests. *Source:* NTSG Report 2005.

[10] Traders from Sikkim can now import ready-made garments, shoes, quilt/blankets, carpets and local herbal medicines from the TAR of China. Before the notification, the import list was restricted to 15 items such as wool, goat cashmere, yak tails, sheep skins, horses and salt. Source: Nathu La trade gets wider, *The Telegraph*, 9 May 2012, Online URL: http://www.telegraphindia.com/1120509/jsp/siliguri/story_15467618.jsp#.UX5Oq6JgeTk, accessed on 5 July 2012.

Uttarakhand and Himachal, which are further complicated by unsettled border issues and topographical disadvantages in those regions. In sum, political mistrust and inertia continue to be major factors influencing the nature and pace of cross-border trade along the Sino-Indian border regions.

Similarly, India's trade with Nepal and Bangladesh also suffers due to political deadlocks which result in a negative 'image formation' for India which is alleged to have a dominating presence in these regions. While an unsettled border and migration issue has led to widespread illegal trade along the Indo-Bangladesh border (as discussed in Chapter 6), trade relations with Nepal have been marred by India's perceived involvement in the regime-change issues (discussed at length in Chapter 7). The same is, however, not true for China, in relation to its other neighbours, which has been hard-pressed to improvise the economic growth of its bordering regions due to political exigencies and has extended its clout unmatched by India, in the other countries of South Asia.

Border Trade between China and Its Other Neighbours

The nature of China's cross-border trade or its good neighbourhood policy (*zhoubian zhengce*) exhibits two broad phenomena: China aims at using its border trade for the overall growth of its underdeveloped western regions (*wending zhoubian*)[11] and also uses its cross-border trade as an instrument of strengthening the use of its currency internationally as well as regionally.[12] To achieve the first objective, China has promulgated projects such as the Western development campaign (*xibu da kaifa*) for Tibet, Xinjiang and south-western Yunnan, which have lagged behind the more prosperous eastern provinces. On the other hand, the launch of the renminbi (RMB) cross-border trade settlement scheme symbolizes its commitment to the second objective.

---

[11] Su Yuanming, an official at the regional commerce department of the TAR government, told the official Xinhua News Agency that the government would invest more in boosting cross-border trade — 'Such cross-border cooperation [with India and Nepal] is conducive to Tibet's economic development and the overall growth of China's underdeveloped western regions'.

[12] 'Leveraging China Reforms: New Opportunities in Cross-border trade', Online URL: http://www.citigroup.com/transactionservices/home/corporations/docs/leveraging_china_reforms.pdf, accessed on 14 March 2013.

Altogether, China's presence in its South Asian neighbourhood has been far more aggressive than India's presence. This is evident in the infrastructure construction being done to connect these regions with China at a rapid pace. China is using both soft power and hard power tools to reach out to these countries. For instance, China's ambassador to Kathmandu, Yang Houlan, was recently pictured in a traditional Nepali cap and silk scarf, digging with a spade to symbolize the laying of the foundations of a new dry port near the Tibet border.[13] China's TAR shares an approximately 1,414-km border with Nepal, making it essential to maintain stability on the border for other economic activities to be carried out and also to make Nepal adhere to its 'One-China Policy'.

For precisely this reason, China is determined to enhance its economic relations with the country enabling it to be effectively used as a transit for South Asia. The growing economic engagement is visible in the increase of the trade volume by 80 per cent in a single year from 2009 to 2010 (US$744 million).[14] China has introduced a zero-tariff facility for over 4,000 Nepalese goods and has signed a number of contracts worth US$20 million in military field and promised to build a military base on the Tibetan border.[15] The construction of the Golmud–Lhasa road is another case in point. Simultaneously, ouster of many Tibetan refugees who traverse to India via Nepal is an example of the growing Chinese control in Nepal.

However, China's engagement with Nepal has become a matter of much debate. While some elements within Nepal perceive China's influence as benevolent in terms of investments and opportunities, others point out China's largesse as a larger foreign policy tool envisioning Nepal's dry ports and roads as a doorway to the huge markets of India.[16] China's investments in its neighbourhood are strongly supported by a domestic expansion of

[13] Deepak Adhikari, 'China eyes India trade by boosting spending in Nepal', AFP, 13 March 2013, Online URL: http://www.tibetsun.com/news/2013/03/11/china-eyes-india-trade-by-boosting-spending-in-nepal, accessed on 27 March 2013.

[14] Bhavna Singh, 'China's Nepal Focus #3431', 14 July 2011, Online web URL: http://www.ipcs.org/article/india/chinas-nepal-focus-3431.html, accessed on 18 August 2012.

[15] Other Chinese projects include a US$1.6 billion hydropower plant which is expected to end power outages that extend to 14 hours a day in winter and a 22-km stretch of road in central Nepal connecting the country's southern plains with the Tibetan county of Kyirong, to form the shortest motorable overland route between China and India.

[16] Deepak Adhikari, op. cit.

infrastructure networks. In Tibet alone, the government recently announced it would spend 50 billion yuan (US$7.5 billion) in the five-year plan on highway construction, increasing the length of highways from 58,000 km to 70,000 km by 2015.

Similarly, in the context of its expanding relations with Pakistan and the Central Asian neighbours, development of its Xinjiang province is a priority. China has been expanding the Karakoram Highway (KKH) (undertaken as a collaborative with Pakistan's national highway (NH) authority) which connects Kashgar to Gwadar and further west and announced several special economic zones to make the cities in Xinjiang a hub for Central Asian trade. There are also suggestions to build a railway network along the KKH for establishing East-West and North-South trade corridors in the regions. It has undertaken several key projects in the field of energy, airport and road construction as well as economic incentivization for foreign investment in the region. It should also be noted that besides the development of its backward regions, China's policy towards its western neighbours is also heavily guided by its need for resources such as oil and gas which are available in plenty in this region.

On the eastern side, China's involvement in Myanmar has been quite apparent. But the investment in Myanmar by China in terms of loans and infrastructure development presents a scenario where its engagement has often been termed as 'unwelcomed interference' and as creating a vicious cycle of dependency. China's support and guidance in building ports and railroads has come to be associated with neo-colonist designs in this part of the world. Thus, while India suffers from a lack of goodwill in the region stemming from its image of a 'big burly dominating elder brother', China also receives mixed responses from its neighbours. The difference, however, lies in the manner of approach that these two big giants adopt in trying to attain their national objectives with reference to their smaller neighbours.

South Asian Trade Corridor: A Viable Solution or Chimera?

Several attempts have been made from time to time to initiate a sub-regional arrangement for boosting trade in South Asia. Most recently, the upgradation of the South Asia Preferential Trade

Agreement (SAPTA) into South Asia Free Trade Area (SAFTA) agreement in 2006 brought about a possibility of a larger framework for enhanced trade networks between the countries in the South Asian region. This was believed to have made way for an eventual establishment of a customs union by 2015 and an economic union by 2020. It was envisaged that SAFTA would lead the growth in intraregional formal trade from US$11 billion in 2007 to US$40 billion by 2015 (RIS 2008).[17] However, in reality, South Asia is far from realizing its trade potential in either formal trade or cross-border trade. One of the critical factors preventing South Asia from achieving its full potential is the absence of regional transit trade for which India is largely blamed while China is believed to have set a high priority to this.[18]

The Indian political leadership and business communities have often voiced their commitment to developing and strengthening regional cooperation in trade and connectivity. For instance, during the India chapter of the World Economic Forum, the Indian Commerce and Industry Minister Anand Sharma highlighted the role of economic complementarities in abetting a South Asian regional economy. While B. Muthuraman, vice-chairman of Tata Steel and president of the Confederation of Indian Industry (CII), said that 'new commercial corridors linking the emerging markets in Asia, Africa and Latin America, spurred largely by the rising demand in fast-growing China and India for raw materials and energy to fuel development are on the rise. These will enhance South–South trade and investment'.[19]

Yet, these commitments have not become manifest on ground due to political misgivings and imbalanced trade relations. The Chinese government has set a high priority on the resumption of trade through India through sub-regional arrangement along

---

[17] Prabir De, Sachin Chaturvedi and Abdur Rob Khan, 'Transit and Border Trade Barriers in South Asia', Chapter 6, *World Bank Publications*, Online URL: http://siteresources.worldbank.org/SOUTHASIAEXT/Resources/223546-1192413140459/4281804-1192413178157/4281806-1265938468438/BeyondSAFTAFeb2010Chapter6.pdf, accessed on 23 November 2012.

[18] See the chapter on Bangladesh (Chapter 6) in this volume for a perspective on India's role in the region.

[19] 'Sharma calls for integrating cross border trade in South Asia', *The Indian Express*, 14 November 2011, Online URL: http://www.indianexpress.com/news/sharma-calls-for-integrating-cross-border-trade-in-south-asia/875328/1, accessed on 12 December 2012.

with Bangladesh and Myanmar as it will play a major role in developing its backward regions and provide easy access to the ports of West Bengal and Bangladesh through which it can trade its goods directly to its western region.[20] But for India, though it may help to make its northeast as a gateway to Southeast Asia, it would also relate to the non-economic issue of border settlement on which it remains sceptical of China. China's assertive behaviour, unpredictability along with its non-committal attitude, keeps India wary of Chinese intentions. China's not so credible record in observing international norms also adds to Indian insecurities. The gap between India's core and periphery, mostly its northeastern states, also needs to be bridged before it jumps the bandwagon on regional cooperation.

While the two countries cooperate on issues such as climate change on the global level, at the regional level, they still remain competitors for resources and influence. According to World Energy Outlook, in 2030, the world's energy needs would be well over 50 per cent higher than today. China and India together alone will account for 45 per cent of the increase in global primary energy demand in this scenario.[21] Besides, bilateral differences on the damming of the Brahmaputra River, China's military and economic assistance to Pakistan countering India, China's massive military modernization and its presence in the Indian ocean region while trying to get access to various ports, widely known as the 'string of pearls' strategy, also deter effective regional cooperation.

Both countries are now trying to engage their neighbours in separate forums, avoiding direct contact or confrontation. For instance, India has been trying to build capacity and strengthen its regional commitments through the South Asia Subregional Economic Cooperation (SASEC) programme aided by the Asian Development Bank (ADB) which aims at promoting economic development between Bangladesh, Bhutan, India and Nepal, primarily in the sectors of energy, transport, power, trade and investment in private sector, information technologies, tourism and environment. China is attempting to do the same through initiatives such as the Greater Mekong Sub-region (GMS) which

[20] Sumedh Lokhande, 'India-China Relations Potentials of Cooperation and Dissonance', Online URL: http://chaurahha.wordpress.com/tag/border-trade-connectivity/, accessed on 7 January 2013.
[21] Ibid.

comprises Cambodia, Vietnam, Laos, Myanmar and Thailand. A similar conundrum exists for the two regional powers as well as the other South Asian countries in opting for multilateral or bilateral cooperation when connectivity issues are considered.

Connectivity in South Asia: Bilateral and Multilateral Imperatives

Land and maritime connectivity play a crucial role in scaffolding the trade and cultural linkages that exist between the two countries or two regions. Not only does it bolster the physical mechanisms for exchange of resources, ideas and manpower, but also creates a network of goodwill and influence that can augur better ties among nations. If connectivity is disrupted, it has immediate consequences for trade; for this reason, many scholars argue that in most cases the proportion of trade over shorter distances increases in relation to trade over longer distances. Thus, it is imperative for trade and transit for which the States in South Asia have been investing in roads, railways and air networks at an unprecedented pace.

So far, India's main focus has been to reconnect its remote northeast with the policies at the centre. It is distressing to see that while railway networks existed connecting all of northeast and Kolkata earlier, today there is no such service. Similarly, the bus services from Kolkata to Dhaka and the Haldia port are in disarray. Through its oft-quoted LEP, it aims to bring the economies of the Seven Sister States at par with the rest of India. It is also seen as the most important element of connectivity between India and its East Asian neighbourhood.[22] This includes the revival of the old routes along with construction of new ones. For instance, India has already constructed a road linking Tamu with the railhead at Kalemyo which connects Mandalay (Myanmar). In addition, construction of new roads such as the Ledo and Kunming roads that connect northeast through Myanmar with Thailand will be essentially in India's interest, and thus, India should strive hard for its revival. Similarly, the

---

[22] *Connectivity Issues in India's Neighbourhood* (New Delhi: Asian Institute of Transport Development, 2008), iv.

Stilwell road which is now in disuse can be revived for better connectivity with south-western regions of China.

The hesitation on grounds of military or security threats does not really hold grounds as seen in China's case which has vastly improved its connectivity along the border areas.[23] If the Indian defence forces were to argue that improving connectivity in these regions would open a way for easier access and entry for Chinese troops, so it could be hypothetically argued about Chinese roads in Tibet and Xinjiang or other adjoining south-western provinces. However, any intrusion or violation of sovereignty will not depend on the availability of better infrastructure, rather would be guided by the presence or lack of credible conventional deterrents. Thus, India needs to realize the significance of better connectivity to emerge as a true global power.

On the other hand, the developments in infrastructure and connectivity on the Chinese side have been spectacular. Its investments in port facilities among the South Asian neighbours ensure a continued supply of the raw materials needed for its spectacular growth along with other strategic advantages. For instance, the Gwadar facility provides China a forward base to monitor US and Indian naval activity in the Indian Ocean besides providing access to the Middle East. China's aid and assistance to Bangladesh as a major supplier of arms is aimed at using it as a staging post for the Malacca Straits. Similarly, its involvement in Sri Lanka as a major source of military equipment is guided by the aim to use Hambantota against its strategic vulnerabilities in the Indian Ocean. The opening of the Kathmandu–Kodari highway and several transit trade posts along with the Beijing–Lhasa railway line (which is being connected with Nepal) has tremendously boosted China's trade with Nepal.

The Kunming initiative and the GMS are examples of China's desire to tap the markets of South and Southeast Asia. These are aimed at creating economic interdependence between China and Association of Southeast Asian Nations (ASEAN) through an extensive road and railway network.[24] Thus, through these projects, China has been able to increase imports of Chinese goods

[23] 'China plans Tibet-Xinjiang rail links', *The Hindu*, 8 March 2011, Online URL: http://www.thehindu.com/news/international/china-plans-tibetxinjiang-rail-links/article1517925.ece, accessed on 12 February 2013.

[24] *Connectivity Issues in India's Neighbourhood*, op. cit., xv.

through borders with Bangladesh, Bhutan, Myanmar and Pakistan while importing major energy resources for its growth. It has also recently announced high-speed railway networks joining Central Asia, ASEAN countries, India and Pakistan and also Europe, which could possibly emerge as potential geostrategic game changers in the region.

China has also quickly utilized air connectivity to achieve its strategic aims. While air connectivity has been on the wane between India's centre and its northeast, China has not only managed to increase the number and frequency of flights plying between its centre and coastal regions but also extended its reach beyond its south-western provinces to Nepal, Bangladesh and Myanmar. China's three leading airline companies—China Eastern, China Southern and Air China—all operate passenger flights to Kathmandu.[25]

Nepal has shown keenness to participate in regional initiatives to upgrade the infrastructure and connectivity in the region for its own rapid development, while Bangladesh has been more than eager to expand ties with China to benefit from trade and the expansion of Yunnan–Kyaukphyu link to Chittagong. However, discerning from the earlier discussion, most of these efforts are restricted to bilateral arrangements, and there has not been any notable achievement at the regional level in South Asia. It is thus important for these countries to overcome local and persistent conflicts which hamper growth and increase regional disparities and engage in multilateral frameworks which augment economic integration and political amicability. The Asian Highway Link, Asian Railway Network and a Natural Gas Pipeline Grid under the leadership of Bay of Bengal Initiative for Multi-Sectoral Technical and Economic Cooperation (BIMSTEC) provide one such opportunity.

The future of trade and connectivity is undeniably interlinked, and there has to be wholehearted involvement of all countries in South Asia to make regional integration successful. There has to be increased involvement of Nepal, Bangladesh and Myanmar in the formal trade of the South Asian sub-region and greater control

---

[25] 'China's Tibet sees booming trade with Nepal, India', *Xinhua*, 28 October 2012, Online URL: http://news.xinhuanet.com/english2010/business/2010-10/28/c_13580195.htm, accessed on 26 March 2013.

of the informal trade through legalizing cross-border arrangements. Traditional routes have to be revived for international trade, along with connecting and constructing new routes. Tourist potential of the backward regions has to be effectively utilized because they make the least controversial element of human connectivity. As brought out in the chapters of the volume, simplification of bureaucratic and procedural requirements will enable growth of trade and connectivity at a relatively quicker pace and facilitate positive economic interactions.

Besides, strengthening of trade and connectivity in the South Asian region requires the convergence of interest between the local communities residing along the border areas with that of the state policy and vision so that their concerns are timely addressed. Their participation will be of immense significance for expanding international trade along with cross-border exchanges. It is also essential that along with physical connectivity through roadways, railways and airways, the cultural connectivity through tourism[26] and intercommunity linkages through technological and communication facilities need to be augmented as well. Developing cross-border cooperation in the power, energy and telecommunications sectors for overall growth of all countries provides the rationale for better economic ties, but how far these countries will be able to rise above narrow political and sovereign issues remains to be seen. The role of regional institutions such as South Asian Association for Regional Cooperation (SAARC) and Bangladesh–China–India–Myanmar Forum for Regional Cooperation (BCIM) will also remain constrained, lest the South Asian neighbours learn to peacefully collaborate for mutual gain.

---

[26] For instance, persuading China to open the relatively safe route of Leh–Demchok–Kailash Mansarovar for the Indian pilgrims.

About the Editors and Contributors

Editors

D. Suba Chandran is a Director at the Institute of Peace and Conflict Studies (IPCS), New Delhi. His primary areas of research include Pakistan's internal security, Afghanistan and Jammu and Kashmir. He is currently working on 'Indus Water Governance' — a study aimed at improving the process of water governance and addressing the concerns of various sub-regions in the Indus Basin region. He is also working on 'State Failure in South Asia', especially focusing on the stability–instability curve, and testing the hypotheses of cyclic failure and functional anarchy. He is the author of *Limited War: Revisiting Kargil in Indo-Pak Conflicts* (2005), editor or co-editor of several books and articles and has widely published in the regional and national media. He is also an Associate at the Pakistan Study Research Unit (PSRU), University of Bradford, and has been a Visiting Professor at the Pakistan Studies Programme, Jamia Millia Islamia, New Delhi.

Bhavna Singh is Country Coordinator for the V-dem Project by the University of Gothenburg, Sweden, and Former Senior Research Officer, Institute of Peace and Conflict Studies (IPCS), New Delhi. She is a Doctoral candidate at the Chinese division on the Centre of East Asian Studies, Jawaharlal Nehru University, New Delhi. Her work focuses on Chinese nationalism, sub-nationalisms and China's foreign policy with regard to the USA, Japan and South Asia. She is particularly interested in separatist and sub-national tendencies in the regions of Xinjiang, Tibet, Taiwan and Inner Mongolia. She is the author of the book *China's Discursive Nationalism: Contending in Softer Realms* (2012) and has written for several esteemed journals such as the *Economic and Political Weekly, Mainstream Weekly, Nam-today, World Focus, Epilogue* and the *China Daily*. She was part of the youth exchange delegation between China and India in the year 2008 and was nominated to the 'Taiwan Study Camp for Future Leaders of South Asia' in 2010.

Contributors

N. Vijaylakshmi Brara is an Associate Professor at the Centre for Manipur Studies, Manipur University, and is currently involved with research in the field of polity, society and economy of Manipur and its interactive dynamics with South Asia and the rest of northeast India. She is the author of *Politics, Society and Cosmology in India's North–East* (1998). She has written extensively on gender issues in Manipur, religious movements and the status of women in institutional power sharing. She has published several reports with the National Commission for Women as well as the North East Region Community Resource Management Project (NERCORMP). She was a principal researcher with the Indira Gandhi Centre for Arts, Institute of Social Sciences and Centre for Human Resources, all in New Delhi. Her main areas of research interest are developmental sociology, cultural anthropology and gender studies, and she has been involved in the study of the northeastern regions of India for more than a decade.

Muinul Islam is a Professor at the Department of Economics, University of Chittagong, Bangladesh. He was the Director General (on deputation), Bangladesh Institute of Bank Management, Dhaka, Bangladesh, from 1998 to 2001. His areas of interest include economic development and planning, public finance, migration and refugee studies, environmental economics, international trade and participatory action research (PAR). He has authored several books, including *The Poverty Discourse and Participatory Action Research in Bangladesh* (2009), *A Profile of Bank Loan Default in the Private Sector in Bangladesh* (2010) and *Economic Integration in South Asia: Issues and Pathways* (2010).

Teiborlang T. Kharsyntiew is presently an Assistant Professor in the Department of International Relations, School of Global Studies, Sikkim University, Gangtok. He is also involved with the School of Policy Studies, Sikkim University, and the Planning Commission's 11th Plan Mid-term Appraisal Report of the Mizoram State. His area of specialization includes Security and Foreign Policy of the European Union. At present, his research interests include global environmental policy and global governance. Dr Kharsyntiew completed his MA, MPhil and PhD from the School of International Studies, Jawaharlal Nehru University, New Delhi.

Uttam Lal is an Assistant Professor in the Department of Geography and Natural Resources Management, Sikkim University. He holds a PhD from Jawaharlal Nehru University, has published research articles and presented research papers in national and international seminars. He is currently working on a book titled *Environment and Society of Kinnaur*, expected to be published soon. He has been the recipient of CSIR Junior as well as Senior Research Fellowships. He was part of a team working on Space Application Center (SAC), Ahmadabad, and Indian Space Research Organisation (ISRO) sponsored project on 'Desertification in the Three Watersheds of Leh and Kathua in J&K and Lahaul in Himachal Pradesh'. He has also carried out extensive field-based research work in Kinnaur and Spiti in Himachal Pradesh as well as high-altitude field-based study in Gangotri–Gaumukh, Uttarakhand. His areas of academic interests include Himalayan environment, economy and culture.

Nishchal N. Pandey is a Director of Kathmandu-based Centre for South Asian Studies, teaches at Department of Conflict, Peace and Development Studies of the Tribhuvan University, Kathmandu, and is Chief Advisor of the Sangam Institute, Kathmandu. He is an international research committee member of the Regional Centre for Strategic Studies, Sri Lanka. Previously, he was Executive Director of the Institute of Foreign Affairs of the Nepal government for eight years. He was also a Visiting Research Fellow at the Institute of South Asian Studies, at the National University of Singapore, in 2006–2007 and an Advisor to the National Planning Commission. Pandey is the author of three books: *Nepal's Maoist Movement and Implications for India and China* (2005), *India's North-Eastern Region:*

Insurgency, Economic Development and Linkages with Southeast Asia (2008) and *New Nepal: The Fault Lines* (2010). In addition, he has edited and co-edited nine other books on various issues concerning foreign and security policies of Nepal, regional cooperation in South Asia, Nepal–India and Nepal–China relations.

Sanasam Amal Singh is a Research Associate at the Centre for Manipur Studies, Manipur University. He has a PhD in History from School of Social Sciences, Manipur University. He worked on the project fellowship 'The Meitei Calendar — Rites and Rituals' awarded by Maulana Abul Kalam Azad Institute of Asian Studies from 2005 to 2006 and as a Field Investigator on the project entitled 'Social, Economic and Political Dynamics in Extremist Affected Areas' from 2009 to 2010. His areas of interest include historical sociology, sociology of inter-ethnic relations, sociology of migration and diaspora, border studies and conflict and development studies. His recent publications include *Social Integration in Early Manipur: Some Aspects in 'Ethnic Relations among the People of Northeast India'*, edited by N. Joykumar (2006), *Globalisation and Krishna Consciousness: An Overview in 'Globalisation and the Changing Scenario of Cultural Interaction Manipur Experience'*, edited by N. Joykumar (2006).

Li Tao is an Executive Director of the Institute of South Asian Studies, Sichuan University, Chengdu, China, and a member of the editorial board of *International Politics*. Her extensive writings focus on ethnic studies (especially Tibetology), social and economic development studies and South Asian studies. Dr Li has 12 publications (written/edited) and some 60 papers on Tibetology and South Asian studies to her credit. She has also directed and supervised some 11 academic research programmes, including 'A Study on the Tibetan Buddhism of South Asian', 'A Study on the Particularity of the Tibetan Areas' and 'Studies on Contemporary Tibetan Buddhism in India'. Professor Li is active in international academic exchanges. She travels widely in Europe, the USA, South Asia, Hong Kong and Taiwan. Dr Li has been awarded the Sichuan Philosophy Social Science Prize (second class and third class), Outstanding Essays in Recent Ten Years Prize (second class) by the National Minority Affairs Committee and honourable prize of Outstanding Research Achievements by the Chinese Academy of Social Sciences.

Index